EDMUND BURKE

EDMUND BURKE

PHILOSOPHER, POLITICIAN, PROPHET

JESSE NORMAN

WILLIAM
COLLINS

William Collins
An imprint of HarperCollins*Publishers*
77–85 Fulham Palace Road
London w6 8jb
www.harpercollins.co.uk

First published in the UK by William Collins 2013

1 3 5 7 9 10 8 6 4 2

A catalogue record for this book is available from the British Library

ISBN 978-0-00-748962-6

Endpapers: front, *The House of Commons 1793–94* © National Portrait Gallery, London;
back, *A View of the Tryal of Warren Hastings Esqr. before the Court of Peers,
in Westminster Hall* © Getty Images

Typeset by Palimpsest Book Production Ltd, Falkirk, Stirlingshire
Printed in Great Britain by Clays Ltd, St Ives plc

MIX
Paper from
responsible sources
FSC
www.fsc.org
FSC C007454

Contents

List of Illustrations

p. 18: *Gin Lane*, by William Hogarth, etching and engraving, published 1 February 1751 © The Trustees of the British Museum

p. 39: *Idol-Worship or the way to preferment*, anonymous, etching, 1740 © The Trustees of the British Museum

p. 45: *A literary party at Sir Joshua Reynolds's*, by D. George Thompson, after James William Edmund Doyle, stipple and line engraving, published by Owen Bailey 1 October 1851 © National Portrait Gallery, London

p. 52: *The House of Commons 1793–94*, by Karl Anton Hickel, oil on canvas, 1793–1795 © National Portrait Gallery, London

p. 57: Portrait of Charles Watson-Wentworth, 2nd Marquess of Rockingham, after Sir Joshua Reynolds, oil on canvas, feigned oval, circa 1768 © National Portrait Gallery, London

p. 61: Portrait of John Wilkes, by James Watson, after Robert Edge Pine, mezzotint, published 1764 © National Portrait Gallery, London

p. 85: Portrait of Charles James Fox, by Karl Anton Hickel, oil on canvas, 1794 © National Portrait Gallery, London

p. 98: Portrait of Edmund Burke, studio of Sir Joshua Reynolds, oil on canvas, circa 1769 or later © National Portrait Gallery, London

p. 115: Map of India in the time of Clive, in Charles Colbeck (ed.), *The Public Schools Historical Atlas*, Longmans, Green & Co. (London, 1905)

p. 116: *Concerto coalitionale*, by James Sayers, etching, published by Thomas Cornell 7 June 1785 © National Portrait Gallery, London

p. 125: *The political-banditti assailing the saviour of India*, by James Gillray, published by William Holland, hand-coloured etching, published by William Holland 11 May 1786 © The Trustees of the British Museum

p. 127: Portrait of Warren Hastings, by John Henry Robinson, after Lemuel Francis Abbott, engraving, 1832 © Getty Images

p. 130: *A View of the Tryal of Warren Hastings Esqr. before the Court of Peers, in Westminster Hall*, by Robert Pollard (etching) and Francis Jukes (aquatint), after Edward Dayes, etching and aquatint, published by Robert Pollard 3 January 1789 © Getty Images

p. 140: *Smelling out a Rat*, by James Gillray, hand-coloured etching, published by Hannah Humphrey 3 December 1790 © The Trustees of the British Museum

p. 157: Portrait of Richard Burke, by James Ward, after Sir Joshua Reynolds, mezzotint, published by James Ward 5 July 1800 © National Portrait Gallery, London

p. 162: *Thoughts on a Regicide Peace*, by James Sayers, etching, published by Hannah Humphrey 14 October 1796 © National Portrait Gallery, London

p. 166: *Promis'd Horrors of the French Invasion*, by James Gillray, hand-coloured etching and aquatint, published by Hannah Humphrey 20 October 1796 © National Portrait Gallery, London

p. 193: Portrait of Edmund Burke, by James Barry, oil on canvas, circa 1771, reproduced by kind permission from the Board of Trinity College Dublin, Ireland

Introduction

EDMUND BURKE IS BOTH the greatest and the most underrated political thinker of the past 300 years. Born in 1730, he came from an extraordinary period in British history, the age of Samuel Johnson, Adam Smith, Edward Gibbon, David Garrick, Joshua Reynolds and David Hume, all of whom were his friends.

Burke was a philosopher-statesman of the first rank, a lifelong campaigner against arbitrary power and injustice, and a fierce champion of fundamental rights and the Anglo-American constitutional tradition. Endlessly lampooned in this, the golden age of caricature, he is nevertheless a figure for the ages. Some understood his greatness at the time: Dr Johnson once remarked that he did not begrudge Burke's being the first man in the House of Commons, for he would be the first man everywhere.

Burke has been all but ignored in recent years, or reduced to a clutch of standard clichés and soundbites. Yet we cannot understand the defects of the modern world today, or modern politics, without him. He is the first great theorist of political parties and representative government, and the first great modern theorist of totalitarian thought. More widely, he offers a compelling critique of what has become known as liberal individualism, and the idea that human well-being is just a matter of satisfying individual wants. To this he joins a perspective with profound implications for many issues now facing policymakers across the globe, including the rise of religious extremism and terror, the atomization of society and loss of social cohesion, the emergence of the corporate state, challenges to the international rule of law, and the nature of revolution itself.

Over his long career Burke fought five great political battles: for
more equal treatment of Catholics in Ireland; against British oppression of the thirteen American colonies; for constitutional restraints
on executive power and royal patronage; against the corporate
power of the East India Company in India; and most famously,
against the influence and dogma of the French revolution. Their
common theme – the inspiration for what W. B. Yeats described
in his poem 'The Seven Sages' as Burke's Great Melody – is his
detestation of injustice and the abuse of power.

In these battles his record of practical achievement was mixed.
He often overreached himself, he rarely exercised real political
power, and he was variously denounced as vainglorious, a blowhard
and an irrelevance. His private life was blighted by debt, which he
was unwilling to relieve by the means of self-enrichment usual for
the time. He offended King George III by his severe criticisms of
royal influence, and by his support for a regency during the King's
period of madness. A man of enormous personal warmth and good
humour, he lost friends and supporters by his near-obsessive insistence on the campaigns of the moment.

Yet in intellectual terms the extraordinary fact is not that Burke
was occasionally wrong, but that he was so often right. Not only
that, he was right for the right reasons – not through luck but
because his powers of analysis, imagination and empathy gave him
an extraordinary gift of prophecy. Thus he anticipated many of the
effects of British rule in Ireland; the loss of the American colonies;
the overreach of the East India Company; and the disastrous consequences of revolution in France. Modern conceptions of social
capital and human well-being have their proper place within his
thought, and his vision of community, free institutions and civic
virtue still has profound and unrecognized implications for politicians today. Lord Randolph Churchill, father of Winston, once
summarized Disraeli's life as 'Failure, failure, failure, partial success,
renewed failure, ultimate and complete triumph.' The same might
be said of Edmund Burke.

There are many reasons for the recent neglect of Burke. He is not an executive politician, like a Pitt or a Peel, and his story is more one of intellect and imagination than of political achievement. His thought is multifarious and scattered across a vast array of pamphlets, speeches and letters, from which it must be quarried by the patient scholar. He is a master of English prose but remains somewhat alienated from current literary or academic debates, in part because he was a working politician, and so perhaps a victim of the distaste that politics often inspires. And he deliberately withholds himself: as he wrote at the age of sixteen to his best friend Richard Shackleton, 'We live in a world in which everyone is on the catch, and the only way to be safe is to be silent, silent in any affair of consequence, and I think it would not be a bad rule for every man to keep within what he thinks of others, of himself, and of his own affairs.' Burke's speeches, his writings and even his letters are notably short on confidences, gossip or personal colour. This is far removed from the modern confessional style.

Moreover, although few more quotable writers have ever existed, Burke himself and his ideas resist brief summary. Even sympathetic readers have seen him as an enigma or a contradiction. They have struggled to understand how he could be both a supporter of the American colonists and a critic of the French revolution; how he could staunchly argue for the established order, yet defend dissenters and Catholics and alienate the Crown; how he could both dismiss abstract rights and insist upon the importance of rights within the rule of law.

For their part, his many critics have accused him of incoherence, hypocrisy, even madness. In particular, for Thomas Paine, and then Karl Marx, Burke is a placeman, a paid propagandist and an apologist for aristocracy and privilege. Such claims were echoed in the twentieth century by the influential historian Lewis Namier and his followers, who generally took a narrow and cynical view of Burke's achievements as a thinker and statesman. Even today, it is striking how much the philosopher Alasdair MacIntyre, for example, owes intellectually to Burke, even while he belittles Burke's ideas. Those who attend to Burke's life often detect inconsistency, because they ignore the deeper consistency of his thought.

But on the other side of the argument such has been Burke's status, especially among conservatives, that his life has regularly been co-opted for political purposes. In the 1830s Disraeli claimed to identify a Tory line of succession including Burke and culminating by implication in himself, only to exclude Burke (and Peel) after he was refused office by Peel in 1841. In the USA, Presidents Woodrow Wilson and Theodore Roosevelt were happy to count Burke their ally, as did a generation of anti-communists during the Cold War and again after the fall of the Iron Curtain. And at a far less exalted level, one way to read the present book is as a modern *Appeal from the Old to the New Whigs* (sic).

Burke has been well served by his biographers over the years, including James Prior and John Morley in the nineteenth century; Philip Magnus, Carl Cone, Russell Kirk, Stanley Ayling and Conor Cruise O'Brien in the twentieth; and most recently F. P. Lock. To them the present volume owes an enormous debt of gratitude, and to Lock's authoritative two-volume study of 1998–2006 in particular. The same is true of the work of many scholars listed in the Acknowledgements, Notes and Bibliography.

This book is not a work of primary research, though it incorporates some important recent discoveries. Rather, it is a personal interpretation of Burke's life and thought, which draws heavily on my own background in philosophy and experience as a working politician. It seeks not merely to present Edmund Burke as a man, and to trace his life against the astonishingly rich tapestry of eighteenth-century society, but to make the case for him as a statesman and thinker. It is short and inevitably selective, and this risks underplaying both conflict and development in Burke's ideas; but its argument is for a deeper coherence. Somewhat unusually, the book is structured in two parts, Life and Thought, so that the interested reader can enjoy his life for its own sake, and engage with Burke's thought with the wider context of his life and society already in hand. My hope is to start to do for Edmund Burke what others have done for Adam Smith over the past thirty years: to recognize him publicly as one of the seminal thinkers of the present age.

The political theorist Harold Laski once said of Burke:

> He brought to the political philosophy of his generation a sense of its direction, a lofty vigour of purpose, and a full knowledge of its complexity, such as no other statesman has ever possessed. His flashes of insight are things that go, as few men have ever gone, into the hidden deeps of political complexity . . . He wrote what constitutes the supreme analysis of the statesman's art.

The purpose of this book is to explain how he came to write it, why it is, and why he and it matter today.

PART ONE

Life

ONE

An Irishman Abroad, 1730–1759

IN THE YEAR 1729 THERE appeared in the city of Dublin a rather
curious publication, by an anonymous author. It did not have the
snappiest of titles: *A Modest Proposal for Preventing the Children of
Poor People in Ireland from Being a Burden to Their Parents or
Country, and for Making Them Beneficial to the Public.* But, its title
apart, in many ways *A Modest Proposal* was the prototype of the
modern policy pamphlet, of a type familiar from present-day think
tanks the world over.

The pamphlet proceeded in the most measured language from
diagnosis to statistical analysis to policy recommendation. Ireland
was then subject to very serious poverty and malnutrition, the
author noted. Careful calculation revealed that the number of new
births far exceeded the level required to replenish the population.
No work existed in handcrafts or agriculture for the mothers, with
the result that the traveller to Dublin found:

> the streets, the roads, and cabin doors crowded with beggars of the
> female sex, followed by three, four, or six children, all in rags and
> importuning every passenger for an alms. These mothers, instead

of being able to work for their honest livelihood, are forced to
employ all their time in strolling to beg sustenance for their helpless infants: who as they grow up either turn thieves for want of
work, or leave their dear native country.

But, the author said, there was a ready-made solution, then as often
now imported from America: 'I have been assured by a very knowing
American of my acquaintance in London, that a young healthy
child well nursed is at a year old a most delicious, nourishing, and
wholesome food, whether stewed, roasted, baked, or boiled; and I
make no doubt that it will equally serve in a fricassee or a ragout.'
Not only were one-year-old children good food; they had other
uses as well: 'Those who are more thrifty (as I must confess the
times require) may flay the carcass; the skin of which artificially
dressed will make admirable gloves for ladies, and summer boots
for fine gentlemen.'

Jonathan Swift's pamphlet is one of the most brilliant sustained
satires in the English language, a masterpiece of moral indignation
which effortlessly ridiculed targets ranging from the new vogue for
statistics to contemporary attitudes towards the poor. But the
economic and social facts he described have never been questioned.

This was, precisely, the Ireland into which Edmund Burke was
born, on Arran Quay by the River Liffey in Dublin, on New Year's
Day 1730. Dublin then was a place of extremes, in which enormous
wealth coexisted with desperate poverty and, frequently, starvation.
Nor were these evils confined to the city. In an essay of 1748, Burke
and some friends indignantly described the condition of the rural
poor at that time: 'Money is a stranger to them . . . as for their food,
it is notorious they seldom taste bread or meat; their diet, in summer,
is potatoes and sour milk; in winter . . . they are still worse, living
on the same root, made palatable by a little salt, and accompanied
by water.' As for what they wore: 'their clothes so ragged . . . nay, it
is no uncommon sight to see half a dozen children run quite naked
out of a cabin, scarcely distinguishable from a dunghill.'

Fortunately the Burkes themselves lived somewhat more comfortably. Edmund was the third of four surviving children, a sometimes neglected position in a family. It may have been so here, for his brothers Garrett and Richard were eldest and youngest, while his elder sister Juliana was the only girl. The Burkes were likely of Anglo-Norman 'Old English' extraction, originally Catholic and not part of the New English ascendancy which took control of Ireland in the seventeenth century. Edmund's father Richard, probably born in County Cork in the south-west, had long since left the land for the city. He was an attorney, a Protestant and a self-made man who had risen in the law through hard work, described by Edmund's friend Richard Shackleton as 'of middling circumstances, fretful temper and punctual honesty'. His wife Mary Nagle was also from County Cork. But otherwise she could hardly have been more different: a Catholic countrywoman from a genteel but much reduced family of landowners. The Nagles were not merely Catholics but Jacobites, who had supported the claims to the throne of James II and his successors after the revolution of 1688, which brought the Protestant William of Orange to the throne as William III. Forty years later most of their land, and much of their dignity, had gone.

By the 1720s Ireland was in name a country, indeed a kingdom, but in reality an English dominion. The functions of state were controlled by Protestants, generally Englishmen, and directed from London. Access to education and opportunities for advancement were similarly restricted. Catholics were barred from the professions, from jury service and from exercising the vote. A host of other laws oppressed them, from owning firearms to controls on inheritance and land ownership. Much of their land had been taken over by Protestant nobility and gentry, who were not offset in influence by a class of yeoman farmers as in England. The result was huge inequalities of wealth and well-being, compounding and in turn compounded by religious hatred and political instability.

Some have suggested that Richard Burke himself was an apostate, one of many who converted in order to get on. But whether or not

it was Richard or one of his forebears who converted, it is evident
that Edmund grew up as the product of a marriage mixed not
merely by religion but by trajectory and class. He and his brothers
Garrett and Richard were raised as Protestants, Juliana as a Catholic.
Protestantism, the city and social aspiration, it seemed, belonged
to the future; Catholicism and rural life to the past. Loyalties must,
then, be divided. This may be one reason why Burke was to develop
such an extraordinary moral imagination, able to reach out at once
in all directions, to comprehend aristocrat and revolutionary,
Catholic and Protestant, underclass and hierarchy alike.

Home life was not easy, for Richard Burke appears to have been
a man of rigid and unyielding disposition. The will he left at his
death is a mass of small-minded bequests and instructions, almost
designed to split the estate and set family members against each
other. He also had a foul temper. 'My dear friend Burke leads a
very unhappy life from his father's temper,' Richard Shackleton
reported in 1747. '. . . He must not stir out at night by any means,
and if he stays at home there is some new subject for abuse.'

Luckily, here too Mary Burke was quite different from her
husband. Little is known about her. But, as scholars have noted,
Burke's references to his mother are always warm and affectionate,
to his father never so. In adult life Burke notably combined high
principle and personal probity with an open, trusting and generous
disposition towards others, though he also knew how to bear a
grudge. Without diving too deep into psychological speculation, it
is not hard to see his father on the one side, his mother on the
other. As a child Burke spent some time recuperating from illness
with his Nagle cousins in the Blackwater Valley in County Cork,
and studied at a rural 'hedge school' in Ballyduff. The Valley was
beautiful country, which made a profound impression on him; it
may also have laid the foundations for his understanding of Gaelic
culture, and his lifelong sympathy with the plight of the Irish
Catholics under the penal laws.

In May 1741 Edmund, then aged eleven, Garrett (fifteen) and

Richard (seven) were sent away to school. Juliana (thirteen) was kept at home with her parents. Edmund had left Dublin previously, to stay with his mother's family in County Cork and get away from the damp and disease of the city. Now he went for an education. His destination was a small non-denominational boarding school in the village of Ballitore, about thirty miles south-west of Dublin. It was run by Abraham Shackleton, a Quaker and the father of Richard Shackleton, who was to become Burke's greatest early friend.

Abraham Shackleton was a remarkable man, who had taught himself Latin at the age of twenty in order to become a school-master. The curriculum was a traditional one, with a strong emphasis on classical languages and literature, and work was taken seriously. Yet it is clear that Burke quickly settled in, and that Shackleton's influence was a sympathetic one, as much moral as intellectual. In 1757, when Burke had moved to London and was building an early reputation as a writer, he thanked his former schoolmaster, saying 'I received the education, that, if I am anything, has made me so.' Still more strikingly, in a poem on Ballitore, Burke paid generous tribute to the older man: 'Whose breast all virtues long have made their home / where Courtesy's stream doth without flattery flow / and the just use of Wealth without the show'. The warmth of these words vividly contrasts with the extant references to Burke's own father, and there is perhaps even a touch of reproof to his father's temper in the second line.

As a non-denominational school run by Quakers, Ballitore was itself a minor study in contrasts. Its influence on Burke was profound. Not in point of doctrine: the Quakers were dissenters, pacifists and abstainers from alcohol, which Burke never was. But he evidently appreciated the plainspokenness and straight dealing he experienced. The egalitarian ethos of the Quakers may also have left its mark with him in later life: in his support for the underdog, in his lifelong willingness to engage intellectually with others, in his hatred of arbitrary power, in his belief that the social order should benefit all. The mature Burke admired the Quakers' commitment to good and active citizenship. While he did not share their opposition to religious hierarchy and priesthood, his arguments for the established Church were notably based more on institutional authority than on revelation to the elect. When Burke came to consider the American revolution in the 1770s, its values and history were things to which he was already instinctively sympathetic.

In 1744 Burke left Ballitore for Trinity College Dublin. Trinity College was then the only institution of higher learning in Ireland, an avowedly Protestant establishment founded by Elizabeth I in 1592 to train clergy for the Church of Ireland. It was smaller than even the smallest universities today, with between 300 and 500 students, more of them headed into the Church than any other profession. The curriculum, based on the medieval *trivium* and *quadrivium*, was divided into 'humanity' (Latin and Greek texts) and 'science' (including mathematics, astronomy, geography and physics, and finally metaphysics and ethics). There were no facilities for social activities or sports within the college.

The average age at entry was sixteen, so that when Burke entered at age fourteen he was among the youngest students in the college. Academically, he performed well but not consistently so. Awarded a scholarship in 1746 after two days of examination on Greek and Latin authors, he was nevertheless ranked only in the top half of the class overall. For assiduity and diligence, he was ranked in the bottom quarter. The reason why is fairly evident: Burke was not happy either at home or at college. Going to Trinity meant, first of all, leaving the Shackletons and returning to the family home, to foul city air and his father's angry moods. In the classroom, he was younger than his fellows, and obviously bored by the often laborious and pedantic teaching. Matters were made worse by his reliance on his father for financial support, support tied to a legal career which held few attractions for him. Many people make the greatest friendships of their lives at university; of the forty or so of Burke's contemporaries who we know studied with him for four years, it seems that none became a good friend while there.

Burke found his outlets elsewhere, in vast amounts of reading, in friendships outside the classroom, and in writing. His sixty surviving undergraduate letters, all to Richard Shackleton, attest to the breadth of his social and literary interests, as well as to his habit of spending three hours a day in the public library. Burke at this time had been seized by what he called a poetical madness or *furor poeticus*. He wanted to become a poet, and seems to have made his literary debut with a satirical poem, probably published in 1747. But he was an omnivorous autodidact, and he used his letters to experiment with new ideas and topics and literary forms, as well as in-jokes, banter and self-analysis, with Richard as a private and supportive audience.

This instinct for self-improvement also led Burke to play a part in setting up two societies at Trinity. Each combined drinking and conviviality with a serious purpose. The first had four members, and focused on the writing of burlesques or parodies, a very popular genre of the time; the second, named absurdly the Academy of Belles Lettres, had seven members and focused on rhetoric and debate. Neither lasted more than a few months. Both evinced Burke's lifelong clubbability, as well as a restless ambition to spread his wings.

Altogether more serious was the *Reformer*. This was a periodical, which ran weekly for thirteen issues in early 1748. Produced by a circle of friends including Burke, it combined essays on diverse topics with articles about the theatre – and in particular the rather controversial local Smock Alley Theatre, which was run by Thomas Sheridan, father of Richard Brinsley Sheridan, the playwright and Burke's later parliamentary colleague and rival. The essays are unsigned except for the teasing initials B, S, U and Æ. But two contributions by Æ are sometimes thought to possess the stamp of the young Burke. One is devoted to the idea of public spirit, and includes a call for more generous patronage of poetry. The second is a vigorous analysis of rural poverty, which highlights and criticizes the extreme inequality of the age, and insists that the

landowning aristocracy must discharge the responsibilities that
come with property. These were, and would remain, characteristically Burkean themes.

Burke graduated from Trinity in February 1748. After that we
know little of his activities for two years or so. Still under intense
pressure to pursue a legal career, he may very well have worked
in his father's office, which will have done nothing to relieve his
spirits. He may also have been sucked into local politics, and in
particular into a fierce controversy stirred up by Charles Lucas,
a radical who stood unsuccessfully in a highly contentious
by-election to the Irish House of Commons. But we simply do
not know for sure.

What we do know is that Burke went to London in 1750, aged
twenty; and that for him, as for Samuel Johnson and so many others,
this was a crucial turning point. Ireland was his birthplace. One way
or another, Ireland would always be in his thoughts. But Burke had
never felt the joy of a settled life there: not with his family, not at
school in Ballitore, not at Trinity. He never lost his Irish accent. But
he returned to Ireland only three times over the next forty-seven
years. London, and England, marked a new beginning.

The London that Burke encountered was by far the largest city in
the British Isles. Its population of more than 600,000 people in
1750 was roughly one-tenth that of England as a whole, and ten
times that of the next-largest city, Bristol. It was a place of squalor
and stench, with huge overcrowding and only the most rudimentary
sanitation. Pigs and fowl often lived in urban cellars. Diseases such
as smallpox, typhoid fever and dysentery were rampant, with periodic outbreaks of influenza. The results were death and deformity,
which hit the urban poor the hardest but left no family untouched.
Barely one child in three survived childhood.

By way of antidote, people turned to gambling, cockfighting and
the like, and above all to drinking gin. The latter, mixed with fruit

cordials, was embraced on such an epic scale that the average annual consumption across the whole of England in 1743 was well over two gallons a head. When Burke arrived in London memories were still fresh of the notorious Judith Defour and, thanks to William Hogarth's print *Gin Lane* (see overleaf), would remain so. It was she who in 1734 had strangled her own two-year-old daughter and sold the new petticoat the girl had been given at the parish workhouse in order to pay for gin. Five Acts of Parliament were required to bring the craze under control.

There was no established police force, and though a widely admired new system of street lighting had been introduced two decades earlier, it was only partially effective. It is not surprising, then, that crime and petty disorder were widespread, arson and looting not unusual. Riots were sometimes seen as a means for an urban underclass to even the score, and could offer rich pickings to people in desperate poverty. Violence lay everywhere below the social surface.

And yet, and yet. Britain was then undergoing what has been called the first sexual revolution, as public and official attitudes softened towards such matters as premarital sex, adultery and prostitution, and new norms of behaviour emerged. In the 1650s barely 1 per cent of births had been outside marriage. By 1800, however, a quarter of first-born children were illegitimate. It was an age of remarkable sexual freedom, and London in 1750 was at the centre of it. In part as a result, the capital saw a burst of sustained population growth that would double its population in three generations.

People did not go to London without good reason, for the city was a place of excitement, wealth and opportunity. It was the metropolis for an early trading empire stretching from Barbados and Boston to Bengal. It was a financial centre that supplied capital and liquidity at low interest rates to Britain's fast-growing entrepreneurial, industrial and commercial classes. It was a crucible of new ideas, and political controversy fuelled by newspaper and pamphlet wars. And like the country as a whole, it was celebrated

on the continent as the home of the liberty of the individual, the land of the theatre and the pub, a place where monarchical authority had been made subject to law and freethinkers could dissent without the endless fear of reprisal. Voltaire had famously asked, 'Why can't the laws that guarantee British liberties be adopted elsewhere?' Why indeed? The contrast with the absolute monarchy and social and religious hierarchies of France was manifest.

Above all, as it grew richer London was ever more a centre for the arts and culture. The British Museum was founded in 1753 as the world's first 'universal museum': a national institution, owned by neither Church nor monarch, open to all at no charge, and dedicated not merely to Britain but to human culture and the world as such. Paintings too were starting to find their way out of the great houses and into the public realm. In 1746 the Foundling Hospital began to show works by contemporary artists, though it would be twenty-three more years before the new Royal Academy could emulate the Paris Salons with its first Summer Exhibition.

Handel's late oratorios date from this period, and his *Music for the Royal Fireworks*, written to celebrate the end of the War of the Austrian Succession, had its first performance in 1749 in Green Park with 12,000 in attendance. The celebrated actor David Garrick took over the Theatre Royal, Drury Lane, in 1747, and made it one of the greatest theatres in Europe. Poems and plays coursed through the city, many of them moralizing parodies and satires, which were enormously popular. The novel, then in its infancy, had recently been galvanized as a literary genre by *Pamela* and *Clarissa*, two works of Samuel Richardson, who had come to London from Derbyshire in 1736; and still more by Henry Fielding's *Tom Jones*, a tale which combined acid social commentary with a self-aware assertion of the value of fiction itself.

Nothing, then, was impossible in London. It was filled at that time with a spaciousness, a sheer energy in human ambition that is hard to imagine even today. The effect on the young Burke, far from home for the first time, must have been overwhelming and electric.

Burke enrolled in the Middle Temple in May 1750. At that time the four Inns of Court were colleges-cum-professional associations, where would-be barristers received instruction in the law. They were a necessary entry-point to a career at both the Irish and the English Bar, and most Irish students opted for the Middle Temple, composing roughly a quarter of its total numbers. The demands were not onerous, and no examination was required to be called to the Bar. Instead, the students needed to eat dinners for eight terms and one vacation, and complete nine exercises, from which they could pay to buy their way out. Most did.

It was a narrow, dry and practical education, requiring scrupulous attention to precedents, and Burke seems to have hated it. A few years afterwards he wrote, 'He that lives in a college, after his mind is sufficiently stocked with learning, is like a man, who having built, rigged, and victualled, a ship, should lock her up in a dry dock.' In a later unfinished essay on the laws of England, he said, 'the study of our jurisprudence presented to liberal and well-educated minds, even in the best authors, hardly anything but barbarous terms, ill explained; a coarse but not a plain expression; an indigested method; and a species of reasoning, the very refuse of the schools'. Nothing could be further removed from his own belief in extensive learning – or from the bustle and energy of the city outside.

But there were three serious drawbacks to his hostility. For the young man with ambition the law was itself a well-trodden path to fame, fortune and social advancement. Moreover, without a legal qualification Burke had no professional direction, or practical means to provide for himself. And finally, a decision to give it up would put him on an emotional and financial collision course with his father. Whatever the tensions between them, Richard Burke had been more than good to his son. He had paid Edmund's way through four years of Trinity College, though this was not strictly necessary for the Bar, and then a further five years in London. He was, in the most literal sense, heavily invested in his son. And what to do instead?

Little wonder, then, that Burke seems from his letters and poems to have had bouts of recurrent ill-health in 1750–2. He recuperated, avoided the big question and saved money by going on extended journeys with a new friend, William Burke. 'Cousin Will' had the same surname as Edmund, but may in fact have been little or no relation at all. He was perhaps a little younger, and had been educated at Westminster School and Christ Church, Oxford, before heading to the Middle Temple and the Bar. Twenty-five years later Burke described Will as someone whom he 'tenderly loved, highly valued, and continually lived with, in an union not to be expressed, quite since our boyish years'. Will was to prove a lifelong friend to Burke, but in many ways a disastrous one: a boon companion and a route to preferment, but also an adventurer, a financial burden and a source of embarrassment and scandal.

All this lay in the future, however. For now, Edmund's travels took him to Bath, then a highly fashionable resort whose spa waters were a magnet for the infirm and well connected, and to Dr Christopher Nugent. Nugent had been an early acquaintance, an Irish Catholic with a medical degree whom Burke may originally have consulted on medical grounds. Like Abraham Shackleton, he was both wise and sympathetic: there is a magnificent painting by James Barry of Nugent as an older man, in which he somehow comes across as at once modest, intensely reflective and yet non-judgemental. Like Shackleton, he exercised a profound and lasting influence on the young Burke, who explicitly credited him as the cause of his recovery in a poem: "Tis now two autumns since he chanced to find / a youth of body broke, infirm of mind / he gave him all that man can ask or give / restored his life and taught him how to live.'

'Taught him how to live' – best of all, Nugent had a daughter in her late teens, Jane, who quickly caught the young man's fancy. Burke was an Irish transplant with literary ambitions, then in the process of alienating his only source of financial support. By no stretch of the imagination could he be described as a catch, not least since Jane was herself a Catholic. He was no Adonis, either, to judge by later pictures; and had no known patrons or social advantages. What he did have was warmth, energy and talent, albeit a talent then confined to his personality, private letters and occasional writings. The beautiful thing is that this was all she needed. It was a love match, and would remain so over forty years of marriage.

Jane herself is hard to glimpse in her own right, then or later. Abraham Shackleton described her rather prosaically as 'a genteel, well-bred woman of the Romish faith [whom Burke married] neither for her religion nor her money, but from the natural impulse of youthful affection and inclination, which guided his choice to an agreeable object, with whom he promised himself happiness in a married state'. Burke himself begins with effortless condescension, in a passage from a eulogy written while they were still courting: 'her stature is not tall. She is not made to be the admiration of everybody, but the happiness of one.' But he soon yields to unfettered admiration: 'She has all the delicacy that does not exclude firmness. She has all the softness that does not imply weakness . . . her voice is a low soft music . . . To describe her body, describes her mind: one is the transcript of the other . . .' And he ends, rather piteously, 'Who can know her, and himself, and entertain much hope? Who can see and know such a creature, and not love her to distraction?' Even by the ironic standards of the time, this is the language of true love.

In 1755 Burke took the momentous decision not to pursue a career at the Bar, deepening the breach with his father, who had supported him quite handsomely to that end. Richard Burke's sense of moral and financial injury was evidently fanned by his son's continuing lack of direction in life. Edmund wrote to his father, 'it grieves me deeply to think that . . . your suffering should be at all increased by anything which looks ill-judged in my conduct . . . In real truth in all my designs I shall have nothing more at heart than to show myself to you and my mother a dutiful, affectionate and obliged son.' Instead he threw himself into writing and thinking, and into forming the social connections necessary to get on in life. He had written essays and perhaps journalism on his long retreats with Will. Now he produced four substantial works in quick succession.

It is not given to us to predict the course of our own existence on Earth; we are forever groping forward. We may look back at our past lives with a clarity that is unachievable in earlier moments, and still more is this true for the biographer, who has the mixed blessing of hindsight. Nevertheless, though Burke can hardly have suspected it, these four early works start to lay out the deep framework within which his later thought takes shape. Each deserves a close examination.

The first of them was *A Vindication of Natural Society, or A View of the Miseries and Evils arising to Mankind from Every Species of Artificial Society, in a Letter to Lord ******** by a late Noble Writer*, published in May 1756. Sometimes ignored or written off as a piece of late juvenilia, the *Vindication* was in every way an extraordinary debut. It was written anonymously, with the goal of attacking the religious ideas of Lord Bolingbroke, whose posthumous collected works had recently appeared. Bolingbroke had been a Secretary of State under Queen Anne, and had negotiated the Treaty of Utrecht in 1713, ending the War of the Spanish Succession, in which the Duke of Marlborough had curbed the territorial ambitions of the French in northern Europe. Notoriously, he was a 'deist' who dismissed claims of religious revelation as mere superstition and regarded the clergy as charlatans. Instead, he argued in favour of 'natural' religion, to which all rational people could in principle have access and without the need for any Church hierarchy.

Burke profoundly disagreed with these views. But rather than confront them openly, he does so indirectly and through irony. On its face, the *Vindication* is a staunch defence of Bolingbroke; underneath, it ridicules his views. Civilization is overrated, the argument ostensibly goes. So-called civilized society has really meant vast slaughter by humans of humans throughout history, the abuse of power, and slavery for the poor and weak. We would, then, be better off as a society in a 'state of nature', without a sovereign authority or civil institutions. As in politics, so in religion: better a return to a pure and natural religion than the dishonesty and exploitation induced by religious sophistication and mysticism. To these Bolingbrokian themes, Burke added a pitch-perfect impersonation of Bolingbroke's imperious authorial voice. Coming at a time when the British constitution and British society were widely admired across Europe, it must have seemed obvious to Burke that readers would get the joke.

Except that many of them didn't. The *Vindication* was generally well received, but some critics thought its arguments entirely sincere. Worse, some saw it as a lost work by Bolingbroke himself; this view was especially popular in America. The misunderstanding was sufficiently marked that Burke felt compelled to add a preface of explanation to the second edition the following year, which made clear that the work was meant ironically. Yet the illusion persisted: even as late as the 1790s, the work was being cast back in his teeth as evidence of inconsistency, while social criticisms that he regarded as fanciful were being taken quite seriously by radical writers.

Nevertheless, the *Vindication* is a remarkable work. It is no more than an extended essay in length. Yet it combines sweeping history with political analysis of despotism, aristocracy and democracy, and mordant satire with vigorous and heartfelt condemnation of social evils. Though it slightly misses its target, it is marked throughout by enormous stylistic flair. Its themes – distrust of abstract thought, celebration of human history and civilization, belief in established institutions – remained with Burke to the end of his life. And as we shall see, its deepest targets were yet to be revealed. This, then, is no mere piece of juvenilia.

The *Vindication* also marked the beginning of a relationship that was to prove very important to the young Burke, with the London bookseller and publisher Robert Dodsley. Dodsley had risen through his writings from domestic service as a footman to become one of the foremost publishers of the day, with a wide circle of friends which included Alexander Pope, Thomas Gray and Samuel Johnson, whose famous *Dictionary* he had helped to finance. He gave Burke a modest fee income from writing, as well as a degree of access to literary London; in return Burke offered him all of his early literary projects, and continued the relationship with his brother James after Dodsley himself retired in 1759.

The next of these projects was to make Burke's early reputation. Again, its title did not spare the typesetter: *A Philosophical Enquiry into the Origin of our Ideas of the Sublime and Beautiful*. But in other ways it was a very different work from the *Vindication*. The *Enquiry* is a study in aesthetics and psychology. What is the source of our emotions, or 'passions'? Why do certain works of art or nature elicit in us the feelings that they do?

Questions of taste, indeed of what if anything 'taste' itself was, fed into and in turn were fed by the rapid spread of British commerce in the early eighteenth century, and the growing international trade in works of art. First debated in ancient times, they had been squarely placed in the public mind by a provocative set of articles by Joseph Addison in 1712 in his influential periodical, the *Spectator*. In the previous year Lord Shaftesbury had argued that taste was a kind of internal sense, which operated as naturally and immediately as the external sense of sight: it was impossible to see something beautiful and not see it, naturally and immediately, *as* beautiful. Addison took the opposite tack. For him taste was the result of judging what arises in the imagination, for example when seeing material objects such as landscapes or human bodies. The effect of these contrasting views is that Shaftesbury has difficulty explaining how material objects can be beautiful in themselves, independently of any mind to judge them so. In contrast, Addison struggles to show why, if material objects are beautiful, the imagination is necessary for them to be seen as such.

In the following decade these questions were taken up by the great Irish-Scottish philosopher Francis Hutcheson, who defended and extended a version of Shaftesbury's theory of inner sense. Shaftesbury, Addison, Hutcheson . . . these were no inconsiderable figures. And as even these brief descriptions hint, aesthetics is a notoriously difficult and slippery subject, beset by conceptual ambiguity and by the simple fact that different people often have different tastes, and that these can change over time: in the words of the late, great S. J. Perelman, 'de gustibus . . . ain't what dey used to be'. So it was brave in the extreme for Burke at the age of twenty-seven to venture into print on this topic. Still more so when one reflects that the work had apparently been completed four years earlier, at the tender age of twenty-three. The *Enquiry* is not a deeply philosophical work. But it had great influence at the time, has been widely read ever since, and develops themes that last long in Burke's own thought.

In tone, the work is quite unlike the *Vindication*. Gone is the mock-ironic, the hint of sneer. Instead we have Burke speaking directly to us, in a measured, engaging and sometimes intimate way. He proceeds from common experience, offering conclusions in a semi-scientific spirit, diffidently or confidently as evidence and intuition demand. He offers, not a rehash of previous work, but a positive theory of his own. And there is the occasional moment of (possibly inadvertent) humour: one of the book's many sections is magnificently entitled 'Proportion not the Cause of Beauty in Vegetables'.

Overall, the tone is quietly assured. It is evident to Burke that humans have a certain nature of their own, for they are commonly struck in the same circumstances by the same pains or pleasures, the same 'passions', feelings and emotions. They take pleasure alike in the smell of a rose, or feel pain from a violent blow, for example. Central to aesthetic judgements and the feelings that accompany them, for Burke as for Addison, is the recreative imagination: the imagination that allows its owner to re-experience all the feelings of a moment, or to extend experience into an understanding of new things and places and people. But Burke does not restrict the imagination to visible objects, and so sidesteps the earlier objection to Addison's account: on the contrary, he is keenly aware of the functioning of the different senses, of touch and smell and taste as well as sight and hearing, and deliberately goes beyond the visual arts to discuss poetry and music, for example.

Burke also improves on Addison by focusing on just two great types of passion: the sublime and the beautiful. These are grounded respectively for him in two basic human instincts, given by God through the workings of providence: the instinct for self-preservation, and the instinct for love. The sublime is what elicits awe or terror or fear. Its marks include enormity, infinity and indistinctness, but also power and the capacity to inflict pain. When humans encounter the sublime directly, be it in an earthquake or a snake, they naturally turn away and seek refuge. But when they encounter it indirectly or at a distance, as in a work of art or in imagination, they can be amazed and delighted. They can be astonished, or aroused to action, by language, poetry and rhetoric.

If the sublime intimidates, the beautiful attracts. Beauty is described by Burke as 'a social quality'; it is not simply what elicits lust between the sexes, but the expression of a social preference for a relationship with a particular mate. More widely, it includes the emotions and instincts that bring people together in general society: these are sympathy, imitation and ambition, again implanted by providence in order to bring human capacities to their fullest expression.

Much of this is speculative and tendentious, to say the least. But through it we can clearly glimpse the writer himself. It would be hard to miss a young man's yearning in passages like this: 'Observe that part of a beautiful woman where she is perhaps the most beautiful, about the neck and breasts; the smoothness; the soft-ness . . . the deceitful maze through which the eye slides giddily, without knowing where to fix, or whither it is carried.' Or later, in considering how the body is physically affected by love:

> The head reclines something on one side; the eyelids are more closed than usual, and the eyes roll gently with an inclination to the object, the mouth is a little opened, and the breath drawn slowly, with now and then a little sigh: the whole body is composed, and the hands fall idly to the sides. All this is accompanied with an inward sense of melting and languor.

This reads more like an erotic novel than a work of philosophy. It is little surprise that the book was later attacked by Mary Wollstonecraft, the great eighteenth-century feminist, for perpetuating a weak and feeble stereotype of women.

The *Enquiry* was published anonymously in 1757, and sold well enough in the right circles for Burke to become quickly and widely known as its author. It became something of a text on the sublime, in succession to the ancient critic Longinus. As a work of aesthetics it impressed one of the great intellectuals and critics of the eighteenth-century, Gotthold Lessing, and two of the greatest thinkers of all time, Immanuel Kant and Adam Smith. It may also have partly provoked William Gilpin into developing his own notion of the picturesque, which combined the sublime and the beautiful in art and nature, an idea which became wildly fashionable later in the century.

But what is perhaps still more striking is that even at this very early stage the *Enquiry* again lays out in embryo an array of themes always later to be identified with Burke. Humans have a distinctive nature, which is not purely subjective but governed by certain general laws; indeed, they are social animals heavily driven by instinct and emotion. The testimony of ordinary people is often of greater value than that of experts. Human passions are guided by empathy and imagination. Human well-being is grounded in a social order whose values are given by divine providence. Human reason is limited in scope, and insufficient as a basis for public morality. There may also be a hint here that, in the words of the American thinker Leo Strauss, 'good order or the rational is the result of forces which do not lend themselves to good order or the rational'. People cannot reason themselves into a good society, for a good society is rooted not merely in reason but in the sentiments and the emotions; this was to prove a crucial precursor to Burke's critique of the French revolution in the 1790s. Overall, then, a coherent, persuasive and strikingly modern set of ideas is already taking shape.

The years 1756–9 were a time in which Burke poured forth a profusion of different writings, mostly unfinished, under his developing relationship with Robert Dodsley. Despite some missed deadlines, these mark his transition from a writer from inspiration to a writer from demand, from something of an intellectual dilettante to a seasoned professional able to master a body of knowledge and set down his views quickly and cogently. They also required prodigious amounts of reading and reflection, deepening an already capacious personal reservoir of knowledge which was to serve Burke well in future years. It has been rightly said that political parties are elected when they are full of ideas, and turned out of office when those ideas run out. In Burke's case, though he was only twice briefly in office, the ideas never did run out.

The next of his early works was *An Account of the European Settlements in America* (1757), in collaboration with his friend Will Burke. This was history and polemic, with a highly topical purpose. British foreign policy since time immemorial could be summarized as the desire to inhibit the emergence and restrain the actions of successive superpowers in mainland Europe, in particular Spain and latterly France under Louis XIV and his successors. Throughout the century the French and British had repeatedly clashed in their colonial expansions, from India to the West Indies to North America. In 1755 the uneasy peace of Aix-la-Chapelle broke down entirely, with the disastrous failure of an expedition by the British commander-in-chief General Braddock to capture Fort Duquesne, in modern-day Pittsburgh. In May of the following year war was formally declared between France and Britain. It would shortly spread across the globe, in what became known as the Seven Years War.

The *Account* summarized the prevailing state of knowledge about the European colonies in North America, covering their history, ethnography, geography, differing cultures and economic conditions. Inevitably, it was a compendium. But it also made an argument: well-regulated colonies mattered to Britain, and by implication were worth fighting for. Not only that: the fading Spanish Empire was less to be feared than French ambition and expansionism. Indeed the fate of the Dutch and Spanish empires gave, the authors held, an object lesson in what not to do. Having taken control of vast swathes of South America, the Dutch and Spanish had largely milked their territories for cash, extracting their immediate mineral resources rather than building sustainable colonies with proper infrastructure and orderly relations with local people. Their leaders had grossly abused their powers through self-enrichment. The result was colossal short-term wealth, followed by odium, failure and decline. Overall, the policy was trenchantly dismissed: 'In government, tyranny; in religion, bigotry; in trade, monopoly.'

The Burkes' own position combined free trade with a belief in the social order and an emphasis on institution-building. Monopolies were to be avoided and oligopoly discouraged. Regulation and economic incentives should be set to enhance the public good over the long term. Promising infant industries could properly be supported by public subsidy while they were being established. The colonies should be encouraged to specialize, and develop compet-itive advantage where they could; and they should be allowed to export in their own right to foreign markets. But they should continue to be prevented from importing, in order to protect Britain's status as the source of higher-value finished goods.

We do not know the exact division of labour of the *Account*. It has been suggested that most of the hard work, and in particular that of compilation and summary, was done by Will, while its intellectual thrust, shape and power of generalization came from Edmund. But this may well be unfair, since Will was evidently no intellectual slouch. What we can say is that it too contributes to the body of Burkean ideas so far advanced in the *Vindication* and *Enquiry*. We have a common human nature, the *Account* avers; peoples differ crucially in their history, character and manners; what institutions and culture they develop make a huge difference to their well-being and success; the Christian religion is generally a civilizing force; great leaders are marked by their capacity for hard work and unselfish public service; divine providence creates opportunity, and the chance for failure to redeem itself.

The *Account* was a success. It ran through several editions and was translated into Italian, French and German. It also gave William a start in life, and he was appointed in 1759 to the British administration in the recently captured island of Guadeloupe, where he began an ill-starred and occasionally illegal career as a fortune-hunter. Edmund, meanwhile, had moved on to the last of his early literary projects for the Dodsleys. Having demonstrated a talent for historical writing in the *Vindication* and the *Account*, he now aspired to write nothing less than a short history of England – in under two years.

The first half of the century had seen at least five multi-volume narrative histories of England. Yet the feeling persisted that genius was somewhat lacking in this area, especially compared to the French and Italian masters, and that what was needed was a shorter treatment combining depth and accuracy. The philosopher David Hume – later well known to Burke – had started to meet the first requirement in 1754, and would soon be acclaimed for it. But his *History* was a massive affair in six volumes. Burke now proposed something radically different: just one-quarter as long, balancing narrative with analysis, and eschewing vast reams of scholarly research on the one hand and Bolingbrokian speculation on the other.

In this, as in much else, he was heavily influenced by the French thinker Montesquieu, in his words 'the greatest genius, which has enlightened this age'. Montesquieu argued that history was governed by general causes, constrained by 'the nature of things', be that physical geography or human custom and law. The result was an approach which emphasized key themes working themselves out through time, illuminated by carefully chosen examples. The experimental nature of Burke's work may be hinted at in its title, *An Essay towards an Abridgement of English History*. But the book was never completed. It extends only as far as 1216, the passage of Magna Carta and the death of King John; and it was not published until 1812, some time after Burke's death.

Even so, the *History* is of great interest and value in understanding Burke. Its shape is broadly chronological, surveying in turn the ancient Britons, the Romans, Saxons and Normans. Each of them is treated in terms of their distinctive institutions and character or 'genius'. This gives the work an occasional touch of *1066 and All That*, of post-hoc-propter-hoc-ism in which historical contingency and luck are downplayed in favour of predestination and 'the English story'.

But the *History* is kept from this, or, worse, from the trite or pedestrian, by its many saving graces. One grace lies in its stylistic brio, starting from the opening chapter, which sweeps the reader majestically across the main facts of Europe's geography and their relation to its history. Another lies in Burke's flair for journalistic colour and the telling detail. A third lies in its deep engagement and sympathy with the cultures under examination, including those underplayed by others; thus Burke discusses at length the customs and institutions of the ancient Britons, paying particular attention to the Druids, 'the priests, lawgivers, and physicians of their nation'. Infusing the whole is a dynamic, emergent Whiggish sense of liberty.

And it is extraordinary to record that, even at this early stage, Burke is already exploring ideas about political parties in the *History* that he does not publish until 1770, as we shall see.

The *History* is also marked by Burke's insistence once again on the importance of providence, allowing him to avoid the intellectual trap of treating Montesquieu's historical laws as deterministic certainties. And then there is the sheer persuasiveness of the book's deeper argument. English history, English culture and English law did not begin with the Normans, the rest being dark ages; nor indeed with the Romans; the English are thus a heterogeneous and mixed people; in general, institutions matter more than individuals; custom, habit and manners are distinct from law, and often superior to reason; the present and future are conditioned, though not determined, by the past. These are, already, familiar and distinctively Burkean themes.

In the *Enquiry*, Burke had written, 'Those which engage our hearts, which impress us with a sense of loveliness, are the softer virtues; easiness of temper, compassion, kindness and liberality; though certainly these are of less immediate and momentous concern to society, and of less dignity. But it is for that reason that they are so amiable.' This is Jane Nugent to the life, as one might expect in an essay on beauty and the emotions, written in early courtship. Edmund and Jane had married in March 1757. Jane's Catholicism cannot have pleased Edmund's father, but the couple adopted the Anglican rites for the marriage ceremony.

In the following year, the Burkes had two children, Richard in February and Christopher in December. Christopher's namesake Dr Nugent had decided to move to London, and this probably helped them to establish a home together – first in Battersea, in those days a village on the southern outskirts of London, and then on Wimpole Street. Wimpole Street now lies in the centre of London. At that time it was on the northern edge, with open fields beyond. Burke always loved the countryside, and may have deemed it healthier for his young children. The household waxed and waned. As well as immediate family, for several years it included Dr Nugent and his son Jack. Edmund's brother Richard also lived for long periods with him and Jane, as did Will Burke between his travels. There was, in addition, a never-ending stream of visitors and house guests.

Burke now had a wife, a family, a home, and a burgeoning literary reputation. What he did not have was an income. The *Vindication* and the *Enquiry* attracted modest fees; he and Will shared £50 for the copyright of the *Account*; and the *History* would have earned £300 if it had been completed (though in fact the project petered out in 1762). But these were small sums, at a time when a gentleman aspired to live on not less that £300 a year. More was needed, and rapidly.

Accordingly, he turned in two directions: to journalism and, less directly, to public life. In April 1758 Burke contracted with the Dodsleys to edit, write for and produce the *Annual Register*. Over the previous decades there had been an explosion in newspapers and print journalism, first dailies and more recently monthlies with the launch of the *Gentleman's Magazine* and the *London Magazine* in the 1730s. Various annuals had also been published, epitomizing each year's events. The *Annual Register* attempted something new: not merely to be an authoritative and highly readable account of the year, but to add to that documentary record a wide range of other material of general interest. Its first part thus comprised a long piece of instant history, describing the main events of the year and placing them in a wider context, and a diary containing factual material culled from the newspapers, including births and deaths, speeches by the King, summaries of Acts of Parliament, and human-interest stories.

The distinctive second part was more lively. It included scientific reports, reviews, essays, poetry, history, health and how-to tips, recent discoveries, archaeology and 'Characters' – character sketches

of contemporary and historical figures, short biographies and anecdotes. Controversy was not sought out, but there was no attempt
at balance for the sake of it. Some of the new material may not
have been by Burke himself, but as editor he controlled the whole.
The *Register* was, and was intended to be, thought-provoking,
eclectic, lively and extremely wide-ranging – an extension of Burke's
own mind. It was a success from the first. Despite some gaps, and
even a period with two competing versions, it is still published
today.

For Burke himself, however, the *Register* was a mixed blessing.
It paid a salary of £100 a year, which was badly needed, but not
enough for any real security. It gave him editorial experience, and
a position, but not one of any great public dignity or status. And
it immersed him in current events, though it proved to be hard
work over the seven years in which he was operationally in charge.
Yet it had other clear virtues. It allowed him to build up a small
team of friends and supporters, including in later years Walker
King and French Laurence, who became his editors and literary
executors. It enabled him to spread his ever-expanding moral and
intellectual sensibility over a vast range of British and European
thought, including Samuel Johnson, Adam Smith, the Scottish
philosopher Thomas Reid, Rousseau, Voltaire and his beloved
Montesquieu, as well as a host of lesser names. And finally it gave
him further modest currency within literary, and in time polite,
society.

It was at about this time, probably in 1759, that Burke took his
first tentative steps towards the world of politics. His entrée was
via an introduction to William Gerard Hamilton. Hamilton was
just a year older than Burke. Educated at Harrow, Oriel College
Oxford and Lincoln's Inn, he had inherited a large fortune and
been elected to Parliament for Petersfield in 1754. He has gone down
in parliamentary lore as 'single-speech' Hamilton, after his maiden
speech in 1755 on the Address, the speech from the throne which
always opens a new session of Parliament. But this epithet does

Hamilton an injustice: he in fact made a second speech, his last, the following year.

In an age where the parliamentary gene pool was small and social position much admired, Hamilton had successfully attached himself to Henry Fox, who had hugely enriched himself as Paymaster of the Forces. Through Fox, Hamilton was quickly appointed to serve under Lord Halifax at the Board of Trade. An ambitious man, he was looking for a secretary and personal assistant, and engaged Burke to that end, probably on a salary of £300 or so a year. That was three times Burke's salary from the *Register*.

At a stroke, then, the arrangement provided a good income and insight into the heart of government. All was set fair; the storms were to follow.

TWO

In and Out of Power, 1759–1774

THE BRITAIN TOWARDS WHOSE SUMMIT Burke now set his course was a country in a state of extraordinary excitement. Politically, it had enjoyed a remarkable degree of stability for over forty years, stability established and personified in the formidable figure of Sir Robert Walpole, now generally regarded as its first Prime Minister, and sustained by his immediate successors. Walpole was a Whig: that is, one of those who supported the constitutional monarchy established after the Glorious Revolution of 1688–9, in which the Catholic James II had fled into exile, and Parliament had confirmed William of Orange from the Netherlands as King William III. On the other side of the political divide were the Tories, the landowners who supported James II and his successors, and who generally defended the prerogative rights of the Crown.

Personal pre-eminence in Westminster was nothing new, but in Sir Robert Walpole it found perhaps its greatest ever exponent. He was a man of enormous political subtlety and energy, a master of detail dedicated to three simple ends: the extension of British trading influence and economic strength; his own complete control of the different organs of government; and the continued political defeat of the Tories.

These three goals Walpole amply achieved. War was in general avoided, the national debt reduced, taxes kept low and colonial trade managed to the benefit of the mother country. After the death of Queen Anne in 1714 Toryism went into a long decline; discredited by the Jacobite rebellion of the following year, it started to collapse, yielding to what came to be known as the Whig supremacy, a process only enhanced by a second failed rebellion in 1745. It was far from inactive, bubbling away in town and country, in the constituencies and in Parliament. But only in 1760 did it start to reappear in government.

In 1720 the South Sea Company, which held the monopoly of trade with South America, collapsed amid a frenzy of financial speculation. In the aftermath it became clear that there had been rampant bribery and insider trading in its shares. Many establishment figures were touched by the scandal, which extended to members of the Cabinet; Walpole himself had invested latterly with reckless enthusiasm, but had managed to escape censure and financial ruin. Having served a few years earlier as First Lord of the Treasury, ultimately in charge of the nation's finances, he was appointed to that post again in April 1721 and set about consolidating his personal power. Supported by the immense wealth of the Duke of Newcastle, he was able to place himself at the centre of a vast network of influence stretching from King George I – and his mistresses – to the Church of England, the City of London and many of the great families. This influence was maintained after the accession of George II in 1727.

Walpole made it his settled principle that every appointment to Church or state, however insignificant, should be conditional on loyalty to Walpole himself. Where patronage did not suffice, bribes and electoral sweeteners were deployed instead, on a prodigious scale. A famous caricature of the period, *Idol-worship, or the Way to Preferment* (opposite), shows him astride a great gateway and baring a pair of enormous buttocks, which men line up to kiss before going through. There was no need even to show Walpole's face, so clear was the inference.

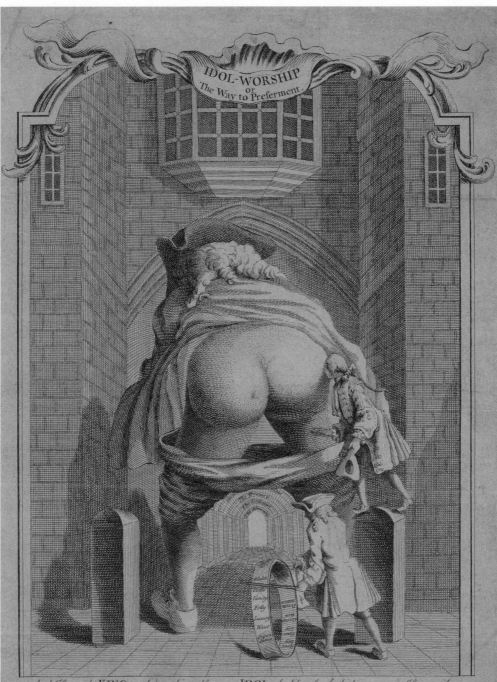

IDOL-WORSHIP
or
The Way to Preferment.

And Henry the **KING** *made unto himself a great* **IDOL**, *the likeness of which was not in Heaven above, nor in the Earth beneath; and he reared up his Head unto ỹ Clouds, & extended his Arm over all ỹ Land; His Legs also were as ỹ Posts of a Gate, or as an Arch stretched forth over ỹ Doors of all ỹ Publick Offices in ỹ Land, & whosoever went out, or whosoever came in, passed beneath, & with Idolatrous Reverence lift up their Eyes, & kissed ỹ Cheeks of ỹ Postern.*

Walpole did not cease to exercise political influence after he left office in 1742; his machine lived on through Newcastle and his brother Henry Pelham. But the increasing need for vigorous leadership in the Commons brought an energetic Whig politician, William Pitt, to the fore. Unlike those of Walpole and his successors, Pitt's family connections were only distantly aristocratic. The family fortune had been made with the East India Company by his grandfather, Thomas Pitt, a governor of Madras whose discovery and sale of an enormous diamond caused him to be known as 'Diamond' Pitt. William was close to his grandfather, and imbibed from him the lessons that Britain's greatness relied on aggression in controlling overseas trade and colonial expansion, and that nothing was impossible to an individual of outstanding personality and energy.

Over time, and despite frequent bouts of illness, Pitt made himself into such an individual: an orator of extraordinary power able to instil in his audience, and in the country at large, the conviction that his was the voice of destiny. Reckless, insecure, bombastic, capable of manic bouts of work lapsing into frequent periods of lassitude, Pitt was determined to exercise power not through any faction or network, but in his own name and through sheer force of personality.

Pitt joined the government in 1746, over the deep objections of George II, and in due course became an ostentatiously upright Paymaster General. His moment came in 1756, when the calamitous early stages of the Seven Years War, and in particular the loss of Minorca to the French, thrust him to centre stage. His famous, and utterly characteristic, remark to the Duke of Devonshire dates from this time: 'My Lord, I am sure that I can save this country, and that no-one else can.' Astonishingly, Pitt made good this claim. He took personal control of the war, targeting overseas trade, and French trade in particular, across four theatres: the West Indies, North America, Africa and India. Each saw vigorous action. An alliance with Prussia on the European mainland freed up British troops to support the navy in Pitt's 'blue water' strategy. French plans to invade Britain were cut off by a blockade of their fleets in Brest and Toulon.

The year 1759 proved to be one colossal triumph after another, for Britain and for the Great Commoner, as Pitt was now known. Guadeloupe was captured, and Dakar. French Canada fell to General James Wolfe after a brilliant night attack on Quebec. Sweetest of all, the French navy was at last forced to put to sea. The Toulon fleet was destroyed by Admiral Boscawen, that of Brest by Admiral Hawke off Quiberon. The country rejoiced. 'Our bells are quite worn threadbare from ringing for victories,' wrote Horace Walpole, son of Sir Robert and man of letters, late in the year. Pitt, it seemed, could do no wrong.

But military triumph was succeeded by political instability. In 1760 King George II died, and – his son Frederick having died unexpectedly in 1751 – his grandson ascended the throne as George III. The new King was young, restless, highly judgemental and widely suspected of being under the malign influence of the Earl of Bute. He shared with Pitt a desire to govern without the need for party or faction. But the two men had fallen out some time earlier, and it was only a matter of time before Pitt departed, as he did in 1761. Nine further years of political turmoil and turnover in government were to follow.

Among the King's early changes, Lord Halifax was moved from the Board of Trade and sent to Dublin as Lord Lieutenant of Ireland. William Hamilton accompanied him, now promoted to Chief Secretary; and with him went Burke, leaving the family to follow later. It was Burke's first trip home since leaving Ireland in 1750, and he cannot have relished seeing his father again. To soften the blow, he sent him a copy of the *Enquiry* via an intermediary, and received back a message of thanks and forgiveness, and even a remittance. But the wound was never to heal fully, for Richard Burke died before seeing his son again. It was a sad ending to their relationship, but perhaps a relief as well.

Burke's stay in Dublin was unremarkable, except for an outbreak of rural terrorism by a group known as the Whiteboys, after their white smocks. These protests arose from poverty and protest at high rents and arbitrary evictions. Initially non-violent, Whiteboy tactics were hardened by the scale and savagery of the response by Protestant landlords and the Dublin authorities, which sent in a force of militiamen. This killed some protesters and captured others. It was followed by what was widely seen as the judicial murder of the main suspects by hanging. This was Burke's first exposure to organized protest and its violent suppression, and his sympathies were heavily on the side of the Catholic underclass. All the more so since the victims included Father Nicholas Sheehy, an opponent of the penal laws and relative of Burke's by marriage, who was tried three times in relation to the Whiteboys and finally hanged, drawn and quartered in 1766.

In 1763 Hamilton was promoted again, this time to the valuable sinecure of Chancellor of the Exchequer of Ireland. For his part Burke accepted a grant, or 'pension', of £300. His feelings were equivocal, however, combining gratitude to Hamilton with a chafing desire to maintain a degree of independence. Pensions were common, but almost always regarded as the result of political corruption and patronage, still more so since the jobbery of Walpole (one of Dr Johnson's *Dictionary* definitions of a pensioner is 'a slave of state hired by a stipend to obey his master'). What made things worse was that Burke's pension was on the Irish Exchequer, not the English, at a time when such pensions were a particular focus of grievance among Irish politicians, including some of his own friends. Burke knew well how little his countrymen could afford him; and claims of undue Irish influence, indeed of popery and Jesuitry, were to dog him later in public life.

In retrospect, it was inevitable that Burke and Hamilton would split. Their personalities were quite different: Burke passionate, committed and warm, Hamilton cool, indolent and sarcastic. Burke was blossoming, Hamilton controlling. Matters were not helped when Hamilton fell out with his new Lord Lieutenant, the Earl of Northumberland, and was dismissed in May 1764. On returning to Ireland he appears to have sought to retain Burke under an exclusive lifetime contract of service. Burke, who had greatly disapproved of Hamilton's conduct in Ireland, rejected the offer as 'a sort of domestic situation' and resigned his pension. Nothing could be more rebarbative than such a role to his free-ranging mind, need for self-expression and nascent political ambitions. By February 1765, amid some rancour, they had parted.

Always prickly about his personal integrity, after the breach with Hamilton Burke felt it necessary to circulate a note among his friends clearing himself of any fault, but setting terms for them as well: 'I never can . . . submit to any sort of compromise on my Character; and I shall never therefore look upon those, who after hearing the whole story, do not think me *perfectly* in the right, and do not consider Hamilton as an infamous scoundrel, to be in the smallest degree my friends.' At a time when personal reputation counted for much, laying out the facts may have seemed only prudent. It had a theoretical basis too, in Burke's developing view that party and political leadership were properly anchored in good character. But it was also unfair to Hamilton, neurotic and alienating. As he grew older, Burke's own essential goodness would shine through on many occasions. But under pressure of events his belief in it would harden into unconquerable self-righteousness, and occasionally self-deception. He gained devotees, but lost many would-be friends and political allies as a result.

All this was in the future, however. For the most part, Burke's friendships at this time were flourishing. Ability and luck had brought him to the very heart of one of the greatest gatherings of talent ever witnessed. This included the Scottish philosopher, historian and notorious infidel David Hume, who on a visit to London gave Burke a copy of the *Theory of Moral Sentiments* by his friend Adam Smith. Burke responded with a letter of thanks to Smith and published a very favourable review in the *Annual Register*, leading to an acquaintance. Then there was the painter Joshua Reynolds, later to found the Royal Academy, who was an intimate of Burke's for more than three decades. He in turn presented Burke with a portrait of their close mutual friend, the actor David Garrick, then leading a revolution to replace bombast and declamation in the theatre with more realistic styles of acting.

But the centre of literary debate would in time become Dr Johnson's Club, or simply 'the Club'. In general, it has been well said that the eighteenth century was the age of the club. There were clubs to meet almost every conceivable social need, personal interest or human contingency. If Joseph Addison is to be believed, they included clubs for the surly, the ugly and the flatulent; and even a Lunatick Club set up by a group of Essex farmers, which met at the full moon. And there was a roster of clubs catering to aristocratic debauch. One such was the infamous Hellfire Club, another 'the Most Ancient and Most Puissant Order of the Beggar's Benison and Merryland, Anstruther', an all-male sex club much patronized by the lawyers, businessmen and clergy of Fife, and in particular by the Earls of Kellie. The clue is in the title, 'Merryland' being a popular codeword for the female body.

Despite its perennial association with Dr Johnson, the Club seems in fact to have been the inspiration of Reynolds. Founded in early 1764, it was devoted to conversation, and met originally every two weeks at the Turk's Head tavern in Soho, in the centre of London. Its nine founding members spanned the arts and included, as well as Burke and Reynolds (known as 'Romulus', after the founder of Rome), Burke's congenial father-in-law Dr Nugent, the Irish playwright and fellow Trinity alumnus Oliver Goldsmith, the music critic Charles Burney, the classical scholar Bennet Langton and of course Samuel Johnson himself. A print by George Thompson

(after James William Edmund Doyle; see previous page) of a literary party at Sir Joshua Reynolds's house in 1781 doubtless conveys something of the atmosphere: Johnson is holding forth to Burke, watched by Reynolds and Garrick. Burney and the Corsican patriot Pasquale Paoli look on. Boswell, Goldsmith and the poet Thomas Warton have been relegated to the background.

Even among the members of the Club, Johnson was a towering figure, in height and presence and accomplishment. The self-made son of a Lichfield bookseller, he had survived low birth weight, scrofula, smallpox and tuberculosis – maladies which scarred his features, left him partially deaf and blind and gave him a disturbing array of tics and convulsive gestures – to become one of the greatest men of letters of that or any age. There are, it has been noted, few literary genres to which Johnson did not make a foundational contribution, including journalism, fiction, poetry, criticism, satire, biography, the essay, travel writing and, of course, lexicography. But it was the publication of his *Dictionary of the English Language* in 1755 that turned him into a nationally celebrated figure.

Johnson had met Burke some years later, and clearly enjoyed the latter's flood of conversation, saying 'he does not talk from a desire of distinction, but because his mind is full'. The relationship matured over time, so much so that Johnson was apt to repeat that 'If a man were to go by chance at the same time with Burke, under a shed, to shun a shower, he would say: "This is an extraordinary man." If Burke should go into a stable to see his horse dressed, the ostler would say, "we have had an extraordinary man here."' It was a handsome tribute, especially since Johnson was no flatterer.

Nevertheless, the relationship between Johnson and Burke was never an entirely easy one. It was not helped by political differences – Johnson was a devout Tory, Burke a Whig – or by the sometimes scheming James Boswell, who oscillated between the quest for political favours from Burke and the gossip's tendency to retail

Johnson's occasionally cutting private remarks. No, the two men had different styles: Johnson possessed of a lapidary wit and a natural genius for quotation, Burke more prolix, carefully building up comic or tragic detail in his speeches to devastating effect. And as so often with two big beasts at the table, there was perhaps an undercurrent of competition. As an out-of-sorts Johnson once said, 'That fellow calls forth all my powers. Were I to see Burke now, it would kill me.'

But Burke's connections were increasingly social and political, as well as literary. They included several opposition Whig politicians, including William Fitzherbert and Lord John Cavendish, the charismatic Charles Townshend and the Buckinghamshire landowner Lord Verney, to whom Will Burke had become very close. In 1763 an ill-starred ministry led by the Earl of Bute had finally fallen, over the supposedly concessionary terms of the Peace of Paris which ended the Seven Years War, and George III was forced to treat with two men he detested, George Grenville and the Duke of Bedford. Two years later the political merry-go-round took another turn, and they too left office. For his part, Pitt remained disenchanted and aloof. The King then asked the Marquis of Rockingham, as leader of a large parliamentary faction, to form an administration, with Newcastle alongside him and the Duke of Cumberland acting as the King's *éminence grise*.

Burke must have been at a low ebb at this time, for his second son Christopher died between the ages of five and six, probably in 1764. We know virtually nothing about the circumstances of his death, but its effect can only have been to focus Burke's love and attention on his surviving boy, Richard. Still more so if, as seems possible from Burke's letters, Jane then had a miscarriage, and perhaps even another. The couple may have been coming to the very sad conclusion that there would be no more children.

But the effect of Rockingham's elevation was to hand Burke the first of two huge strokes of luck. Rockingham had only just engaged him as his private secretary, despite the protestations of the aged Duke of Newcastle, who denounced Burke in soon-to-be familiar terms as a closet Catholic and a Jacobite. But Rockingham ignored the Duke, and Burke was thus catapulted from near-obscurity into the very cockpit of power. The new administration took office on 15 July 1765, and Burke started work the following day.

The second bit of luck was better still, for Will generously waived his own political ambitions temporarily and persuaded Lord Verney to allow Edmund to stand for Parliament for Wendover, a 'pocket borough' in Verney's personal gift. For Burke, the way was now clear to a political career.

The new government's first priority concerned the American colonies. For decades, these had been allowed to prosper in an atmosphere – it would be too much to call it a policy – of more or less benign neglect. The exception was trade. Colonial affairs, in America as elsewhere, were managed along strictly mercantile lines: the colonies existed to generate raw materials and import finished goods, the mother country to manufacture those finished goods and derive the extra value thereby added, the goods themselves always to be carried in British ships. The counterpart of this trade was that American merchants were perennially short of hard currency, and so perennially indebted to financiers in the City of London. From a British perspective, it was an immensely convenient and lucrative arrangement, sustained by each side's general ignorance of the other.

But events now conspired to change this. Over the course of the century, the modest American colonial population of some 200,000 had doubled, then doubled again, and again. By 1765 it stood at not quite 2,000,000. It had been swelled by immigration, much of which was not English, but Scottish, Irish, French and German, to say nothing of those at the margins of society seeking to escape the law or gain a new life. Thomas Paine would later be one of these, emigrating to America in 1774. Many of the new immigrants felt no great love for the Westminster Parliament.

The Seven Years War had ended in triumph for Britain, and the further extension of its early colonial empire around the world. In the long term, this would bring vast profits. But the war's immediate effect was a drastic depletion of the Treasury. The national debt nearly doubled, from £70 million to £130 million. Taxes, totalling some 15 per cent on a country gentleman's estate, were regarded as unfeasibly high. Something had to be done. Grenville's response was to limit expense by restraining westward expansion and seeking to end the long-running border war with the American Indians; to enforce the Navigation Acts, limiting foreign trade competition and forcing the colonies to pay higher prices, especially for sugar; and to raise revenue directly from the Americans, via a new Stamp Act on legal transactions, passed in 1764.

Within the increasingly fractious colonies, the result was uproar, resistance and the first signs of rebellion. The urgent question for the new government in 1765 was, therefore, what to do about the Stamp Act. To enforce it would be ruinously expensive, while compromise would likely please no one. Rockingham therefore opted for outright repeal, a view in which he may have been influenced by Burke, whose memorandum urging repeal has survived. To save face and give itself a measure of political cover, the ministry added a Declaratory Act, which insisted on Britain's right in principle to tax the colonies, even if that right was not exercised. The move worked, and both Acts were voted through. But it proved to be a short-term expedient; the colonists had been informed that the Declaratory Act would not be exercised, and their reaction later to further taxes was to prove extreme.

Meanwhile, Burke needed to get elected and take his seat in Parliament. Wendover at that time had just 250 electors – the modern constituency has around 70,000 – most of whom were Lord Verney's tenants and therefore disposed to vote as instructed. The sitting member was induced to retire, but there was still the formality of election. In keeping with the time, this was accompanied by an extended bout of mass inebriation. It was not to Burke's taste, but he got the job done. As he wrote to his Irish friend and mentor Charles O'Hara on Christmas Eve of 1765, 'Yesterday I was elected for Wendover, got very drunk, and this day have an heavy cold.'

Facing the chamber of the House of Commons itself was another matter, however. The chamber itself has been rebuilt twice since Burke's time, once after the great fire of 1834 and then after bomb damage sustained in the Second World War. On the latter occasion, at the specific insistence of Sir Winston Churchill, care was again taken to make it too small for the membership. In Churchill's words, 'The essence of good House of Commons speaking is the conversational style, the facility for quick, informal interruptions and interchanges ... [This] requires a fairly small space, and there should be on great occasions a sense of crowd and urgency . . . a sense of the importance of much that is said and a sense that great matters are being decided, there and then, by the House.' The chamber thus measures a rather modest 68 feet by 46 feet, and contains only 427 places for 650 MPs. Yet the eighteenth-century chamber was smaller still, at about 58 feet by 33 feet or 300 to 350 places for 558 MPs, an even smaller percentage. It functioned effectively simply because many county members only rarely attended.

The sense of enclosure was increased after 1707, when Sir Christopher Wren remodelled the chamber, bringing the ceiling down and installing galleries supported by columns along both sides. Then as now, such a confined space is infinitely removed from the empty caverns of the great modern democracies. In it politics becomes, literally, hot and personal. Today the chamber of the House of Commons is the only air-conditioned public space in the Palace of Westminster, and a blessed refuge from a steamy summer day. In Burke's time it must have been stifling.

Then as now, the members faced each other. The seating reflected the institution's earliest origins in St Stephen's Chapel; for in an

English chapel the congregants look across the aisle, not towards the altar as in a church. The Speaker and clerks sat, wigged and gowned, at the east end beneath three high windows. Senior ministers wore full court dress, with swords; the sartorial contrast with backbenchers was such that it caused something of a stir when large numbers of them lost office in 1782 and the Rockinghamites appeared in the Commons from court, bedecked in blue, with swords, lace and hair powder. But, ministers apart, there was no dress code as such: members wore hats, boots, sometimes spurs, and often carried sticks. They talked among themselves, ate fruit or nuts, and not infrequently slept in the chamber; but they were forbidden to smoke or read. Without the microphones and tiny speakers dotted around the modern chamber, members needed formidable powers of vocal projection if they were to make themselves heard.

Since Walpole's time the modern custom had arisen that government ministers would sit on the front bench on the Speaker's right, and by the 1770s senior opposition figures sat on the bench directly facing them. But – there being as yet no political parties in the modern sense – other members sat individually or in groups as they chose. Burke normally sat, with other Rockinghamites, on the third row behind the opposition front bench, close to a pillar and not far from the Speaker's chair. That was close enough to be fully engaged in the cut and thrust of debate, but distant enough to underline the group's independence in opposition.

There followed the awful initiation of a maiden speech. Some of life's terrors are inevitable, others self-inflicted, and among the latter there are few to compare with the task of making a maiden speech in the House of Commons. To dull the pain, both for the speaker and their audience, the convention has arisen in recent times that maiden speeches should be short, pleasant and uncontroversial. They often take place late at night, in minor debates, when few MPs are present and the chamber is becalmed. The new member sings the praises of their predecessor, however evil or incompetent, and takes those present on a light and ideally brief tour of the constituency, before identifying some worthy cause as their one true political ambition. Rare and brave is the MP who deviates from this primrose path.

Things were very different in Burke's day. A maiden speech was a political statement, of course; but it was also a social one, in which the ambitious novice sought to cut a certain figure, regardless of his – and it was always 'his', until the twentieth century – personal origins. Most importantly, it was a first presentation of political force. In the days before round-the-clock media coverage, political debate focused on the chamber of the House of Commons. Moreover, a really controversial Bill hugely increased attendance, from 200–300 members to over 400, most of the extra being county members, of more independent mind. There being relatively little 'whipping' or party discipline to speak of, none of the present party lines to take and no national political organizations to take them, effective oratory could make a huge difference. Careerists heeded the MP Hans Stanley's advice: 'Get into Parliament, make tiresome speeches; you will have great offers; do not accept them at first, then do: then make great provision for yourself and family, and then call yourself an independent country gentleman.' But, given the stakes, many MPs simply could not bring themselves to make a maiden speech at all. The great historian Edward Gibbon was one such, in a political career of nine years; the poet Andrew Marvell was another, a century earlier. More than half the 558 members never spoke at all on public matters.

Burke took the plunge on 17 January 1766. This was no primrose path. The occasion was the stormy debate on repeal of the Stamp Act, the chamber packed and rancorous – Karl Anton Hickel's painting of Pitt addressing the Commons after news of the French declaration of war in 1793 conveys something of the atmosphere (see opposite). But not only did Burke speak once; he spoke again, and once more, and then frequently on subsequent days. There were no official, full or accurate records of debates at that time;

the great crisis of whether or not the Commons would permit public reporting of debates only occurred in 1771. But even so it is clear that Burke was extremely effective. No less an authority than the Great Commoner himself weighed in: after a speech in February it was remarked that Burke 'received such compliments on his performance from Mr Pitt as to any other man would have been fulsome, but applied to him were literally true and just'.

Under other circumstances this might have been the beginning of a long friendship between the older and the younger man. In fact the opposite was the case. Shortly afterwards Burke went on a mission to see Pitt at his house in Kent. He sought to persuade the older man of the merits of a free port in Dominica, but also to ask on Rockingham's behalf whether and how Pitt might be prepared to return to government. The mission underlined the fragility of Rockingham's government, and his increasing reliance on his secretary. But in hindsight it was exceedingly ill judged, for even the most cursory understanding of Pitt's character would have made clear that this supreme egoist was not about to discuss such issues with a mere parliamentary whippersnapper. Pitt dismissed Burke in the most cutting terms, and sent him away with a flea in his ear. The result was to create bad feeling between them, magnified by Burke's increasing view that Pitt was in fact a bombast who lacked any real intellectual substance. When the Younger Pitt took office some fifteen years later, Burke's view of him may already have been coloured by a degree of familial antipathy.

The Rockingham administration fell in July 1766, after little more than a year. It was undermined by the inexperience and incompetence of its ministers, by Rockingham's unwillingness to treat with the followers of Bute, whom he regarded as mere placemen for the King, and most of all by the opposition of Pitt. Pitt had denounced the Stamp Act as unconstitutional, as asserting a right to tax colonists who were not represented in the Commons, a position which earned him wild popularity in America. Now he turned around and distanced himself from Rockingham and his followers, through a general denunciation of political parties and factions as such. The King, who similarly despised parties, took the hint and invited Pitt himself to form a government. This Pitt did from the House of Lords as the newly ennobled Lord Chatham, a transformation from Great Commoner to Noble Lord which earned him enormous public ridicule and opprobrium.

Burke's reaction, as so often, was to turn to his pen. The result was *A Short Account of a Late Short Administration*. At just 750 words, it was less a political pamphlet than a squib, a brief piece of instant history designed to present a favourable image of the departed ministry's year in office and its achievements. The Rockingham administration had brought calm to the Empire, the argument went, and placed British trade upon a settled basis. It had preserved the constitution, and enhanced the liberties of the subject through a prohibition on general warrants and against the seizure of personal papers. In particular, Burke was at pains to contrast the Rockinghamites' uprightness with the forces ranged against them: 'With the Earl of Bute they had no personal connection . . . They neither courted nor persecuted him. They practised no corruption . . . They sold no offices. They obtained no reversions or pensions . . . for themselves, their families, or their dependents [sic]. In the prosecution of their measures, they were traversed by an opposition of a new and singular character; an opposition of placemen and pensioners.' These were not purely personal remarks; they gave a glimpse of a new conception of the very idea of a political party.

Burke had hopes of being given a position within the new administration, but these were ended by Chatham himself. The experience strengthened his conviction that his future belonged with Rockingham, whether in opposition or in government. Chatham was visibly ageing; it could surely only be a matter of time before Burke and his patron were back in office. But while his personal influence had grown with Rockingham, a huge social gulf still separated the two men. Rockingham was one of the very wealthiest men in England. Rich in his own right, he had married an heiress and inherited Wentworth House, now Wentworth Woodhouse, a home of such stateliness that it has 365 rooms (more or less; no one has ever succeeded in counting them definitively) and, at 606 feet, an east front with the longest façade of any house in Europe. He had large properties in Northamptonshire and County Wicklow, as well as vast family estates in Yorkshire. Burke, by contrast, was struggling to maintain a modest household in London.

At first glance, it is easy to see Rockingham himself just as a dilettante given over to racing and gambling, the twin passions of the day, and he was often so described. But in fact he was rather more than this. A retiring man, he was no public speaker and was plagued by illness, including a debilitating venereal disease picked up on a visit to Italy, which may have rendered him sterile; there was no third Marquis. But he had great personal charm, a certain personal nobility – to be seen in his portrait, after Reynolds (see opposite) – and a remarkable capacity to inspire loyalty in his followers, who included great Whig aristocrats such as the Dukes of Richmond and of Portland in the Lords, and fifty or so MPs in the Commons. He began to set a pattern among his political set, combining moral principle with a consistent adherence to a set of core policies, and political patronage and financial support. Burke was a mere salaried secretary. But over time he assumed a crucial role within the Rockingham Whigs, moving them away from factional politics and shaping them organizationally and intellectually into the prototype of the modern political party.

In the meantime, Burke continued to yearn for financial security and social status. He had always been close to Will Burke, regarding him as a member of his household. These ties had been deepened still further by Will's magnanimity in securing Edmund a seat in Parliament from his friend Lord Verney. Now they extended into financial speculation. Will had started to invest 'on margin', using money borrowed from Verney, in shares in the East India Company.

Immense sums were involved – as much as £49,000 at one point. There is no evidence that Edmund was aware of the details of Will's scheme, or had any direct involvement. But they and his brother Richard had long had a 'common purse', whereby they shared mutually in each other's gains and losses. So Edmund was seriously exposed to Will's financial dealings.

For a while, all went well. In May 1767, the East India Company raised its dividend, for the second time in eight months, to the giddy heights of 12.5 per cent. In the previous year Will had estimated his own gains at more than £12,000. So Edmund may have felt few qualms in purchasing Gregories, a handsome Palladian country house with an estate of some 600 acres of mixed land near Beaconsfield in Buckinghamshire. Its cost was £20,000, almost entirely funded by loans and mortgages, including a loan of £6,000 from the ever-willing Lord Verney, again arranged by Will.

Given Burke's background and evidently slender means, the purchase was a source of wonderment to his friends, and of gossip and slander to his enemies. But he loved the countryside, and now set himself to become a successful farmer on scientific principles. The house also brought with it a magnificent collection of paintings and sculpture. Boswell noted seven landscapes by Poussin on a visit, and a sale catalogue of the estate in 1812 included sixty-four paintings – including four by Titian, five by Reynolds and one by Leonardo da Vinci – fifty marbles and twelve drawings. Some of these works were added by Burke, including most likely the Reynoldses and a large Poussin sent by his protégé James Barry from Rome.

The new property was close to London, a crucial merit for the working politician of the day. But best of all it would give him the respect then accorded to men of property. As one admirer remarked, 'An Irishman, one Mr Burke, is sprung up in the House of Commons, who has astonished every body with the power of his eloquence, his comprehensive knowledge in all our exterior and internal politics and commercial interests. He wants nothing but that sort of dignity annexed to rank, and property in England, to make him the most considerable man in the Lower House.' That was precisely the point. Gregories would make Burke a gentleman.

But his new status came at a high cost. Mortgages at that time could be called in at six months' notice, the estate was far from paying its own way, and the Burkes did not live frugally. Moreover, through the common purse, they were acutely exposed to changes in the value of East India Company shares. Nemesis inevitably followed. There had been stock market tremors, notably in 1766 when Chatham announced a parliamentary inquiry which was seen as a transparent attempt by government to annex a portion of the company's profits. But three years later events in India caused a sudden panic, and the price of East India Company shares fell 13 per cent. The effect on the over-extended Will Burke was catastrophic: from being handsomely ahead, he and Verney now faced a joint debt of £47,000, and were themselves the hapless creditors of other East India speculators whose holdings had crashed. Richard faced similar ruin. Despite – sometimes because of – numerous other money-making schemes over the years, the two adventurers would die in debt. For his part, Edmund Burke would spend the rest of his life with money troubles. Members of Parliament could not be arrested for failure to pay their debts; but failure to get re-elected carried with it the imminent possibility of debtors' prison.

The Chatham administration started badly and ended worse, having dragged on despite parliamentary defeat and the chronic illness of its principal; its parting gesture was to pass the Townshend duties on American imports of items such as paint, paper and tea, which only stoked the fires of rebellion among the colonists still further. The government was taken over by the Duke of Grafton, only to be reconstructed yet again under pressure from the Rockinghamites ... in collaboration with none other than Chatham himself. With these endless changes, the country seemed close to being ungovernable, all the more so as a tide of radical petitions flooded in complaining bitterly of parliamentary corruption, incompetence and the growing subordination of ministers to the King.

Burke was indefatigable throughout. In addition to his secretarial duties, he was writing, canvassing for petitions and speaking in Parliament wherever possible. It has been estimated that over the period 1768–74 he was the third most active speaker in the House, rising more than 400 times on a wide range of topics, especially on trade policy and his growing concern at the abuse of the King's prerogative powers. Around him, the Rockinghamites and their leader were reluctantly having to acknowledge, and even embrace, the fact that theirs might be a protracted parliamentary exile.

Radicalism was in the air. But in the 1760s it also had a specific cause célèbre: the case of John Wilkes. In giving him a vicious squint and a prognathous jaw, nature had not been kind to Wilkes (see opposite). But he had overcome these impediments to procure himself a notorious reputation as a hell-raiser and philanderer; he boasted that it 'took him only half an hour to talk away his face' with a woman. He also had a positive genius for constitutionally valuable mischief-making, a vaulting ambition frustrated by lack of patronage, and a great hatred for the Earl of Bute. In 1763, now an MP, Wilkes obtained an advance copy of the King's Speech, and he denounced it and its presumed author Bute in his radical (and violently anti-Scottish) weekly, the *North Briton*. He had previously accused the Archbishop of Canterbury of buggery, and called the Bishop of Gloucester's wife a professional prostitute. He had even suggested that Bute's influence extended to taking George III's mother as his mistress. This, however, was the final straw.

The King's response was to instigate a criminal charge of seditious libel, and have the government issue general warrants in which Wilkes and his collaborators were not named. Forty-nine people were arrested, including Wilkes himself. He was sent to the Tower of London, his home ransacked for incriminating materials, and papers removed. He then counter-sued for trespass and to secure his own immunity as an MP to libel claims under parliamentary privilege. Both actions were successful. Over a series of cases, Wilkes was able to establish both the illegality of general warrants and the

R.E. Pine pinx.   *J.ᵒ Watson fecit*

John Wilkes, Esq.ʳ

Published according to Act of Parliament 1764.   Price 5ˢ

now basic principle that the English courts were under no obligation to defer in law to so-called 'reasons of state', advanced by
government in the cause of political expediency.

Wilkes, however, was only just getting into his stride. In the same
year, his political enemies published an erotic burlesque of Pope's
Essay on Man attributed to him called *An Essay on Woman*. Among
other things, the poem neatly summarized what seems to have been
Wilkes's own personal credo: 'Life can little more supply / Than just
a few good fucks, and then we die.' It was condemned as blasphemous
and obscene by the House of Lords, and Wilkes, who had been
wounded in a duel, escaped to Paris to recover and avoid imprisonment. He was convicted *in absentia* of obscene and seditious libels
early in 1764, and declared an outlaw. Four years later, however, and
under some pressure from his French creditors, Wilkes made a
dramatic return to England and was elected to Parliament for
Middlesex, amid wild scenes of mob hysteria and rejoicing. He
surrendered himself, waived parliamentary privilege and was sent to
jail, whereupon some of his supporters were killed by troops at a
riot in St George's Fields, on the site of the present Waterloo Station,
not far from Parliament. As if this was not enough, a succession of
expulsions from and re-elections to Parliament now followed, which
only succeeded in embarrassing the authorities still further and
cementing the words 'Wilkes and Liberty' into the popular mind.

Even then Wilkes was not finished. As an MP, he burnished his
radical credentials by denouncing British policy in America, and in
1771 fought a successful campaign to prevent the suppression of
reports on parliamentary debates. The loss of trust in our ancient
institutions, and specifically in Parliament, is often regarded as a
modern phenomenon. But Wilkes reminds us that this is not so. In
less than a decade, he had almost single-handedly thrown Parliament
into grave disrepute, shining a searching light on its corruption,
authoritarianism, dependence on the Crown and willingness to
suppress the common-law freedoms of the citizen. He had galvanized
the press, organized political societies and mobilized the mob.

To Burke, Wilkes was at best a mixed blessing. Personally, he found him 'a lively agreeable man, but of no prudence and no principles'. There was little in common between them temperamentally, or much politically, since Burke was no radical. In many ways Wilkes was an embarrassment and, worse, a highly effective one. The Rockingham Whigs shared his criticisms of overreaching Crown prerogative and British policy towards America, and during their brief year in power Parliament had banned both general warrants and the arbitrary seizure of personal papers. But they were deeply uncomfortable about any alliance with such a notorious blasphemer and libertine. Burke himself deplored the use of general warrants, and pressed in the public interest for three years for a parliamentary inquiry into the killings in the St George's Fields. But nothing could have been more hostile to his developing conception of principled political opposition, or to his deep belief in the value of the social order, than Wilkes's willingness to whip up crowd hysteria and pander to the mob. That way led to revolution.

It was in this context that Burke framed one of his most famous and enduring essays. In 1768–9 he had written – perhaps with William Dowdeswell, the Rockinghamites' leader in the Commons – *Observations on a Late Publication Entitled 'The Present State of the Nation'*. Two years later he published *Thoughts on the Cause of the Present Discontents*. The first is a long and carefully argued pamphlet, now somewhat unjustly ignored; the second is a classic of political thought, which has been rightly read and re-read by succeeding generations. Together, they mark Burke's transition to political maturity.

The *Observations* is Burke's first real political pamphlet. In purpose, it is a counter-attack. In late 1768 William Knox, a follower of Grenville, had published *The Present State of the Nation*, which set out a vigorous defence of Grenville's trade policy, and an attack on Rockingham and his followers for betraying that policy and the interests of the nation. In response, Burke does not simply resort to the political stock-in-trade of deflection, denial and insult. Rather,

he makes a lengthy argument on the merits, backed up with a host
of detail, statistical tables and evidence. The subtext was clear. The
Rockinghamites were right on the facts and right on the principle,
and they stood ready to serve when the ministry collapsed, as it
surely would. But more than that: as a party they had the capacity
to articulate policy based on fundamental political principle, which
could as a result outlast the vagaries of the moment, and become
the basis for loyal and yet energetic opposition.

Much of the *Observations* is dry stuff indeed, though towards the
end it moves from evidence and rebuttal to a vigorous defence of
the Rockingham ministry along the lines of the *Short Account*.
Throughout, however, Burke demonstrates his ability to combine
specific detail with Olympian generalization. Thus a discussion of
imports from Jamaica and the malign effects of the Stamp Act yields
the timeless Burkean insight that 'politics ought to be adjusted, not
to human reasonings, but to human nature; of which the reason is
but a part, and by no means the greatest part'. Or take Burke's
magisterial repudiation of Grenville's proposal for the American
colonists to be enfranchised and their representatives sent 3,000
miles to London. This he denounces as constitutional folly, in terms
that have resonance today: 'Has he well considered what an immense
operation any change in our constitution is? How many discussions,
parties and passions it will necessarily excite; and when you open
it to inquiry in one part, where the inquiry will stop?' In a favourite
metaphor, Burke likens the British constitution to an old building,
which 'stands well enough, though part Gothic, part Grecian, part
Chinese, until an attempt is made to square it into uniformity. Then
it may come down upon our heads altogether, in much uniformity
of ruin; and great will be the ruin thereof.' In its scepticism about
human reason, and its respect for tradition, for what is given, the
thought is deeply conservative. In language, it is biblical.

In *Thoughts on the Cause of the Present Discontents*, published
anonymously in April 1770, Burke turns from economic to social
disorder. The return of Wilkes in 1768 had spread panic in official

circles, generated huge public excitement and cast the authorities generally in the worst possible light. But Burke does not analyse popular grievances simply in their own terms. Rather, he develops an elaborate conspiracy theory, in which their ultimate cause is to be found in the extension and consolidation of royal power.

This was potentially dangerous territory, even for someone protected by parliamentary privilege, and Burke prudently follows the convention of the time that the King can do no wrong. Instead he attributes to the 'King's Friends', an alleged Court faction of shadowy advisers, the importation from France to Britain of a Double Cabinet: a parallel administration designed to control the workings of government from the inside. This has as its counterpart an attack on other sources of power; notably, he accuses the Court faction of seeking to destroy potential opposition within Parliament through patronage, and by constant changes of administration. Given all these offices and pensions, it was little wonder that the Crown could not live within the ample financial means voted to it by Parliament.

Rhetorically, Burke's argument was highly ingenious. It allowed him to retell recent political history as an unconstitutional attempt by George III to escape the constraints imposed by the Glorious Revolution in 1688–9 and accepted by monarchs thereafter. It offered a delicious hint of foreign intrigue, reminiscent of the influence of Louis XIV over Charles II and James II. And its analysis had a plausible and deeply satisfying twist in the tail. Far from being unwelcome to the King's friends, Burke argues, the advent of Wilkes offered them an extraordinary opportunity, for it actively assisted their project of undermining Parliament, and securing more power for themselves in the ensuing crackdown.

The *Thoughts* thus contained an elaborate conspiracy theory. One might think this a thin rationale for political immortality, especially since the theory of the Double Cabinet has since been largely exploded by historical research. How, then, has it achieved its status as a classic of political thought?

As in the *Observations*, the reason lies in the final third of the

book. Formally, Burke dismisses radical solutions like shorter parliaments and a 'place bill', which would remedy excesses of patronage
by excluding holders of lucrative offices or pensions from the
Commons. He also disavows specific remedies of his own. In fact,
however, he has nothing less than a complete re-engineering of
party politics in mind. He insists that power can never be properly
exercised by an individual, however distinguished, for any great
length of time. Practically, then, the only solution is a principled
assertion of the power of the House of Commons, through political parties: 'Government may in a great measure be restored, if
any considerable body of men have honesty and resolution enough
never to accept Administration, unless this garrison of *King's men*,
which is stationed, as in a citadel, to control and enslave it, be
entirely broken and disbanded, and every work they have thrown
up be levelled with the ground.' In other words, parliamentarians
should band together on principle to destroy what Burke insisted
was the King's network of patronage.

If that fails, then the only backstop can be at the ballot box:

> I see no other way for the preservation of a decent attention to
> public interest in the Representatives, but [by] *the interposition of
> the body of the people itself*, whenever it shall appear, by some
> flagrant and notorious act, by some capital innovation, that these
> Representatives are going to over-leap the fences of the law, and
> to introduce an arbitrary power . . . nothing else can hold the
> constitution to its true principles.

In a mixed constitution, then, all sources of power are constrained:
MPs hold the government to account, but they must themselves be
held accountable by the people if the constitution is to work its magic.

But, Burke argues in a brilliant move, this balance in turn rests
on a crucial distinction. For faction is not party. Factions are group-
ings of the moment, which exist to take power and to exercise it.
Those forming Burke's 'considerable body of men' are not a faction.

No, they are a political party; that is, they are 'united, for promoting by their joint endeavours the national interest, upon some political principle in which they are all agreed'. The test comes when such a group is evicted from office. Founded on self-interest, factions will tend to disperse. Parties, however, will sustain themselves and their membership – on principle and shared values, on mutual commitments and on personal loyalties and friendship – until the opportunity to exercise power returns.

There is a risk of circularity here: to the conspiracy theorist, lack of success can itself be a form of self-justification, and an excuse for inertia. Nevertheless, it was a matter of deep political principle that the Rockinghamites should be able to sustain themselves as a party in opposition, and they had learned how to do this, with some difficulty, since 1766. So it was not surprising that they saw themselves as almost the sole repository of political virtue, and came to refer to the *Thoughts* as 'our political creed'.

The *Thoughts* was a significant *succès d'estime*. It quickly ran through four editions, and made Burke, now forty years of age, into a national figure. More than 3,000 copies were printed, and it was widely debated in the press. As a political call to action it was a failure: too intricate and theoretical to be really effective, it was neutered when publication coincided with a rare lull in Wilkes-related scandal. As a basic credo for the Rockingham Whigs, it was a vital statement of shared belief. As political analysis, it remains of enduring importance today.

But by mid-1770 Burke's own mind was elsewhere. Jane had fallen ill and was confined to her bed for two months, perhaps as a result of a miscarriage. Worse, just as the *Thoughts* was published there had also appeared a detailed, accurate and highly personal article about him in the *London Evening Post*. In general Burke accepted public scrutiny; he could do no less. But this was different: 'Hitherto, much as I have been abused, my table and my bed were left sacred, but since it has so unfortunately happened, that my wife, a quiet woman, confined to her family cares and affections, has been dragged into a newspaper, I own I feel a little hurt.' What made it worse was that the original source was a well-meaning account by his oldest friend, Richard Shackleton, which had fallen into the wrong hands. In it Shackleton had claimed that Burke was 'made easy by patronage', unintentionally inflicting a wound; and what was worse, he had revealed that both Burke's mother and wife were Roman Catholics. Coming at a time when Irish grievances were rapidly on the rise, this could only excite and succour Burke's political opponents.

In other ways, this period was more hopeful. In December 1770 Burke was chosen by the Assembly of the colony of New York to act as their agent in London, a role which paid well – £500 a year, or roughly that of a middle-ranking official – and kept him closely in touch with colonial affairs and issues relating to trade with America. He expanded the farm at Gregories, and invested money he did not have in new techniques and experiments under the influence of the agriculturalist Arthur Young. He also made a very happy visit to France in 1773, travelling to Auxerre with his son Richard, then fifteen, placing the boy with a local family named Parisot in order to teach him some French, and also establishing a lasting link which would feed Burke much useful information in due course about the first years of the revolution. Returning via Paris, Burke visited Versailles, where he saw the young Dauphine, Marie Antoinette, an experience which would later be immortalized in his *Reflections on the Revolution in France*.

However, it was with revolution in America that the government, and Burke, were to be increasingly concerned. The Rockinghamites had learned to survive in opposition during the Chatham and Grafton ministries. But their morale was sustained by the regular change in administration, and by hopes of a return. In January 1770, however, George III had after ten years at last discovered in the Tory Lord North a Prime Minister in whom he could repose his trust. It was a fateful choice.

North was likeable, flexible, deferential, a patriot and a moralist in his private life, all high recommendations to the King. What he was not was a great leader. In 1773 Parliament passed the Tea Act, which allowed the East India Company, which had built up a vast surplus of tea in Britain, to export tea to America for the first time. At North's insistence this tea bore a symbolic tax of three pence per pound, a last remnant of the highly unpopular and now discarded Townshend duties, left in part specifically to remind the American colonies of Britain's right to tax them. Even including this tax, however, East India Company tea was cheaper than other imported tea, and cheaper than smuggled Dutch tea. The effect of the new Act, then, was immediate and comprehensive: at a single stroke it united all sections of American opinion, nationalist and loyalist, commercial and illicit, against the new imports. On 16 December, after a lengthy stand-off in Boston harbour with the colonial author-ities, and a raucous meeting of some 7,000 local citizens, rebels disguised as Mohawk Indians boarded three ships at night – all of which were American, not owned by the East India Company – and dumped 342 cases of tea from them into the harbour.

The 'Boston tea party' scandalized Parliament and British public opinion alike. With feelings running high both in the country and on the backbenches, Lord North and his ministers prepared draconian measures to crack down on the colony of Massachusetts and the port of Boston, and reassert their control. Both in principle and in his well-remunerated role as the British agent of the New York Assembly, Burke's sympathies lay with the colonists. As the storm clouds of revolution gathered, in April 1774 he made the first of two great speeches designed to bring Parliament back to its senses, to vindicate – yet again – the policy of the Rockingham government, and to set out a proper long-term basis for relations between Britain and America.

Burke devoted enormous time and trouble to his 'Speech on American Taxation', anticipating its later publication. In it he traces the odious tea tax back through a tortuous history of varied and sometimes contradictory policy: imposition of the Stamp Act by

Grenville; its repeal under Rockingham; renewed taxation via the Townshend duties, passed during the chaos induced by Chatham's temporary absence from politics; and their partial withdrawal in turn under North, leaving only the odious tea tax behind. Describing his opponents in the most generous terms, he is nonetheless perfectly clear in attributing to them the blame for Britain's ugly predicament, in terms at once impassioned, ironic and magisterial. Though he does not say as much, the whole episode amounts for him to a case history in which failed policy derives from a failed approach to government itself.

Experience and not abstract ideas, Burke insists, is what counts:

> Lord North asserts, that retrospect is not wise; and the proper, the only proper subject of inquiry, is 'not how we got into this difficulty, but how we are to get out of it.' In other words, we are, according to him, to consult our invention, and reject our experience. The mode of deliberation he recommends is diametrically opposite to every rule of reason and every principle of good sense established amongst mankind.

The Stamp Act marks a profound and disastrous shift in policy, Burke argues, in attempting for the first time to derive revenue from America itself, over and above the revenue naturally deriving from its growth and Britain's control of trade through the Navigation Acts. America could never be governed effectively without a recognition that Americans were freeborn Englishmen abroad, to whom the tea tax was a grave insult: 'No man ever doubted that the commodity of tea could bear an imposition of three pence. But no commodity will bear three pence, or will bear a penny, when the general feelings of men are irritated, and when two millions of men are resolved not to pay.'

The only solution was to build 'a rampart against the speculations of innovators', embrace 'a spirit of practicability, of moderation and mutual convenience', and repeal the tea tax. But this in turn required Britain to return to an earlier and fundamentally different conception of empire: as non-coercive, commercial and based on shared interests and identity, not on attempts at control and retribution. Only thus, and through a far more selective exercise of national power, could Britain reconcile imperial sovereignty with imperial dominion. But without such a shift, Burke predicts, there will be disaster in the American colonies. 'Will they be content in such a state of slavery? If not, look to the consequences. Reflect how you are to govern a people who think they ought to be free, and think they are not . . . such is the state of America, that after wading up to your eyes in blood, you could only end just where you begun.' It was an early demonstration of his gift of prophecy.

The 'Taxation' speech signally failed to secure the repeal of the tea tax. Published in January 1775, it and its sister speech on 'Conciliation' with America are gems of historical analysis and statesmanship. But they also marked a small but important watershed in political communication. Speeches by parliamentarians had been published before, but these were some of the earliest occasions on which they had been self-consciously used to build a basis of knowledge and shared education within politics, a reputation outside Parliament and indeed – such was the interest that they attracted in America – a degree of international renown.

This was all to the good. But in April 1774 Burke was having difficulty in securing a platform even in his own country. A general election was imminent, but his patron Lord Verney had been all but destroyed financially by his speculations in the East India Company. Verney's pocket borough at Wendover was a valuable asset, which would undoubtedly be put out to bid. The result was that Burke had nowhere to stand for Parliament. Disaster stared him in the face.

THREE

Ireland, America and King Mob,
1774–1780

IN EARLY 1774 EDMUND BURKE was facing an imminent and enforced departure from the House of Commons. But characteristically his first reaction was to think not of himself but of William. Thanks to his ever-generous patron Lord Verney, William Burke had been elected for Great Bedwyn in Wiltshire in 1766. But Lord Verney's finances were now such that this seat too would be lost; and as William had graciously given way to Edmund in 1765, so he should have the priority now. All the more so since no seat meant no immunity from prosecution, and so no protection from his numerous and pressing creditors. At Burke's urging William was duly enabled to stand for Haslemere in Surrey, but was defeated. Judgements were soon filed against him in the Court of King's Bench.

For Burke himself the parliamentary landscape was considerably more complicated than it had been in 1765. In the modern era, it is a truism that no two constituencies are quite alike. Various in their political geography and party affiliation, constituencies also widely differ in the volunteer associations which select and adopt candidates, and then – it is hoped – campaign for them to win office. Surprisingly often the result is to form a long-term bond of loyalty and affection, which ties MP and constituency together through political thick and thin. Sometimes, however, the counterpart of a 'safe' seat, with a solid majority already in place, is a constituency association only too aware of its power to choose the MP – and willing to choose another if the current incumbent does not toe the line on its favoured issues.

Eighteenth-century constituencies were quite different, owing far more to individual patronage and informal groups of supporters than to local party organization. The most famous of them today are perhaps the 'rotten boroughs' such as Dunwich, which had fallen into the sea, or Old Sarum, long owned by the Pitt family, which had three houses, seven voters – and two MPs. But this caricature does a disservice to the fantastical complexity of the electoral structure that had grown up by the 1770s. At that time Parliament had 558 members, comprising 489 from England, 45 from Scotland and the balance of 24 from Wales. Ireland had its own Parliament until 1800 so there were no Irish seats at Westminster, though some MPs with Irish connections sat in both places.

The English seats were heavily weighted towards the south and south-west, especially sea ports: Cornwall alone had forty-four Members of Parliament, and it and its four neighbouring counties of Devon, Dorset, Somerset and Wiltshire contained roughly a quarter of the seats. London, by contrast, had 10 per cent of the whole population, but only ten seats; Nottingham and Newcastle, then both large and important towns, had just two seats each. Birmingham and Manchester had none.

The most important English constituencies were the forty counties, which returned two members each, chosen by 'forty-shilling freeholders', or those with freehold property worth £2 or forty shillings per year. The property qualification had originally been introduced in 1430, but three and a half centuries of inflation and exception-making had reduced the effective threshold and so greatly enlarged the voting population. However, the counties, while prestigious, were vastly outnumbered by the 203 cities and boroughs, from which a total of 405 MPs were elected (there were also four university seats). These city and borough seats ranged from near-universal male franchise through those controlled by local corporations to 'burgage' boroughs, where votes were attached to local properties, known as burgages, which could be bought and sold in order to achieve electoral control. At a time when voting was by open ballot, corruption was less than is often portrayed but nonetheless endemic by modern standards, and it varied by seat: undue influence could be exercised by landlords instructing tenant voters, by bribing a local corporation or simply by owning or controlling enough burgages.

For Burke, then, the options were limited. A county seat was out of the question for the son of a Dublin attorney, which was lucky because the generally wide franchises made elections, especially contested elections, prohibitively expensive to all but those with the wealthiest supporters. At the very least, voters expected to be lavishly wined and dined, or 'treated', by the different candidates. Treating remains an electoral offence today, but only if alcohol and meat are involved – it is an oddity of English law that vegetarians and teetotallers cannot be treated. In the eighteenth century, however, treating was endemic, and since elections often took weeks to conclude, the cost could be ruinous. In fighting for Chester in 1784 the Grosvenor family paid for 1,187 barrels of ale, 3,756 gallons of rum and brandy, and over 27,000 bottles of wine. These were pretty heroic numbers for a seat with just 1,500 voters.

An inebriated electorate was pliable in other ways too, albeit sometimes with disastrous results. George Selwyn, MP for Gloucester, wrote in 1761 that:

> Two of my voters were murdered yesterday by an experiment which we call shopping, that is, locking them up and keeping them dead drunk to the day of election. Mr Snell's agents forced two

single Selwyns into a post chaise, where, being suffocated with the brandy that was given them and a very fat man that had the custody of them, they were taken out stone dead.

The most famous example of electoral expense is perhaps that of Yorkshire, where William Wilberforce's two opponents in the bitterly contested election of 1807 each reputedly spent £100,000, or more than £6 million today; Wilberforce topped the poll, but out of a total of nearly 24,000 votes only 850 finally separated the three candidates. By comparison, the average election budget allowed by law for a parliamentary candidate in the final month of the 2010 general election, including all staff, office and equipment costs, campaign literature, merchandise and advertising, was approximately £12,000 – less than the cost of a single TV advertisement in a US congressional election. At the local level at least, there is extraordinarily little 'money power' in modern British politics.

To return: matters were further complicated from 1707 until the early twentieth century by a law which required those accepting an office of profit from the Crown to resign and fight a by-election. The principle was clear: ministerial office rewarded an MP personally and would likely distract him from the zealous duty of care owed to his constituents, so they were entitled to refuse him leave to accept. In practice, however, this discouraged good MPs in marginal seats from accepting office, and occasionally unhorsed those who did accept, as Winston Churchill found to his cost in 1908. It also all but ruled out those in county seats from doing so, since a by-election meant another round of enormous electoral expense. The result was that county seats were rarely contested, often divided up by agreement between prominent local families, and occupied by landed gentlemen with decidedly independent views. This only added to their prestige.

A 'pocket' borough, however – not quite 'rotten', but with a small enough number of votes to be effectively controlled by a local landowner or magnate – hardly offered a legitimate platform for

someone who aspired to be a statesman. So in the face of an imminent general election, it was with some reluctance that Burke
approached his patron Rockingham, and then at Rockingham's
behest was elected for the borough of Malton in Yorkshire on 11
October 1774. However, on the very same day he was summoned
post-haste to stand for Bristol, where one of the declared candidates
had suddenly withdrawn.

Unlike Malton, Bristol was a huge prize: the second city in Britain,
an economic powerhouse and an 'open borough' whose wide franchise would confer legitimacy and independent authority. It was
rich, and dominated not by a leisured gentry but by merchants
who had made their money in trading with Ireland and America.
For a politician like Burke, deeply engaged in trade issues and
already vociferously opposed to taxing the American colonies, it
seemed a perfect fit. So thought Richard Champion, a porcelain
manufacturer and one of Bristol's many influential Quakers, who
had become his campaign manager. After a bitter and personal
three-way fight lasting twenty-three bibulous days, in which Burke
was denounced as a stooge, a papist and a friend to aristocratic
tyranny, he was elected on 3 November as one of two members
behind Henry Cruger, a radical. It was as the member for Bristol,
and not for Malton, that Burke was returned to Parliament in 1774.

Burke's victory speech was expected to be formal, deferential
and platitudinous; instead he turned his 'Address to the Electors
of Bristol' into what has become a hallowed account of political
representation itself. Over the previous century the idea had sprung
up in radical circles that Members of Parliament could and should
be bound by instructions from electors as to how to vote. For how
else could electors know that their wishes were being heeded? What
was to prevent an MP, having been elected, from doing exactly as
he pleased? The same cry is frequently heard today.

Speaking first, Cruger pledged himself to be guided by his constituents' instructions. Burke, however, simply destroyed the idea at
source, in words that have resounded down the ages.

Certainly, Gentlemen, it ought to be the happiness and glory of a representative to live in the strictest union, the closest correspondence and the most unreserved communication with his constituents . . . It is his duty to sacrifice his repose, his pleasures . . . to theirs; and above all, ever and in all cases to prefer their own interest to his own.

Yet deference could go only so far; indeed, too much would be self-defeating. Burke continued:

But his unbiased opinion, his mature judgement, his enlightened conscience, he ought not to sacrifice to you; to any man, or to any set of men living. These he does not derive from your pleasure; no, nor from the Law and the Constitution. They are a trust from Providence, for the abuse of which he is deeply answerable. Your representative owes you, not his industry only, but his judgement; and he betrays instead of serving you, if he sacrifices it to your opinion.

In the interests of their constituents, then, Members of Parliament must have, and must be allowed to have, independent minds: 'Authoritative instructions, mandates issued, which the member is bound blindly and implicitly to obey . . . these are things utterly unknown to the laws of the land, and which arise from a fundamental mistake of the whole order and tenor of our Constitution.' MPs, then, should not be held hostage simply to advocates of particular issues or interests.

Moreover, such an approach to politics mistook the character of Parliament itself:

Parliament is not a congress of ambassadors from different and hostile interests . . . Parliament is a deliberative assembly of one nation, with one interest, that of the whole; where not local purposes, not local prejudices ought to guide, but the general

good, resulting from the general reason of the whole. You choose
a member, indeed; but when you have chosen him, he is not a
member of Bristol, but he is a member of Parliament.

These were stern, even foolhardy, words from a newly elected MP
to an electorate tempted by radicalism, and they carried with them
a hint of trouble to come. But the present moment carried troubles
of its own. Lord North had been vindicated at the election with a
comfortable majority, reflecting the popularity of his harder attitude
towards America. Rockingham's followers, in contrast, are estimated
to have fallen in number from fifty-five to forty-three MPs. Amid
allegations of divided loyalty and even betrayal they were increasingly stigmatized as 'friends of America', as relations with the colonies further deteriorated. Rockingham himself was becoming
withdrawn, while his group was further undermined by the death
in February 1775 of William Dowdeswell, its leader in the Commons
and in-house expert on financial matters. The wider opposition
was split, with Chatham as erratic and uncooperative as ever in
the Lords.

Burke chafed at the enforced inactivity. Lacking the position to
lead his party or his nation, his reaction was again to quarry out
from within himself the intellectual leadership that the situation
demanded, and offer it to those in authority. The result was his
'Speech on Moving his Resolutions for Conciliation with the
Colonies', delivered on 22 March 1775. Its message was plain and
bold:

The proposition is peace. Not peace through the medium of war;
not peace to be hunted through the labyrinth of intricate and
endless negotiations; not peace to arise out of universal discord . . .
[or] to depend on the juridical determination of perplexing questions . . . It is simple peace, sought in its natural course and in its
ordinary haunts. It is peace sought in the spirit of peace.

Britain had a choice between peace and war, between conciliation and coercion, between submission – yes, submission – to colonial demands and an over-insistence on its own sovereign rights. It must choose conciliation.

Why so? Burke starts by highlighting the enormous growth in trade with the American colonies. This was all but equal to Britain's entire global trade only two generations earlier. Meanwhile the colonies had grown, he estimated, to contain some two million people of European extraction, plus slaves and others totalling 500,000 more. In a brilliant stroke, he argues that the use of force is not merely ineffective or self-defeating, but self-contradictory. It is inevitably temporary: 'a nation is not governed which is perpetually to be conquered'. It is uncertain of success, and leaves no alternative if it fails. It destroys what it seeks to protect, for America is not a foreign enemy, but part of Britain:

> I do not choose to consume its strength . . . because in all parts it is the British strength that I consume . . . I do not choose wholly to break the American spirit; because it is the spirit that has made the country. And finally in logic, the British Empire has been founded, and made rich on a policy of benign neglect to which the use of force is the direct antithesis.

But for Burke the decisive consideration is not America's population or commercial strength; it is the American spirit itself. One cannot hope to govern a nation without knowing its character, and 'In this character of the Americans a love of freedom is the predominating feature . . . This fierce spirit of liberty is stronger in the English colonies, probably, than in any other people of the earth.' America was first colonized by Englishmen who left their country in the exercise of freedom, and took with them English ideas and English principles. Their idea of liberty was specific and concrete, not abstract, expressed in their popular assemblies and their resistance to taxation; and it was invigorated by dissenting religion, which opposed established temporal authority as such. 'All Protestantism . . . is a sort of dissent. But the religion most prevalent in our northern colonies is . . . the dissidence of dissent, and the protestantism of the Protestant religion.'

Nor was this all. Indeed, three other specific factors sustained the American spirit. In the American South, according to Burke, the prevalence of slaves only made the colonists more jealous of their freedom and status. Moreover, the American people as a whole, and especially their legislators, were imbued with a study of the English common law, so much so that almost as many copies of William Blackstone's authoritative legal overview, the *Commentaries on the Laws of England*, were sold in America as in England. 'This study', Burke noted, 'renders men acute, inquisitive, dexterous, prompt in attack, ready in defence, full of resources . . . They augur misgovernment at a distance, and sniff the approach of tyranny in every tainted breeze.' Finally, there was the small matter of the 3,000 miles of sea separating the colonies and Westminster. No empire could rule the extremities as it did the centre. 'The Turk cannot govern Egypt . . . as he governs Thrace . . . The Sultan gets such obedience as he can. He governs with a loose rein, that he may govern at all.'

What, then, was to be done? The causes of that proud spirit could not be removed or oppressed. These were Englishmen abroad, with English ideas, English language and English laws: 'We cannot falsify the pedigree of this fierce people, and persuade them that they are not sprung from a nation in whose veins the blood of freedom circulates . . . your speech would betray you. An Englishman is the unfittest person on earth to argue another Englishman into slavery.' Britain would never receive any tax revenue from America, for it could not be coerced, and any attempt to coerce it would fail. A narrow obsession with Britain's rights ignored not merely its national responsibilities but its imperial interests.

No, the only solution was conciliation. That meant the temporary indignity of agreeing to the colonists' demands, but it also meant measures to restore mutual confidence, now so badly damaged, and to renew America's commercial stake in the Empire. Part of the genius of the British constitution lay in its ability to absorb new interests, and spread to new regions the benefits of its social order and rule of law. But such measures should be offered not in a captious spirit, but in one of openness and accord: 'Genuine simplicity of heart is an healing and cementing principle . . . Magnanimity in politics is not seldom the truest wisdom; and a great empire and little minds go ill together.'

At the end of the speech, Burke set out his programme for conciliation in the form of fifteen propositions, framed as motions to Parliament. The power to tax the colonies should be given up and relocated within the colonies themselves; the highly offensive Coercive Acts, which closed the Port of Boston and suppressed the charter of Massachusetts, should be repealed; and the power of American popular assemblies, rather than the colonial governors or the King, to appoint judges should be formally recognized. It is notable that Burke deliberately did not seek to amend the Navigation Acts, widely regarded as the foundation of British trade power; or the Rockinghamites' own Declaratory Act, by which Britain maintained, without asserting, its general rights to legislate for America, as the sovereign power.

Burke spoke for two and a half hours, and sat down to a note of congratulation from Rockingham. But the Commons remained set on teaching the Americans a lesson, and ignored him. His first and utterly innocuous motion, a mere statement of fact, was defeated by 270 votes to 78. Acknowledging the strength of sentiment, Burke did not push the other motions to a vote or 'division' of the House, and Britain took another step towards war with America.

Yet the 'Speech on Conciliation', like Burke's earlier 'Speech on Taxation', is a small masterpiece, which retains its power to this day. It is an Irishman's love letter to the American spirit – that is, to the spirit of the English and of English institutions expressed in and through America. Part poem, part sermon, part homily, it is wise and prophetic, a work not merely of political thought but of political statesmanship. It looks both backwards and forwards: backwards, to a nuanced historical argument about the sources of British commercial and constitutional success; forwards, to a non-coercive conception of empire based on shared identity and institutions – especially the rule of law – which would prove hugely influential in the century to come.

Could Burke's proposals, if enacted, have saved Britain from the disastrous conflagration of the Revolutionary War? It is impossible to say. They could not have prevented the first acknowledged exchanges, since the battles of Lexington and Concord took place less than a month after the speech. The wider momentum towards war on both sides was already significant, and Burke's measures implied a change of policy and approach so drastic that the North administration would surely have fallen, and necessarily so, before they could be implemented. But what we can say is this: in March 1775, some fifteen months before the Declaration of Independence, conciliation might conceivably have led to peace. Without it, as Burke foresaw, war was all but inevitable.

Over the next five years the Rockinghamites remained a coherent group. But they were caught in a political bind; castigated as pro-American when some early successes rallied British public opinion in support of the war, they were denounced still more after General Burgoyne's defeat at Saratoga in 1777, which acted as a trigger for France to enter the war against Britain, followed by Spain and later the Netherlands. Rockingham himself remained passive, oscillating between politics, ill-health and the racecourse. Dowdeswell was dead, the Duke of Richmond preoccupied with the registration of his French peerage, and other key figures unavailing. In more meritocratic times the group's leadership in the Commons would more naturally have fallen to Burke. Instead it went to Lord John

Cavendish – an MP, not a peer, his being merely a courtesy title – who represented the family and interests of the Duke of Devonshire. But Lord John's greatest interest lay not in politics but in fox hunting.

Burke apart, by far the most interesting figure to emerge at Westminster in the 1770s was the young Charles James Fox. Fox had entered Parliament in 1768 at the age of just nineteen and quickly established himself as a formidable orator. He then twice joined the North ministry, and twice resigned on mainly personal grounds. These erratic actions did not endear him to the Prime Minister, or to the King, who found much to object to in the young man's lifestyle. By 1774 Fox was moving slowly and with some mutual distrust towards the Rockingham Whigs.

As his Stuart forenames suggest, Fox had distinctly Tory origins, being a direct descendant on his mother's side of Charles II. He was the son of Henry Fox, who had held several senior offices of state, made a fortune from public office as Paymaster General, and yearned without repose or success for an earldom. Well educated and highly intelligent, the young Fox was the epitome of the spoiled child, who found it impossible throughout his life to control either himself or those around him. Of no one was Oscar Wilde's quip more apt, that he could resist anything except temptation. His father lavished political connections, money and worldly wisdom on the boy, including a trip to Paris in 1763, in the course of which he lost his virginity at the age of fourteen to a certain Madame de Quallens. There followed a desultory period at Oxford, which he left without taking a degree, and a grand tour on which he met Voltaire and Gibbon and formed close links with the French nobility, including the Marquis de Lafayette. These links were later to exercise a huge influence over Fox during the French revolution.

Fox was dissolute, unprincipled and a notorious gambler and spendthrift who squandered an enormous fortune before he was thirty. He was so hairy at birth that his father likened him to a

monkey; in caricatures he is generally depicted as corpulent and
unshaven, with a five o'clock shadow and enormous bushy eyebrows.
Having been one of the leading 'Macaronis' in his youth – a fashionable fop in the French style – in middle age he cut a rather
slovenly figure in the Commons. A painting by Hickel of 1794 (see
opposite) shows the decidedly portly Fox dressed in buff and blue,
the colours of Washington's army, which he adopted in the 1770s
in support of the American revolutionaries. Someone further
removed from the publicly austere and committed Burke could
hardly be imagined. Yet despite these differences, and a gap of
nineteen years in age, they formed a close and enduring friendship.
Fox recognized the older man's depth and wisdom, while for his
part Burke wrote in an exuberant moment that Fox was 'one of
the pleasantest men in the world, as well as the greatest genius that
perhaps this country has ever produced'.

Casting around at this time for a means to make an impact, the
Rockingham group contemplated the idea of seceding altogether
from politics, to demonstrate the dismay and contempt they felt
for policy towards the colonies, and their refusal to give that policy
any appearance of sanction. Ever more aware of the power of the
printed word, Burke was a keen supporter of this idea, provided it
was framed in a suitably dramatic way and announced alongside
a public manifesto. To that end he drafted an 'Address to the King'
which tried rather unsuccessfully to combine deference to the
monarch with sulphurous criticism of his ministers. In fact,
however, the whole attempt at secession was a minor fiasco. The
group decided against an Address and its MPs began a partial
boycott of Parliament in February 1777. This received little public
attention. Early on, Fox decided – alongside Sir George Savile, an
independent country gentleman – to break the boycott in order to
oppose North's highly contentious attempt at partial suspension
of the ancient right of habeas corpus, creating further confusion.
After a few weeks the whole thing collapsed. It was no way to run
a nascent political party.

To make matters worse, Burke's increasingly numerous detractors in Bristol pointed out that non-attendance at Parliament made it impossible for him to represent them. The radicals in particular were angry that the Habeas Corpus Act and other measures oppressing the rights of the individual had not been vigorously opposed. They were right, since the Rockinghamites' secession was a dead letter from the off; and this in turn reinforced the impression of a distant and dilatory MP, a view given further currency by Burke's unwillingness to accept instructions, to take part in local events or even to visit the constituency.

Burke was in fact quite energetic within Westminster on behalf of Bristol. Nevertheless, in the course of his six years as its MP he made just two visits to the city. Even given that he was one of two members at the time, this is a record which would be unthinkable today, when a good constituency MP will be locally active virtually every week of the year, and a poor one every month. His response to the increasing local mutterings of discontent was to write a long *Letter to the Sheriffs of Bristol*, which was published in May 1777. This restated in somewhat more radical language much of the argument of the 'Speech on Conciliation', with a trenchant critique of the American conflict as amounting to a civil war, whose domestic effects in coarsening public opinion and encouraging the official suppression of dissent Burke noted with alarm. Tucked in alongside this was a rather slender defence of his conduct during the Rockinghamites' secession, a brief paean of praise to the city of Bristol, and a denunciation of those who issued blanket condemnations of all politicians as wicked and corrupt regardless of the facts. The *Letter* marks a useful further development of Burke's central argument. As an apologia for his own mistakes, however, it was – and remains – distinctly unpersuasive.

Many Bristol merchants had originally been delighted to attract someone with Burke's national profile and clear opposition to taxation of trade with America. But as a war mentality set in, they increasingly questioned these judgements, and they were especially critical of Burke's renewed interest in the affairs of Ireland, and his desire to lift the many burdens which Britain imposed on Irish trade. Liberalizing their trade with America, a vital export market, was one thing; liberalizing it with Ireland, not many miles away and a major potential competitor, was quite another.

Despite a long period of relative calm in Anglo-Irish relations between 1714 and 1760, Ireland had continued to struggle socially and economically. Much of the harshly anti-Catholic legislation of the two previous centuries had been reversed after the Restoration, only to be significantly and vigorously extended after William III's victories in 1689–91. Dissenters fared little better. In 1792 Burke summed up the Penal Acts with heavy irony in a *Letter* to his friend the Irish politician Sir Hercules Langrishe, as 'a machine of wise and elaborate contrivance, and as well fitted for the oppression, impoverishment, and degradation of a people, and the debasement in them of human nature itself, as ever proceeded from the perverted ingenuity of man'. Among other things, Catholics were barred from public office, could not buy land except on a lease of less than thirty-one years and were forbidden to vote, teach, inter-marry with Protestants, bear firearms or own a horse worth more than £5. The last provisions reflected a deep fear among the Protestant minority of the potential threat from an armed and mounted Catholic militia.

In trade, Ireland remained subject to the punitive Navigation Acts, which discriminated against foreign competition with British manufactures and required as much economic value as possible to be added within Britain itself. The Acts therefore prohibited vital Irish wool exports except to Britain, banned the domestic manu-facture of woollen items and prevented Irish ships from trading with the colonies.

The long-term effects of these policies were predictable and disastrous. With no prospect of economic gain, Ireland's lush and fertile fields remained underdeveloped, its agriculture rudimentary. Its absentee landlords stayed in England and sucked rent out of the country. There were two serious famines, in 1730 and 1741, and food shortages would have been still worse had it not been for the rapid and widespread take-up of potato cultivation. Despite starvation and emigration, the population had still doubled to some four million people, creating the dreadful conditions described by Swift in *A Modest Proposal* at the start of this book. But power remained in the hands of Westminster, and was jealously guarded locally by the Protestant ascendancy. The Irish Parliament was weak, complaisant and little troubled by elections; during the reign of George II it sat for a single stretch of thirty-three years.

Nevertheless by the late 1760s the economic situation was much improved. Irishmen, even Catholic ones, could still make money, and Ireland had recently enjoyed a period of prosperity. Dublin had grown hugely and become a capital city of architectural distinction, spurred on by a sense of colonial insecurity and a desire to outdo London. But this prosperity was brought to a crashing halt by the Revolutionary War and the British blockade of trade with the American colonies. Deprived of American flax seed and the potash used as a whitening agent, the Irish linen trade started to fail. A shortage of manpower for the war caused Britain to withdraw troops from Ireland, leaving the country defenceless against France.

In response, in 1778 the Irish, led by Burke's friends Henry Grattan and the Earl of Charlemont, two national politicians of distinction, mobilized and armed a force of some 40,000 men, known as the Irish Volunteers. The Volunteers were a loyalist force, sworn by oath to the King, and they even included a number of Presbyterians and Catholics. From the outset they were not merely a military but a political force, sharing and debating advanced ideas and demonstrating in 1779 for free trade for Ireland and the removal of tariffs. Their creation, especially amid so much hardship and discrimination, added to the already significant pressure in Westminster for reform. With the American colonies seemingly on the brink of independence, any inklings of revolution in Ireland, or secession from the Empire, served to concentrate English minds wonderfully.

For Burke, Ireland was undoubtedly a place of deep and mixed emotions. As a *novus homo*, a man of aspiration and talent seeking to make his name in England, he had long suffered from the generic abuse of the Irish as Catholic mountebanks and adventurers seeking the daughters and fortunes of the English gentry. And his increasing prominence drew specific opprobrium upon him: he was denounced as 'Edmund Bonnyclabber', a Jesuit, indeed one supposedly educated at the notorious (to Protestants) seminary of St Omer in France. In caricatures he was standardly depicted as a thin and severe figure wearing the cassock and cornered hat, or biretta, of the Jesuits, sometimes with a potato or a rosary and almost always with spectacles. The imagery was cunningly chosen: it made him instantly recognizable, it hinted at sophistry and lack of political vision, it contrasted superbly on the page with the fat and hirsute Fox and it drove home an impression of someone remote, legalistic, censorious and above all *foreign*.

Having spent time in Ireland while working for Hamilton in the early 1760s, Burke had visited the country again in 1766, in part to settle a small estate in County Cork which he had inherited from his brother Garrett. The tenants were some Nagle cousins, whom the new landlord treated with generosity; the property did not generate much income, and still less when Burke's charitable gifts – remarkable given his own acute shortage of funds – were deducted. But the unfairness of Catholic farmers being sustained through the grace of their Protestant landlord relatives could hardly have been lost on him. One result was his unpublished 'Tract on the Popery Laws' of about this time, which contained a vigorous denunciation of the laws as imprudent, ineffective, unjust and oppressive.

Burke had not returned in the ensuing decade. But Ireland seems rarely to have been far from his thoughts. In 1773 he was instrumental in organizing opposition to Dublin's attempt to repair its difficult financial position through a new tax on absentee landlords. This, he argued, was contrary to the principles of free trade that should govern the Empire, and would only increase Ireland's isolation. While Burke's own Irish income was too small to generate a genuine conflict of interest, it was perhaps not irrelevant that several Whig magnates had enormous annual incomes from their Irish estates. In the case of his patron Rockingham that amounted to a princely £15,000 a year. Political beliefs and personal interest thus ran in usefully concurrent channels.

Given his background and history, then, it is no surprise that Burke was deeply involved when in 1778 the North administration finally buckled and moved to relieve the pressure on Irish trade. The same was true when Sir George Savile and Lord Richard Cavendish, both Rockingham Whigs, moved the repeal of some of the Penal Laws restricting Catholic ownership of property. Burke's Bristol constituents, however, were not impressed. The decline in trade with the US had hit many of them hard; now one of their own MPs seemed to be undermining their business and supporting their Irish competitors. Emotions in the city ran high, causing Samuel Span, the Master of the Society of Bristol Merchant Venturers, founded in 1552 and the leading local guild, to write to both of the city's MPs indicating the merchants' alarm and demanding their support.

Cruger, predictably, complied. Burke did not. Instead he gave Span and his fellow merchants a brief but impassioned lesson in economics, in two open letters later published as a pamphlet. Ireland did not pay equal tax to England, he conceded, but it paid all that it could bear. Only through economic growth could it be enabled to pay more, and any such economic growth would immediately redound to the benefit of the Bristol merchants. That growth required the ability to trade freely, and it should not be begrudged the Irish, for it was a mistake to see trade as a fixed quantity: 'It is hard to persuade ourselves that every thing which is *got* by another is not *taken* from ourselves.' Jealousy of Ireland was thus not merely indecorous and impolitic, but economically unwise. In a characteristic dictum, Burke declared, 'Indeed, Sir, England and Ireland may flourish together. The world is large enough for us both. Let it be our care not to make ourselves too little for it.'

As for himself, it was very natural for people to believe the worst of their MP, in Bristol as elsewhere. But in fact, Burke insisted, he was acting in his constituents' interest. It would be easy to court their goodwill, but in a contest between truth and popularity, he opted for truth. If he had acted against his avowed principles,

> I should have lost the only thing which can make such abilities as mine of any use to the world now or hereafter; I mean that authority which is derived from an opinion that a member speaks the language of truth and sincerity . . . that he is in Parliament to support his opinion of the public good, and does not form his opinion in order to get into Parliament, or to continue in it.

Thus Burke affirms his willingness to speak truth unto power. His Bristol friends admired the sentiment. But they worried, with justification, about the seat.

Repeal of the restrictions on trade with Ireland was launched, faltered and was finally pushed through by North amid much bitterness. The Dublin Catholic Committee was grateful for Burke's efforts on behalf of Irish Catholics and voted him a gift of £500, which Burke refused with a request that it go to support local education.

In truth, Burke was not, did not see himself as and took pains not to appear specifically pro-Catholic; but he was filled with a profound hatred of injustice and of the abuse of power. And he went further than this. At a time when religious toleration was still a highly contentious subject, he argued that all the major religions were the products of custom, tradition and 'long and prescriptive usage'. That is, they had grown up within specific communities and secured the assent and belief of those communities over time. As such, Jews and Muslims deserved not merely toleration but the full protection of civil law. The same was true of Presbyterians. But there was a significant exception: atheists should not be so protected. To affirm a disbelief in God was, for Burke, a deliberate move to place oneself outside society itself. It followed, he thought, that atheists should not receive the benefits afforded by society.

As the American war ground on, and in the face of threatened invasion from the combined French and Spanish fleets, tension continued to rise across England. In late 1779 the Yorkshire clergy-man Christopher Wyvill started to agitate for reform, and quickly built up a huge following of petitioners across the country. At first, he focused on 'economical reform', or reductions in government spending and Crown patronage, quickly gaining the support of Rockingham and his followers. To the Rockinghamites, and espe-cially Burke, economical reform was not merely prudent house-keeping. It was a way to restrain the power of the Crown, to reassert the constitutional basis of the monarchy established after 1688, and to strike a blow against the King's Friends and the secret Double Cabinet supposedly identified in *Thoughts on the Cause of the Present Discontents*. So it was with some alarm that they saw Wyvill's movement shear away from the relative calm of econom-ical reform and towards the turbulent waters of shorter parliaments, more equal representation and radicalism. The political tempera-ture rose a few more degrees.

Burke himself had laboured long and hard on specific measures of economical reform, inspired by the French reformer Jacques Necker's success in bringing about an almost balanced budget amid all the excess and waste of the *ancien régime*. On 11 February 1780 he therefore introduced a compendious Bill of reforms in the House of Commons. In these days of hurry and executive control of Parliament, a backbencher introducing a Private Member's Bill will speak in the Commons for ten minutes, or sometimes for half an hour or so. In presenting 'A Plan for the Better Security of the

Independence of Parliament, and the Economical Reformation of
the Civil and Other Establishments', Burke was able to speak for
three hours and twenty minutes, and so to develop a detailed argument. His purpose is clear: not merely to curb spending, waste and
corruption in government, but to restrain the expense and influence
of the royal household itself.

Burke opens with praise of Necker and, more tellingly, of Louis
XVI, the young monarch whose support had made Necker's reforms
possible. He then enumerates 'seven fundamental rules' governing
his own proposals: jurisdictions which encourage oppression or
corruption should be abolished; public estates whose purpose is
patronage or influence rather than revenue should be sold off;
wasteful 'offices', positions which impose cost without proportional
benefit to the state, should be cut, as should those preventing a
clear and unified control of public expenditure; payments should
be made in order of their utility or justice, not partially or in
response to importunity; due process should supplant discretion
in public decision-making; and 'subordinate treasuries', that is separate sources of funds for public expenditure, should be dissolved
and consolidated into the general treasury itself. These principles
hint at the many malpractices which Burke's investigations had
unearthed within government. They retain their value as maxims
of good government today.

Burke then moves on to elaborate each of these seven categories.
Keenly aware that economical reform is never the most beguiling
of topics to any audience, let alone the House of Commons, he
interleaves his critique with moments of great humour. Thus he
ridicules the expense, sovereign jurisdictions, separate establishments and titles of the monarchy:

> Cross a brook, and you lose the King of England . . . coming again
> under his Majesty, though . . . [as] no more than Prince of Wales.
> Go to the North, and you find him dwindled to a Duke of
> Lancaster; turn to the West . . . and he pops upon you in the

humble character of Earl of Chester. Travel a few miles on . . . and the King surprises you again as Count Palatine of Lancaster. If you travel beyond Mount Edgecombe, you find him once more in his incognito, and he is Duke of Cornwall.

Ridicule then becomes farce, as Burke uncovers the real reason why Lord Talbot's earlier attempt at reform of the royal household had failed: 'It was because the turnspit in the King's kitchen was a Member of Parliament! The King's domestic servants were all undone . . . His Majesty's slumbers were interrupted . . . the judges were unpaid . . . the foreign ministers remained inactive . . . the chain of our alliances was broken, all the wheels of government at home and abroad were stopped, because the King's turnspit was a Member of Parliament.' The image of the King as a master of disguise, or jack-in-a-box popping out to surprise the traveller, and the sublime juxtaposition of an imperial government tottering from the wasteful patronage of the royal kitchen bear the stamp of ancient Roman comedy, and its later offshoot the *commedia dell'arte*.

But Burke had more serious targets in mind. The first was to reform the office of Paymaster General, who acted in effect as banker to the army. The Paymaster's job was to receive the sums voted to pay for the army – rarely small, and enormous during wartime – and disburse them as required. It carried the significant potential liability that the Paymaster himself could be held personally liable for any loss of funds or maladministration. But in practice this risk was negligible, since the audit procedures were extremely complex and long drawn out, ending many years after he had left office. And the potential rewards were colossal, since the Paymaster was legally allowed to draw down advances of cash before they were needed, and lend them out at interest for personal profit.

It was little wonder, then, that the Paymastership was keenly sought after. Chatham had famously refused to enrich himself from the post, but it had been a vast fountain of wealth for Henry Fox and for Walpole earlier in the century. The present incumbent was

Richard Rigby, a follower of the Duke of Bedford and a man whom Burke detested as the very model of the unscrupulous and self-interested placeman, who was said to have left the gigantic sum of half a million pounds at his death. It is of some comfort to know that several generations later this fortune was used to endow the magnificent Pitt-Rivers Museum of archaeology and anthropology at Oxford University.

Burke's other goals included abolition of the Board of Trade, a perennial target of opposition politicians over the centuries, and of the office of Third Secretary of State, responsible for the colonies, and specifically America. But more interesting are the obvious targets that he omitted. Pensions were known to be widely abused, as were sinecures within the Exchequer itself, yet Burke proposed only modest changes to them. Politic in seeking consensus, he was also respectful of what he saw as private property, and personally reluctant to deprive any man of what might be his livelihood. More than this, he believed that it was greatly to the benefit of the nation as a whole that long and disinterested public service be rewarded, and so encouraged, with honours and property. His goal was a balance between the twin evils of an ossified aristocracy and a politics of court favourites, drones and placemen eagerly shimmying up the greasy pole.

Burke's caution was well advised. His motion for leave to bring in later legislation went through, the only dissenter being the eccentric Lord George Gordon, of whom more anon. But the specific Bills which he moved in subsequent months failed to pass, with the exception of that concerning the Board of Trade, which was abolished only to be resuscitated a few years later. Burke's measures suffered the triple indignity of being denounced as insufficiently radical by Lord Shelburne, partially co-opted by North and then superseded by the famous motion of John Dunning in April 1780, that 'the influence of the Crown has increased, is increasing, and ought to be diminished', which was voted through a packed House by the narrow margin of 233 to 215 votes on 6 April.

But the speech itself attracted great public interest. It was pirated within the month, and Burke quickly put out an official version. It has long been regarded as one of the finest speeches ever made in the Commons. And rightly so, for in addition to its literary merits it is, like the great speeches on 'Taxation' and 'Conciliation', a work of statesmanship. High-minded, detailed yet comprehensive, it insists on the principles that the executive, and specifically its expenditure of public money, must be held and maintained as publicly accountable to Parliament; that it must be managed prudently; and that self-interest among office-holders must be subordinated to the public good. More than this, it evinces the classic Burkean idea that to be effective reform should be early, cool in spirit and proportionate, governing with the temper of the people. Burke would never be Prime Minister, or even a member of the Cabinet; but this panoramic vision again underlined his suitability for the highest offices of state.

In 1780 Burke was fifty years of age, and at the height of his powers. But what of him in private? Despite his personal reticence, we can catch glimpses: of the bespectacled Irishman with his wig off, who kept his red hair for many years and always spoke with an accent 'as strong as if he had never quitted the banks of the Shannon', in the words of the MP and memoirist Sir Nathaniel Wraxall; of the husband, 'Ned' as the family called him at home, who addressed his wife with the utmost tenderness as 'My dearest Jane', 'My dearest love' and 'My ever dear Jane'; of the father, whom one son's death had left almost too fond of the other, and who adored the company of children; of the host, never free of house guests but always entertaining with an open hand; of the patron, who knew the value of help to a young man, and who supported talented outsiders such as the painter James Barry and the poet George Crabbe; of the clubbable fellow who relished puns and low jokes and conversation, but never quite mastered the art of wit or repartee; of the countryman, who loved nature and rejoiced in his vegetable garden and in 'scientific agriculture'; of the solitary thinker, who did not make close friends easily, who chafed at idleness and was prone to fits of melancholy.

Burke took care not to allow private matters to intrude into his public life, but there was no great gap between the two. And publicly at this time he was in every way a substantial figure: physically substantial, though never corpulent, and intellectually substantial, though still light enough to charm and command an audience. Two portraits, one painted in 1766–70 after Reynolds (see overleaf) and the other in 1774 by Reynolds himself (see cover), show his development; there is an almost tangible hardening, a sense of toughness and purpose in the (now rather damaged) latter painting. By 1780 Burke was a man of significant property, and debt; and he was an orator of huge power and unending invention, so that James Boswell once said, 'It was astonishing how all kinds of figures of speech crowded upon him. He was like a man in an orchard where boughs loaded with fruit hung around him, and he pulled apples as fast as he pleased and pelted the Ministry'; and he was a senior politician, who dared to hope of high office after fourteen long years in opposition, as the North administration undid itself over the war.

It is at around this time that Burke composed a work for which he is still little recognized, his *Sketch of the Negro Code*. This remained in a drawer for over a decade, until it was sent on request to Pitt's Home Secretary and trusted lieutenant, Henry Dundas, in 1792. Burke intensely disliked the institution of slavery: as he says, 'Rather than suffer it to continue as it is, I heartily wish it at an end.' But he felt himself forced to acknowledge the size and pervasiveness of slavery as an institution, its considerable political support at the time and the likely economic impact of its abolition. Accordingly, the *Sketch* is a fairly detailed memorandum outlining a system of regulation designed to improve the transportation, treatment, settlement and education of slaves, as a preliminary to the trade's later outright abolition. Burke shows his mastery of the

facts by including measures to correct abuses: keeping families together, protecting slave property, creating a provision for common-law marriage, and giving slaves limited rights against depredations from their owners, with inspectors answerable to the Attorney General. Once again Burke was ahead of his time; it would not be until 1787, seven years afterwards, that William Wilberforce and Thomas Clarkson founded the Abolition Society, and not until the following year that the Crown appointed a committee of the Privy Council to inquire into the trade. As late as the 1820s, efforts to make slavery more humane echo Burke's recommendations from forty years earlier. The *Sketch* is, then, a small but significant foot-note to modern histories of slavery and its abolition.

At the end of the spring of 1780 Parliament rose, and the govern-ment's thoughts started to turn to the coming general election. But they were interrupted in June by a massive and unexpected outbreak of violence. Partial relief of the Irish penal laws through Sir George Savile's Catholic Relief Act in 1778 had passed off successfully, but a proposal to relax some of the penal laws against Scottish Catholics led to a petition for repeal of the Act, from the same Lord George Gordon who had uniquely voted against Burke's motion on economical reform.

Gordon was another extraordinary eighteenth-century figure, whose erratic personality impeded his advancement first in the navy and then in Parliament. In the late 1780s he was excommu-nicated for defying the Church in an ecclesiastical lawsuit, converted to Judaism and was imprisoned for defamation, before dying of typhoid fever in 1793 at only forty-two. In 1779, however, aged just twenty-eight, he had assumed leadership of the Protestant Asso-ciation. Using remarkable powers of oratory and organization, and drawing on centuries-old fears of papist conspiracy, foreign invasion and absolute monarchy, he quickly built up a large anti-Catholic following.

On Friday, 2 June 1780 a crowd of some 50,000 people assembled in St George's Fields in south London. Led by Gordon, they made their way to Parliament, to present the petition for repeal, by now bearing some 45,000 signatures. These included an estimated one in five adult male Londoners, testifying to the lingering strength and depth of anti-Catholicism at the time. While Parliament deliberated, fighting broke out, and a mob destroyed the chapel of the Sardinian Ambassador in Duke Street. There followed a week of violence, in which the mob raided distilleries, released prisoners from Newgate Prison, made a sustained attempt to capture the Bank of England and rampaged drunkenly around the streets destroying property associated with Catholicism. Wild rumours began to circulate: that the King had been burned to death in Buckingham House, the Queen murdered, Lord North hanged in Downing Street.

Politicians regarded as instigators of Catholic relief were an early target. Sir George Savile's house was looted, Rockingham's London home placed under armed guard, Devonshire House besieged by the mob. The Burkes were living at that time on Charles Street. Burke had received early intelligence that he would be targeted after Savile, and moved Jane and the family and furniture for their protection to the house of General Burgoyne, now home on parole after his defeat at Saratoga, in Hertford Street not far away. On the following day, he dismissed the sixteen soldiers guarding the house to release them for other duties, and 'spent part of the day in the street amid this wild assembly, into whose hands I delivered myself, informing them who I was . . . My friends had come to persuade me to go out of town . . . but I . . . resolved they should see that, for one, I was neither to be forced nor intimidated from the straight line of what was right.' Despite having to draw his sword at one point to keep the looters at bay, he was unharmed. It was a moment of extraordinary personal bravery, coming at the high point of the violence of 'King Mob'.

On 7 June, the army was deployed and the riots brought to an end, with significant loss of life. Some 500 people were shot dead, hundreds more wounded or arrested. Up to thirty of the rioters were later executed, but Lord George Gordon himself, who had been appalled at the bloodshed and had taken steps to end it, was found not guilty of high treason. Burke argued for a policy of clemency for the general mass of those arrested.

In retrospect, it is not hard to see many possible causes of the Gordon Riots. Petitioning movements were raising political consciousness, and support for specific issues, across the country. The war continued to drag on, the country remained at risk of invasion, and radical feeling ran strongly against the North government and in favour of the colonists. Prices were high and money scarce. There was no police force, and politicians and the King were naturally reluctant to bring out the army. Burke was proud to have faced down the rioters. But nothing was to prove more striking to this philosopher of the social order than to see the rapid and near-total collapse of society at first hand, indeed literally on his own doorstep. It was a lesson he would vividly remember a decade later, in the context of the French revolution.

FOUR

India, Economical Reform and the King's Madness, 1780–1789

AS HIS DECADE IN OFFICE had shown, Lord North was nothing if not politically astute. Under the Septennial Act, he was under no obligation to call a general election until 1781, and parliaments at that time were generally expected to run their full course. But noting that the country had reacted with indignation to the Gordon Riots, he brought his plans forward. His decision to dissolve Parliament in September 1780 caught the opposition unawares – and no one more so than Edmund Burke.

If Burke's position in 1774 had been fragile, in 1780 it was highly precarious. True, he was now a figure of national, indeed international, renown. But he had spent six years leading an unsuccessful and unpopular parliamentary opposition to the war in America, fighting to restrain the influence and expenditure of the Crown and latterly struggling to lift the twin oppressive burdens of taxation from Irish trade and of penal law from Catholics and dissenters. This was not a recipe for longevity in Parliament. Worse, he had been given the chance to build an independent political base of his own in Bristol and had not taken it.

The irony was manifest. Burke's 'Speech to the Electors of Bristol' of 1774 had proclaimed in ringing tones that 'it ought to be the happiness and glory of a representative to live in the strictest union, the closest correspondence and the most unreserved communication with his constituents'. Far from the 'strictest union' with his constituents, however, Burke himself had virtually no local organization of volunteers able to canvass or promote him on the ground – or patrons to pay what would inevitably be horrendous election expenses. Far from 'the closest correspondence and unreserved communication' with his constituents, he had positively alienated them by hardly visiting the city and by taking positions, without notice or prior explanation, which they instinctively opposed: on the war, on trade with Ireland, on Catholic relief. Particularly odious to the Bristol merchants, he himself believed, was his support for a Bill to reduce the penalties on insolvent debtors, penalties which then included life imprisonment. By 1780, the other candidates were all better established in Bristol than he was.

The simple truth is that Burke's stubborn streak of pride and self-righteousness made it all but impossible for him to seek the support of his voters on their own terms. In tremendous haste, and after a period of indecision, he withdrew his name in Bristol, a decision whose wisdom was borne out when his rival Henry Cruger was badly beaten at the poll. Burke was disconsolate at his predicament; feeling 'outlawed by the whole nation', he was desperate to return to Parliament, but reluctant to do so for a rotten borough. There followed a rather embarrassing hiatus, while Rockingham was sent various indirect hints of the need to do something to assist his principal lieutenant. Eventually, however, the Marquis got the message, evicted the poor wretch who had just been re-elected for Malton and installed Burke there in a by-election on 7 December.

Despite its unexpected timing, the general election did nothing to strengthen the government's hand. Its most notable result was the arrival in Westminster of William Pitt the Younger. Nevertheless, the new Parliament did mark an important milestone for Burke. It thrust him into the heart of a controversy which was to dominate his work and his life over the next decade, a cause which convulsed public and parliamentary opinion alike and raised profound questions about Britain's conduct abroad, indeed about the nature of empire itself. That cause was India.

Founded by Royal Charter of Elizabeth I in the year 1600, the East India Company had exercised since then a monopoly of all trade between Britain and Asia. The Company started life trading spices and pepper, but over time this expanded to include other high-value commodities such as cotton, silk, saltpetre (used to make gunpowder), tea and opium. So did its commercial reach, which extended to China by the early eighteenth century. By the 1770s it had built up an enormous presence in India, with major trading centres or 'factories' in Bombay and Surat in the west, Calcutta in the east and Madras in the south.

There had been no plan of conquest, no grand strategy. After the death of the Emperor Aurangzeb in 1707, the rapid decline of the Mughal Empire had created a huge vacuum of power, which local princes and foreign trading houses had competed to fill. The East India Company had been eclipsed in trade during the seventeenth century by its Dutch counterpart, the VOC, which had beaten it to the Spice Islands (the modern Maluku Islands, now part of Indonesia). India had been, in effect, a consolation prize. But now the Company saw off the Dutch, as well as Portuguese, Danish and Austrian/Flemish trading competitors, settling into a protracted struggle for commercial and military superiority in the Carnatic region of south-east India with the French Compagnie des Indes.

Similar in name, the British and French companies were in fact

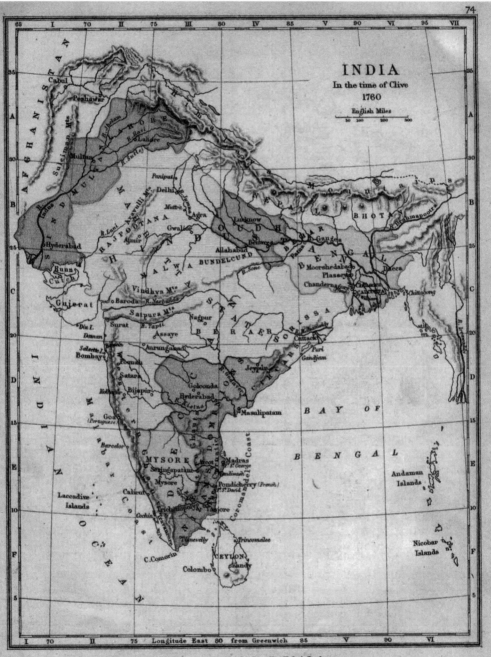

INDIA
In the time of Clive
1760
English Miles

Longmans, Green & Co. London, New York & Bombay.

rather different in nature. The Compagnie was originally funded by the monarch, its shares were narrowly held, and it was consequently short on capital and social connections within France. The East India Company, by contrast, had been capitalized by rich merchants and aristocrats, with no direct government ownership, control or supervision. It had nearly 2,000 shareholders, heavily drawn from the country's political and commercial elite, with more than a third of them living in London or the Home Counties. These men used their significant political influence to defend the Company's commercial monopoly and defeat various attempts at regulation. Their efforts were assisted by the periodic tendency of British governments to get into debt, which in turn necessitated borrowing from the Company.

Trade with the Indian subcontinent accounted for roughly one-fifth of world trade in the early eighteenth century. The Indian trade had long been extremely profitable for the Company, but those profits were raised to almost unimaginable levels as a result of the exploits of Robert Clive. A natural troublemaker who had been expelled by a succession of English schools, Clive entered the Company on the bottom rung in the usual position of 'writer' or junior clerk. Caught up in the running wars of the period with the French, he distinguished himself by his bravery and leadership, a reputation greatly enhanced across Europe by his success in defending the city of Arcot against siege in 1751. In 1757, after a visit to England, he recaptured the Company's vital eastern base, Calcutta, which had briefly fallen to the Nawab of Bengal, before defeating the Nawab directly at the battle of Plassey, laying the foundations for what would later become the Raj. A puppet was installed as the new Nawab. In 1761 the important French outpost of Pondicherry was taken, further consolidating British power along the eastern coastline. The Treaty of Paris two years later restricted the Compagnie des Indes to commerce, not politics, banned its fortifications, limited its garrisons and hastened its decline. The crowning moment came in 1765 when, after a further period in

England, Clive received the firman, or royal decree, from the Emperor granting the British legal title to Bengal itself, and to the neighbouring provinces of Bihar and Orissa as well.

The effect of these actions was to unleash a bonanza of personal enrichment for the Company, its shareholders and above all its local agents. Bengal alone had forty million people at this time, or four times the entire population of Great Britain; it was now effectively controlled by a few hundred Company men. Indian nobles had been quickly elbowed out of the markets after Plassey as the British took over the lucrative trade in betel nuts, salt and opium. But now the Company possessed something far greater: control of the entire tax revenue of Bengal, amounting to some £33 million per year. Clive was thought to have returned to England in 1753 after his triumph at Arcot with £40,000, at the age of just twenty-eight. Seven years later, his fortune was over £300,000. More than ever, India now became the wild east, a dangerous place full of exotic temptation, where young men risked serious disease and death, but from which they could and often did return with vast fortunes. 'Nabobs' – nouveaux riches who had returned to Britain to parlay their wealth into social standing and political influence – became familiar cultural stereotypes at home, and were much envied and lampooned.

But these developments also raised profound moral questions. India was being conquered, and not by Britain but by a private British company. Revenue from mutually beneficial trade was being replaced by revenue from tribute and tax. Clive had been a brilliant commander, but he had not hesitated to bribe, coerce and where necessary deceive Indian nobles and merchants in order to achieve his goals. The battle of Plassey itself had been less a military engagement than a subtle process of dividing the Nawab from his financial backers and military commanders, in particular the army paymaster Mir Jafar, who was bribed to defect at a crucial moment. Once established in power, the British had been brutal in enforcing their control of concessions in Bengal, extorting new rights and tribute and beating or flogging those who opposed them. Self-dealing and private profiteering were rampant. Clive himself had been shocked on his return to see 'a scene of anarchy, confusion, bribery, corruption and extortion', and had sought to institute reforms.

As reports of these practices increasingly reached Westminster, pressure grew for Parliament to take action. But the East India Company had shown itself to be a formidable political power in its own right over the previous century and more. Until the mid-1760s at least, it had in general been an immensely profitable success; its loans had sustained the Treasury in time of crisis; and its dividends had enriched much of the political elite, a fact which created huge and endemic conflicts of interest. Moreover, its power had only increased with the influx of new MPs from among the nabobs. After the 1774 general election there were twenty-six nabob MPs; after 1784 there were forty-five. Mocking the nabobs, or fretting about their values and influence on public life, was one thing. The question now, however, was not simply how far Parliament should condone British despotism in India, but whether it could in fact control it at all.

In 1773 the North government decided to act. Its motivation was as much economic as moral or political. After 1767 the fortunes of the East India Company had gone rapidly into reverse. It had emptied the treasury of Bengal, which was also struggling in the aftermath of famine; it had seen its lucrative American market for tea wiped out by smuggling; and it owed £1.5 million to the Bank of England and the British government. Moreover, the costs of sustaining its military presence remained high. The Company's financial plight was such that it had recently been unable to pay a £400,000 annual subvention to the Treasury, agreed a few years earlier with Chatham to cover the cost of army and navy assistance. After the speculative bubble of 1767–9 its shares had crashed, taking the Burkes and Verney down with them, among many others.

These factors created not merely political pressure but political opportunity. In response, the North government passed the Regulating Act. This capped the Company's dividends at 6 per cent until it repaid its government loans; streamlined its administration under the control of a new Governor General, Warren Hastings, based in Calcutta; established a new Council to whom Hastings would be accountable; and created a Supreme Court, in which British judges would sit, administering English law.

These were sensible reforms, passed without significant parliamentary opposition. But, perhaps surprisingly in view of later events, that opposition included Edmund Burke. Burke had had some familiarity with Indian affairs, through Will Burke's and his brother Richard's calamitous speculations in Company stock with their common purse during the 1767–9 stock market bubble. But he had developed no great expertise on India, and his opposition to the Act came on general grounds, that by regulating a private chartered company it constituted an attack on private property. To Burke, this was robbery in disguise. Indeed he saw the whole matter in terms of his long-time conspiracy theory of the King's Friends and the Double Cabinet: its real purposes were, he thought, to disable a source of opposition to the Crown, to co-opt Company revenues and, by controlling who was allowed to seek their fortune with the Company in India, to increase the Court's powers of patronage.

Four years after the Regulating Act Burke was more directly drawn into the hideously complex world of Indian affairs. The British-sponsored Muslim Nawab of Arcot in the south-east of India had long coveted the little Hindu state of Tanjore. Supported by the Governor in Madras, and with the help of Company troops, in 1773 he occupied Tanjore and annexed its revenues, deposing the Raja. The Company's directors in London repudiated these local actions, however, as in due course did Parliament. Spotting an opportunity, Will Burke was able to get himself sent out to Madras with instructions and letters of recommendation for himself.

In the event Will was left floundering with the failure of yet another of his get-rich-quick schemes. But the episode was a telling one, for it marked a further development in Burke's understanding of India and in his attitudes towards it. As with Ireland, his sympathies and imagination were deeply engaged by Tanjore, and what he saw as the oppression of a small state by a large and avaricious neighbour. He deplored the loss of local customs and traditions in the face of commercial interests, and romanticized the clash as one between virtue and vice. Finally, he noted the Company's unprincipled conduct in Madras and the Carnatic, its increasing power within domestic British politics, and the lack of effective control by either its directors or Parliament. Henceforward, he read omnivorously about India, and poured himself into Indian affairs at Westminster.

Actually doing something about India was another matter, however. Burke's first opportunity to make a genuine impact came in early 1781. The general election had left him smarting from his indignities in Bristol, and with no immediate outlet for his energies he took advantage of his election to a parliamentary select committee charged with reviewing the effectiveness of the new Supreme Court in Calcutta. In setting up the Court, the Regulating Act had failed to define its relations with the new Council, leading to conflict between them. Moreover, the decision to impose English law and British judges had led to great resentment within Bengal itself, especially among Hindus. Burke came to dominate the Committee, which quickly took evidence. Its report led to further reforms, which struck a balance between English law and procedure, Muslim law and Hindu custom. Women's apartments and religious shrines were not to be entered, and beheading was substituted for hanging in capital cases. But the Muslim punishment of maiming was prohibited. Relativism, it seemed, could go only so far.

These were small but important matters. But the fundamental questions were how the East India Company was to be held to account, what parliamentary oversight or control of the Company was appropriate, and, more deeply still, what moral standards ought to be applied to the governance of India at all. To these questions Burke would before too long give his own trenchant and passionate response.

Meanwhile the American war ground on. After several successes over the summer of 1781, the British were disastrously defeated at Yorktown in November, with the loss of 8,000 men under Lord Cornwallis. After that, it was simply a matter of time before the North government lost its majority in Parliament, and in March 1782 North announced that he was stepping down. Distrustful of the Rockinghamites, and filled by intense personal dislike of Fox, the King cast about for alternatives. Lord Shelburne, an Anglo-Irish aristocrat born in Dublin just seven years after Burke, was the clever, wily and ambitious leader of the Chathamite Whigs. A patron of radicals such as Joseph Priestley and Richard Price, he was widely disliked and did not have enough parliamentary support in his own right, while a mixed ministry from among the different group-ings was rejected by Rockingham. Eventually the King was forced to agree: Rockingham would be Prime Minister, with substantial control over appointment of senior ministers; the King would not oppose key legislative measures; and Shelburne and Fox would be Secretaries of State. Other Cabinet positions were shared between the two groupings.

It was a distinctly equivocal victory. The King remained opposed, the Rockinghamites did not possess a majority in Cabinet, and Shelburne was a notoriously slippery political operator. Burke had pressed for an unfettered power for the Prime Minister to appoint his own Cabinet, and for the Cabinet acting collectively to be recognized as the sole source of state power. He had urged Rockingham to refuse office except on these terms, which he had first sketched in his *Thoughts on the Cause of the Present Discontents* back in 1770. The political realities, however, made these ideas impracticable. This was a change of administration without a general election, the King was determined to hold on to power as far as he could, and after all Rockingham is unlikely to have had more than eighty or so followers at most, or less than 15 per cent of a Parliament of 558 MPs. In the eighteenth century this was a formidable political grouping. But it was nothing like enough to dictate terms.

Nevertheless the new government marked, without doubt, an extraordinary moment not just in Britain's political history but in that of the world. Rockingham and his followers had been out of office since 1766. But they had not then fragmented, as factions had fragmented before them. On the contrary, for sixteen years they had maintained a political grouping, a core of shared policies and a coherent political identity. They had, in other words, created the first outlines of the modern political party. Power had now passed entirely peacefully to this party, large numbers of office-holders had been forced to leave, and the new leadership had arrived with well-understood legislative intent.

The Rockinghamites had returned to office, moreover, despite the opposition of the King, and in pursuit of a conception of Cabinet responsibility that has since become the foundation stone of British government. In so doing, they had pushed the country one more step towards a constitutional democracy, and away from a purely personal monarchy. It remains a remarkable and woefully under-recognized achievement; and Edmund Burke was, intellectually and practically, at its centre.

Reckoned by talent alone, Burke should have had a Cabinet position himself. Yet he lost out. He was a commoner, indeed an Irish *novus homo*, at a time when Cabinets were small and almost invariably drawn from the peerage; and there may have been some taint from the well-known financial speculations of Will Burke and Richard Burke. But there were perhaps two other important reasons in the background. Burke's relationship with Rockingham had faded somewhat, and the long years of often futile opposition had taken a toll on his public character. He was not merely passionate and outspoken but becoming tougher, sometimes embittered, and prone to rant. Over time he would acquire the nickname of 'the Dinner Bell', able to clear the Commons benches when he rose to speak. Colleagues who had admired him increasingly saw him as a bore . . . uncollegial . . . unsteady . . . too independent-minded . . . not someone to have round the Cabinet table. It cannot have helped either side that he was so often right.

Instead Burke was made Paymaster General and admitted to the Privy Council, an ancient body of advisers to the monarch, membership of which still carries with it the title 'Right Honourable'. For the first time, he was able to move from his position high on the opposition benches down to the government front bench, and take a seat alongside the new Cabinet, now sporting their blue court dress and swords. Sweeter still in a different way, perhaps, he was elected to Brooks's, a club which had become the social home of the Whigs. The Privy Council was by this time a mainly honorary body, but membership was nevertheless a mark of distinction. And although not a Cabinet position, in many respects the post of Paymaster General was an ideal appointment. Its handsome annual salary of £4,000 was badly needed to pay down Burke's numerous debts, while the role gave him a platform from which to push through his plans to cut waste and patronage, and to reform the Civil List of Crown expenses.

Burke abolished the traditional perquisite of investing public balances for personal gain, which had enriched Paymasters through the ages. He then reintroduced many of the key measures of his 1780 reforms, including abolition of the Third Secretary of State, the Board of Trade and a range of sinecures, and limitations on pensions. The savings proved much less than he had hoped for. But the reforms struck an important blow for limited government, for parliamentary accountability and for further constitutional constraints on the Crown.

The administration was also active on other fronts. It quickly moved to end the war in America, and passed a range of measures granting relief to Ireland. The subordination of Dublin to Westminster was ended, allowing the Irish Parliament to pass its own legislation without British assent; the Irish judiciary was made formally independent; rights of appeal from Irish to English courts were abolished. Burke supported these reforms, but with substantial reservations. They strengthened the Protestant ascendancy, he felt, but would do little or nothing for Catholics. The Popery laws remained in place. The British maintained *de facto* control through the Dublin Castle executive appointed by the Lord Lieutenant and through patronage and land ownership, while he feared that the economic and social subjugation of Irish Catholics would continue uninterrupted. Burke did not describe the atrocities and rebellion that would follow, but he may have sensed their possibility.

But in July 1782 disaster struck the new government. Rockingham – always frail, now exhausted by the strains of office – died after a short illness. For one who had waited so long to return to government, it was a cruel twist of fate; and it is to his everlasting credit that even in extremity he had the kindness and presence of mind to add a late codicil to his will annulling Burke's debts. The King immediately invited Shelburne to form a government. As a result Burke, still grieving at the loss of his friend, mentor and patron, now faced a serious dilemma. He found Shelburne personally and politically rebarbative. But to resign now would be to leave his work unfinished, losing a salary he could ill afford to do without and inflicting economic hardship on the two Richard Burkes, his brother and son, for whom he had found offices within the government. A more politic man – a man of less principle, perhaps, or less imprisoned by principle – would have regarded resignation at this early stage of a broadly reforming ministry as the height of foolishness. Nonetheless, resign he did, following Fox, the new leader, back into the wilderness with a rather reduced group of followers.

During the summer Shelburne pushed on with peace negotiations over America, a process in which the British government was widely believed to have underplayed its hand. As a result, when Parliament reconvened in the autumn, it was increasingly clear that Shelburne himself could not survive in office without support from North or Fox and their followers. In the event, after protracted negotiations the two opposition groups came together in a coalition. The King insisted that Fox was kept away from the Treasury and accepted the new government on sufferance, while looking for alternatives.

The situation was richly ironic. The Rockingham Whigs had fought for the primacy of party over faction. They had remained in principled opposition for sixteen years, twelve of them against North, whom they had regularly denounced for his patronage, opportunism and incompetent handling of the American crisis. Now under Fox they had cast principle aside and were allying themselves politically with their detested foe. A print from the time tellingly shows the Coalition as a band of musicians, all facing in different directions, with Burke on the trumpet (see overleaf). It is hard to imagine that Rockingham himself would have stood for such a marriage of convenience. Little wonder that the new Fox–North coalition was abominated and ridiculed from the outset.

For his part, Burke was back in post as Paymaster, while the two Richards returned as well. Yet even this modest triumph was tainted, for on his return Burke naively reinstated two civil servants, John Powell and Charles Bembridge, who had been dismissed under Shelburne for corruption, and instantly came under attack for condoning embezzlement. Insisting that the men were innocent until proven guilty and disavowing himself of any error, Burke defended them three times in the Commons. But eventually Bembridge was fined and sent to jail, while Powell resigned, later committing suicide. Burke's enemies rejoiced to see the self-proclaimed man of principle and economy brought low, and suggested that his very sanity was at risk. And even his friends had

CONCERTO COALITIONALE

to acknowledge his increasing reputation for extravagant language and political misjudgement.

Once again he overcame adversity by throwing himself into his work, and specifically his select committee on Indian reform. At its best, committee work in the House of Commons involves the patient accumulation and mastery of considerable bodies of specialist knowledge and expert testimony. On the whole, it is little noticed and little credited by the general public. Yet it is a staple of good government, now as then. Burke's committee would in time produce eleven detailed reports, in which he took great pride, and of which the Ninth and Eleventh are still read today. Both were sharp indictments of East India Company policy and practice, in which evidence and poignant anecdote were carefully marshalled to build up a picture of malfeasance and corruption. The Ninth Report surveyed the recent history of the Company, arguing that North's Regulating Act of 1773, which sought to overhaul its management and improve its finances, was inadequate and being widely abused. It then traced the loss of revenue in Bengal to private abuse and peculation; described the unavailing attempts of the directors to prevent misconduct; surveyed specific abuses in silk, opium, saltpetre and the other traded monopolies; and pointed the finger squarely at key figures within the Company. The Eleventh Report then continued the attack, by looking at gifts received by Company employees, arguing that these were illegal and unjustifiable and amounted to corrupt tribute obtained by extortion. Again, it did not shrink from focusing blame on specific individuals.

The principal target of both reports was a man who would occupy much of Burke's life for the next twelve years, almost to the point of obsession. This was Warren Hastings, Governor General in Calcutta since 1773. Burke had first come across Hastings in the context of the Regulating Act. Since then his suspicions had been regularly fed by Philip Francis, who had been appointed to the East India Company's new Supreme Council in Bengal at that time. But Francis himself was a far from disinterested observer. Yet another talented Irishman on the rise, he was ten years younger than Burke and possessed of a far greater skill for social ingratiation, moving from the patronage of Henry Fox to that of William Pitt the Elder, and thence into the War Office under the North government. Today he is widely thought to be the author of the *Letters of Junius*, which in the years 1769–72 excoriated the Grafton administration and its successors for corruption, incompetence and patronage, as well as arousing considerable public anger against the treatment of John Wilkes, the radical reformer.

After Francis moved to India in 1774 he and Hastings quickly discovered a deep mutual antipathy, both professionally and personally. Francis repeatedly tried to thwart and discredit Hastings, and had united the other two members of the Council against him, only for his own credibility to be destroyed by the discovery of his flagrant affair with the wife of a fellow Company man, the spectacularly beautiful Madame Grand, later to become a famous courtesan and the wife of the diplomat and statesman Talleyrand. The hatred between Francis and Hastings culminated in a duel in 1780, in which Francis was wounded. Returning to England in the following year, he dedicated himself to promoting reform of India, bringing Hastings to justice and securing the Governor Generalship in his own name. To these ends, he worked vigorously behind the scenes to feed Burke with his own information and often highly partisan opinions.

Over the summer of 1783 Burke was heavily involved in constructing and drafting what became known as Fox's India Bill. At its heart was an unhappy compromise. It seemed obvious that the Company required greater supervision and control by Parliament, but Burke, Fox and their followers instinctively opposed any extension of the power of the Crown. In the modern era this problem would hardly arise, since the British monarchy generally has little formal political personality independent of Parliament. In the 1780s, however, matters were very different both constitutionally and practically, given George III's particular appetite for political activism, an appetite to which he was about to give considerable indulgence.

Accordingly, the Bill proposed the creation of seven new nominated commissioners, based in London and holding office for between three and five years. These would be appointed only by Parliament, and answerable only to Parliament. The idea was simple: to continue the process of reform by further curtailing Crown powers of patronage. But the Bill itself was far from satisfactory. Not only did it constitute a clear erosion of the rights of the Company – rights made more vivid to contemporary eyes by being those of an institution created by Royal Charter – but there was little reason to think that seven commissioners in London would make any real difference in curbing abuses many thousands of miles away in India. A voyage between the two countries typically took four to six months. The brute facts of geography could not be amended by Act of Parliament.

More controversial still was the Bill's nomination of specific commissioners on fixed terms, which was widely regarded as a hypocritical attempt by Fox to secure for himself and his cronies precisely the kind of patronage for which they had long denounced the Crown. Even if the commissioners were dismissed, it was suggested, they could continue to control the vast wealth and influence of the East India Company for years afterwards. Nevertheless, the Bill sailed through the Commons, supported by a brilliant speech by Burke, in which he described recent abuses by the East India Company under Hastings and their devastating effects on the Indian people, and expounded on the magnificence of Indian civilization, its wealth, its learning, its antiquity, its religious and cultural pluralism, its princes and merchants, agriculture and markets. The Bill and other measures would, he said, be 'a Magna Carta for Hindustan', protecting the rights of individuals and supporting the social order.

Burke ended with a long paean of praise to his friend and companion in arms Charles James Fox:

the rescue of the greatest number of the human race that ever were so grievously oppressed, from the greatest tyranny that was ever exercised, has fallen to the lot of abilities and dispositions equal to the task . . . He well knows what snares are spread about his path, from personal animosity, from court intrigues, and possibly from popular delusion . . . He may live long, he may do much. But here is the summit. He never can exceed what he does this day.

It was evidently heartfelt. But Fox may not have been the only man he had in mind.

Yet all was in vain. The Bill was expected to become law, and opposition to it, despite the formidable number of nabob MPs, had been caught napping by the government's speed of movement. But the King had been and remained implacably hostile to the Coalition. Now he saw his chance. Casting aside constitutional protocol, he actively encouraged his confidant Lord Temple, the son of his former Prime Minister George Grenville, to foment opposition to the Bill in the House of Lords, by stating in terms that 'whoever voted for the India Bill, were not only not his friends, but he should consider them as his enemies'. William Pitt the Younger, who had grandly refused junior office but been appointed Chancellor of the Exchequer under Shelburne, was sounded out as to his willingness to form a government, and offered tactical advice behind the scenes. The Archbishop of Canterbury was instructed by the King to vote against the Bill. The Bishops were mobilized. The result was that the Bill was defeated in the Lords on 15 December 1783 and thrown out amid scenes of high drama on the 17th. On the 19th the King dismissed the Coalition. On the following day William Pitt kissed hands as the new Prime Minister. He was just twenty-four years of age.

With a large majority against him, Pitt was widely expected to last only a few weeks in office. But with astonishing adroitness he cobbled together a Cabinet and manoeuvred himself through the coming months, shrugging off lost votes, dividing the opposition by framing new legislation on India, wooing reformers and the City, and building a public reputation for independence of mind and commitment to the national interest, while telling a few bare-faced lies to Parliament about his own complicity in Fox's downfall. Above all, he was sustained by a tidal wave of royal influence and patronage: office-holders who switched sides stayed in post, wavering MPs were given pensions, while those with a political following got something better. 'They are carrying peerages about the streets in barrows,' said Horace Walpole. Slowly, the numbers started to turn in Pitt's favour.

The King finally dissolved Parliament in March 1784, with public opinion running strongly for Pitt. The result was a triumph for the new Prime Minister. The Coalition lost more than a hundred of its supporters, promptly nicknamed 'Fox's Martyrs', while Pitt registered seventy net gains, enough for a three-figure majority. As for Burke: he had retained his pocket-borough seat at Malton, thanks to the support of Earl Fitzwilliam, Rockingham's nephew and heir. But in every other way the turn of events had been a disaster. Fox had been decisively outmanoeuvred. A compromised but reforming government had been repudiated at the polls. Constitutional precedent had been set aside by the King, and the House of Commons vanquished by the royal prerogative. Patronage held sway. Burke himself was isolated, mocked, humiliated. Twenty years of thought, of argument, of political struggle, lay in total disarray.

Pitt's immediate priorities were to put reform in India and Ireland on as secure a long-term basis as possible, not least to placate his own reforming supporters. For Ireland, he framed a series of Irish Propositions in 1785 which failed in the Commons, eliciting in Burke the same equivocal feelings as had the earlier reforms.

India was a different story, however. In passing his own India Act in 1784, Pitt had hoped to end the controversy over the

Company's abuses, corruption and profiteering. In reality, however, controversy continued to grow, and Burke was its prime mover. The Act was a sensible reforming measure, which further stream-lined Company administration in India, while giving London a degree of direct control. Pitt was in some ways almost as strongly committed to Indian reform as Burke, but he was a far cannier politician. Working with his friend and adviser Henry Dundas, who had made himself an expert on the issue, he secured in advance the crucial support of the Company for the new legislation. The Company's commercial independence was formally left undis-turbed, while in reality it was made subordinate to a board controlled by ministers and privy councillors. The Act remained in place until 1858, when Company rule was ended after the catas-trophe of the Indian Mutiny.

In the Commons Burke was still severely shaken by the election and its aftermath. He gave a wild speech against the Bill, misreading Pitt's intention and denouncing it as an extension of patronage. But he also sought to shape the political agenda, and made clear in calling for papers that he intended to petition for the recall and prosecution of Warren Hastings himself. Hastings was, he said, 'the scourge of India . . . a dreadful Colossus . . . who lorded it over every thing that was great and powerful and good in India, and in England'. Those responsible for the evils of Company rule must be brought to account personally for their actions. Henceforth for Burke that meant the prosecution – many said, persecution – of one man. It would be just, it would have exemplary value *pour encourager les autres*, and it could be used to highlight the Company's secret role in defeating Fox's India Bill and bringing down the Coalition government.

His next opportunity to build support occurred in February 1785, and revisited a previous battleground. Eight years earlier Burke had denounced the Company's role in supporting the takeover of the state of Tanjore by the Nawab of Arcot; now the bills had come due. The Nawab had long been a British client and had been instrumental in fighting off incursions from the neighbouring state of Mysore. In so doing he had incurred huge debts to another key figure in Burke's Indian demonology, Paul Benfield, a Company man with close links to financiers in Madras, who had acted as his adviser. The Company's directors had decided that the various claims for payment should be individually assessed, but this was now overruled by Dundas, who ordered the total amount to be paid off directly out of public funds.

Benfield stood to make the gigantic sum of over £500,000 from a complete settlement of the debts. Earlier he had successfully argued to the directors that his actions were well known to the Company, if not above board, and that they had been highly beneficial to Company and nation alike. In his marathon four-hour 'Speech on the Nawab of Arcot's Debts', however, Burke detected not merely usury at work, but a deeper conspiracy to defraud the public interest, in which the British in India had used debt to grease the wheels of power in India, making private fortunes for themselves through guarantees which would now be met by the Exchequer, that is by taxpayers. There had never been, he charged, an expectation that the Nawab would pay those debts back himself. To this was added a political dimension, in the support which Benfield's influence among MPs had given to Pitt in the election.

All this, however, was merely a preliminary. Burke had been publicly calling for those responsible in India to be held to account since 1782; now he decided to take the matter into his own hands. After an autumn and winter of further intensive work, he announced in the Commons on 17 February 1786 that he was initiating impeachment proceedings against Warren Hastings. Impeachment was an ancient procedure, going back over 400 years; the last one had been in 1746. Originally used as a means by which the legislature could hold individuals in government to account, it had fallen into disuse under the Tudors, before being taken up again in the seventeenth century as a political weapon: the Long Parliament of 1640–51 alone had seen ninety-eight impeachments. The impeachment of Lord

Macclesfield in 1725, however, saw the procedure returned to its proper purpose, as a means to prosecute ministers and officials for abuse of power.

Impeachment proceedings could theoretically be for any crime, but were reserved by custom for 'high crimes and misdemeanours'. They were initiated by MPs, but the trial itself was heard by the House of Lords, with procedures similar to those in a criminal trial. For Burke, the advantages of impeachment were obvious: it was an ancient and hallowed procedure; it could be initiated by him personally; and it could relate to alleged crimes long past or committed in foreign countries. He privately acknowledged from the outset that it was unlikely to secure a conviction: it would be difficult to obtain evidence from India admissible in an English court, and Hastings was supported by the King and had many friends in the government and across the Lords. But the trial would have such a high profile that conviction might not be necessary for success in the court of public opinion. And, he thought, impeachment itself might become a weapon once again against the abuse of power. Bernard Mandeville had taught in his *Fable of the Bees* (1714) that private vices could give rise to public benefit; so might it be here too.

Impeachment had one other important feature: unlike a Crown case, it would be deeply personal, pitting him directly against Hastings, the campaigner against the financial establishment. It is unlikely that Burke saw this as a drawback. James Gillray, the greatest caricaturist of the period, caught the point perfectly in his print *The Political Banditti assailing the Saviour of India* (see opposite). Hastings is ironically depicted as an exotic Indian maharaja-cum-Britannia on horseback, making off with jewels and personal loot. To protect himself he holds up a Shield of Honour against which the austere, barefoot and bespectacled Burke in 'Jesuit' garb and biretta is discharging a blunderbuss. Tellingly, Fox rushes to stab Hastings in the back, while North quietly helps himself to a large bag of rupees for the Revenue. Only Burke faces Hastings from the front.

Pub.d 3.d May 11 1786 by Wm. Holland N.º 66 Drury Lane.

The POLITICAL-BANDITTI assailing the SAVIOUR of INDIA.

What kind of man was Hastings? On balance, history has not demurred from the judgement of Thomas Babington Macaulay, who said 'he had great qualities, and he rendered great services to the State. But to represent him as a man of stainless virtue is to make him ridiculous . . . He must have known that there were dark spots on his fame. He might also have felt with pride that the splendour of his fame would bear many spots.' A lifelong servant of the East India Company, Hastings (see opposite, after a portrait of 1796) had come to India in 1750 as a teenager and worked his way up the hierarchy over more than thirty years. Captured by the Nawab's forces in 1756, he had escaped and then volunteered to join Clive's forces, before the latter retook Calcutta. After the battle of Plassey, Clive arranged for Hastings to be installed as British Resident in the Bengali capital of Murshidabad. After a long visit to Britain in which he fell badly into debt and impressed Dr Johnson, he went to Madras in 1769, before becoming Governor of Calcutta, and then the first Governor General following the 1773 reforms.

Hastings was used to exercising a degree of personal power unknown to any British politician, in circumstances of extreme treachery, complexity and danger. As the impeachment record would show, he had a great deal to answer for in his dealings with various Indian states, which he had successfully manipulated against different threats coming from the west in the 1770s, before extracting prodigious sums of money from the winners. Despite a very different background and experience Hastings had a surprising amount in common with Burke himself: classically educated and a deeply cultivated man, he was a linguist both in Urdu and in the Persian of the Mughal Empire, and the sponsor of the first grammar of the Bengali language. Far from despising the Indians, as would become characteristic of so much of the Raj in the nineteenth century, he had immersed himself in their customs, traditions and religious practices. As Resident in Murshidabad he had incurred the enmity of fellow residents by his attempts to root out corruption and abuse by European traders in Bengal. In Madras, he had

reformed trading practices successfully. In Calcutta, despite vigorous
opposition from the Council, he had greatly improved the administration and finances of the Company in Bengal. Like Burke, he
believed that all good government must go with the temper of the
governed.

Hastings was quite as self-righteous as Burke, but he was also
arrogant. Forced in May 1786 to respond publicly to the first of
Burke's twenty-two articles of impeachment, he made a bad first
impression in denying that there was any case to answer. By June,
with the unexpected support of Pitt, Burke had secured a Commons
majority on the charge that Hastings had overreached himself in
extracting £500,000 from the Raja of Benares. Process was agoniz-
ingly slow, since Parliament did not sit in the summer and autumn.
However, when it resumed in January 1787 a crucial witness gave
way under interrogation on another key charge, that Hastings had
forcibly expropriated the huge sum of £2 million from the mother
and grandmother of the Nawab Wazir of Oudh, and seized,
shackled, imprisoned and starved their two elderly advisers, the
eunuchs of the treasury. The 'Begums of Oudh' and their eunuchs
became instant celebrities as a result. Pitt continued to stir the pot
from a distance, doubtless happy that public attention was focused
on the impeachment rather than on the government; he now waived
his demand that the charges be separately debated. There was a
final vote in April, and Hastings was arrested and released on bail.

The action now moved to a full trial in the Lords, to take place
in Westminster Hall. Westminster Hall, already then 700 years old,
was and is still the greatest jewel in the Palace of Westminster. The
modern visitor can see the very places where Sir Thomas More was
tried in 1535, where King Charles I sat during his trial for treason
in January 1649, and where Churchill's body lay in state in 1965
– there is no plaque to show the location of the trial of Guy Fawkes
in 1606. If walls could talk, truly it would have tales to tell. For
centuries the largest single-span building in Europe, it was begun
in 1097 by William Rufus, the son of William the Conqueror; the

magnificent hammer-beam roof, with its carved wooden angels gazing down, is a later creation and dates back to the 1390s. The Hall was long used by the different Courts of King's Bench, of Chancery and of Common Pleas, and in particular for great state trials. This was once again to be its function.

When Burke opened impeachment proceedings on 13 February 1788, Westminster Hall was a majestic sight (see overleaf). It had been set up as a larger version of the Lords itself, with the throne and royal boxes at the south end, benches for the peers in the centre and long galleries for spectators on each side, hung with scarlet. Two hundred lords had walked solemnly down in full robes from their chamber to sit in judgement. Queen Charlotte and the Princesses were present, as were judges, bishops and archbishops, along with unnumbered ambassadors and a further 200 members of the Commons. Outside, the crowd was kept at bay by the King's Guards. The writer Fanny Burney had long been a friend and admirer of Burke's, only to have second thoughts over the impeachment. Yet she was dazzled by him on her visit to the trial: 'All I had heard of his eloquence ... was answered by his performance ... His satire had a poignancy of wit . . . his allusions and quotations . . . were apt and ingenious; and the wild and sudden flights of his fancy ... had a charm for my ear and my attention wholly new and perfectly irresistible.'

The excitement did not last, and it could not. Burke's impeachment of Warren Hastings was to continue for 149 days, dragged out over seven years. And it was overtaken by news in November that was to rock the entire political establishment to its foundations: the King, it seemed, was going mad.

It had started quietly enough. In June 1788 the King had been somewhat indisposed, and he and the Queen had taken the waters in Cheltenham, marking his recovery with a tour in the west of England. Courtiers had noted with alarm that he had beat time at

a performance of the *Messiah* in Worcester Cathedral as though conducting an orchestra, but put the matter down to natural exuberance. In late October, however, the King's doctor diagnosed him as bordering on delirium; in November he was clearly deranged, at one point descending from his carriage in Windsor Great Park and greeting a tree as the King of Prussia. What added to the irony was that despite a reign so far of almost thirty years the King was just fifty years of age, a man of ascetic habits and self-discipline, indeed a fitness fanatic given to walking and riding many miles at a stretch. Modern medical opinion is divided as to the nature and causes of his illness; some have suggested the genetic disorder porphyria, but recent research has pointed to psychiatric illness. At the time poisoning was widely suspected, some even attributing it to Fox.

Government and opposition alike were now thrust into a constitutional crisis of the first magnitude. If the King were to die, that meant the elevation to power of the notoriously dissolute and thoroughly pro-Fox Prince of Wales. If the King were declared incompetent, however, a regency would surely follow. In either case, the results for Pitt and the government could be disastrous. Pitt therefore temporized, adjourning Parliament and then convening the Privy Council and a Commons committee to question the doctors. At the same time he held his administration together while key members, notably the Lord Chancellor Thurlow, consulted their personal ambition and considered defection to the Whigs. Speculative lists of Whig Cabinet ministers started to circulate in anticipation. Burke's name was not on them.

In stalling for time Pitt was assisted by the incompetence, arrogance and division of the opposition. Devonshire and Portland were away. Fox himself was in Italy in November with his mistress, the redoubtable Mrs Armistead, a former courtesan whose previous conquests had included 'two ducal coronets, a marquis, four earls and a viscount', according to *Town and Country Magazine*, as well as the Prince of Wales himself. Fox had resolved to read only the

racing reports in the newspapers while he was away, but nevertheless heard the news and rushed back to London, only to spend
much of the next three months in bed with illness himself, or
gambling at Brooks's. In his absence the role of intermediary
between Prince and Parliament was played by Richard Brinsley
Sheridan. Sheridan was another Irish transplant, elected to
Parliament in 1780. Twenty years younger than Burke, he had had
a brilliant career as a playwright and theatre manager, writing the
smash hits *The Rivals* and *The School for Scandal*, both of which
immediately became (and have remained) standards of the reper-
toire. Fiercely ambitious, a formidable speaker and legendary wit,
he had attached himself to Fox's more radical flank and ingratiated
himself with the Prince of Wales. Now these relationships came
into their own.

Matters came to a head in a tumultuous parliamentary debate
on 10 December 1788, when Pitt proposed the creation of a further
committee to examine the relevant precedents. Thwarted, ailing,
impatient of detail and filled with a desperate craving for power,
Fox insisted that, given the King's manifest incompetence, the Prince
of Wales be allowed the succession immediately. He had 'no hesitation in declaring that His Royal Highness the Prince of Wales had
as clear, as express a right to assume the reins of government . . .
as in the case of His Majesty's having undergone a natural and
perfect demise'. Above all, the Whigs were committed to the constitutional settlement of 1688–9, which affirmed the supremacy of
Parliament. The irony of a Whig leader now proposing to set
parliamentary process aside in favour of an individual claim to the
throne was too much even for the imperturbable Pitt. He is said
to have slapped his thigh with delight, saying 'I'll unWhig him for
the rest of his life.'

Burke himself had little time for the Prince of Wales. But for
him it was precisely the principles and spirit of the constitution of
1689 that created an automatic right to a regency for the Prince.
The position was a dubious one, and it was not helped by a speech

which misjudged the chamber: intemperate, rambling, filled with bemusing historical allusions, and very hostile to Pitt himself. Worse, after a quiet January in which Burke systematically educated himself on madness, even visiting an asylum of 300 inmates in Hoxton, he renewed the attack in February with a series of violent verbal assaults on Pitt's formal proposals to manage a period of regency. His speech included lurid descriptions of inmates who had supposedly recovered from madness, only to commit suicide, butcher their families or injure themselves. Intended as scholarly contributions to the debate, these were regarded as ill-judged and highly offensive aspersions on the King, who was even then recovering well from his illness. The danger had passed. Pitt was triumphant.

At about this time the MP Gilbert Elliot spoke for many in his description of Burke, now nearly sixty:

> Of Mr Burke, I reverence the character, and . . . I venerate him as a man of uncommon genius. I lament that such a man should be driven . . . to the narrow character of a party advocate . . . he seems at present to be little valued; for he is heard in the house with impatience. Dismiss him, then, to ease; as you would turn out a good old horse to a fertile pasture for life.

Yet even then the thunderclouds of revolution were building over France. The old horse was a war horse, and about to have his finest hour.

FIVE

Reflecting on Revolution, 1789–1797

THE EARLY MONTHS OF 1789 SAW the King regain his sanity and the Regency Crisis recede. Burke prepared to resume the impeachment of Warren Hastings, resisting an effort by Fox in May to recuse himself and halt proceedings. Parliament returned to business as usual.

In France, however, the social order was about to experience a cataclysm. The immediate causes were not far to seek: rising food prices, shortages and hunger. Food stocks were low, a long spring drought had made matters worse, and a freak storm in early July, with hailstones large enough to kill men and animals, had devastated much of the harvest. These evils were not alleviated, indeed they were worsened, by the financial near-collapse of the state, arising from colossal war debts and especially those left by the American Revolutionary War. To such matters were added a host of other grievances: the arrogance of the Court at Versailles, the ineffectiveness of ministers, the feudal structure of land ownership, the rigid authority and impositions of the Church, and a regressive tax system which penalized the poor and privileged the rich. Enlightenment ideas fanned resentment with dreams of political freedom, religious toleration and personal emancipation, while established authority rapidly waned. Even the weather did not help, with a blisteringly hot summer that inflamed tempers still further.

The early architect of financial reform Jacques Necker, long admired by Burke, had been dismissed two years before, only to be restored to office as the crisis escalated. An Assembly of Notables was convened in 1787 to address the worsening situation and concert pressure for tax reform, but with no result. In desperation the King called a meeting of the Estates General for May 1789, its first meeting since 1614. The Estates General was a general assembly, comprising the three great constitutional orders or 'estates' of the nobility, the Church and the people. Summoned to agree tax reform, it quickly became embroiled in a dispute over the powers and voting rights of the Third Estate. In 1614 voting had been not by individual ballot but by orders, a system which privileged the nobility and Church over the vastly more numerous deputies of the people. In June, however, the Third Estate, now calling itself the *Communes*, or Commons, decided to proceed without the other two; then, joined by their more sympathetic members, it resolved itself into a National Assembly, an assembly not of orders but of deputies representing themselves as such. The King tried vainly to prevent the Assembly from meeting, then dismissed Necker again in early July. Paris erupted in chaos and rioting. On 14 July, the mob stormed the prison of the Bastille, a detested symbol of the *ancien régime*. The revolution had begun.

In Britain, the initial reaction to events in France was sanguine, and would remain so for some time. Realists were not generally dismayed to see the country's historic enemy shattered and humbled, while progressives and radicals rejoiced at what they regarded as the triumph of Enlightenment ideals over intolerance and inequality. Fox was exultant: 'How much the greatest event it is that ever happened in the world! And how much the best,' he wrote in July. The revolution was regarded as a brief upheaval, which would quickly yield to good order, indeed a constitutional monarchy. This view was not daunted by the forced removal in October of the French royal family from Versailles into virtual house arrest in Paris;

Pitt himself fatefully declared to the Commons in February 1790 that 'The present convulsions of France must, sooner or later, termi- nate in general harmony . . . thus circumstanced, France . . . would enjoy just that kind of liberty which I venerate.'

For many people, a specific parallel beckoned with the events of 1688–9, when King James II had fled the country and the Protestant Stadtholder of the Netherlands William of Orange had assumed the throne, in what became known as the Glorious Revolution. That revolution was celebrated as glorious because it preserved a Protestant succession without renewed civil war or, in England at least, much bloodshed; Ireland and Scotland were a very different story. In a superstitious age, the fact that almost exactly a century had intervened between the two events seemed a mark of provi- dence itself. As a period of calm ensued in France, these expectations seemed to be fulfilled.

But one man did not share the general optimism. Even before hearing of the events of October 1789 Edmund Burke had expressed deep reservations about the revolution. In November, he received a letter from a young French friend, Charles Depont, soliciting his support for it. Then in January 1790 he read what he regarded as a highly incendiary sermon from a leading radical, the dissenting preacher Dr Richard Price, given at a meeting of the recently formed Revolution Society. Ostensibly on the topic of patriotism, Price's sermon in fact argued that patriotism did not imply any belief that one's own country was superior to others. Instead, Englishmen should see themselves not as rooted in a specific community but as citizens of the world. Price celebrated the French revolution as the proper successor to the Glorious Revolution, itself unfinished, which had given the British people the right to cashier their governors and remove their own monarch from the throne. On 1 November 1790 Burke published his reply, *Reflections on the Revolution in France.*

The *Reflections,* and the works that accompany it, mark one of the greatest late flourishings not simply of any politician, but of any writer or thinker throughout history. They are filled with anger,

indeed outrage. But gone is the aged irrelevance, the embarrassment, the much derided pantaloon of the Regency Crisis. Instead
we have Burke the Celtic *vates*, the seer, inspired by cold passion
and intellectual energy, prophesying the future when all around
are absorbed in fantasy, folly and self-congratulation. This is no
great event, he says, no general harmony, no liberty to be venerated;
it is a catastrophe. It will not lead to good order, or the ideal society
anticipated by the *bien pensants*, the radical intellectuals and their
fellow-travellers. No, the French revolution is not ended. What lie
in store are violence, bloodshed, anarchy, terror and civil war. Far
from settling down, France will spread an international spirit of
sedition that will infect Britain, and the result of its revolution will
be war.

The *Reflections* is a great master-work, which refines and extends
ideas with which Burke had been working for almost thirty years.
These ideas will fill much of the rest of this book, so a brief summary
will suffice here. In form, the work is not a treatise but a long letter
addressed to Depont. As a letter, it enables Burke to mix commentary on events in France with political observations and deep
insights into history, culture and philosophy. He can speak author-
itatively to his young friend, and persuade without seeming to
lecture. An opening shot gives a warning of what is to follow:

> Flattery corrupts both the receiver and the giver . . . I should
> therefore suspend my congratulations on the new liberty of
> France, until I was informed how it had been combined with
> government; with public force; with the discipline and obedience
> of armies; with the collection of an effective and well-distributed
> revenue; with morality and religion; with the solidity of property;
> with peace and order; with civil and social manners.

As the rest of his book makes clear, for Burke the French revolution
in fact fails all these tests.

He turns next to Dr Price's sermon and the attempted parallel with 1688. To Burke this comparison is entirely spurious. The Glorious Revolution was not, he avers, the exercise of the people's supposed right to choose their own monarch. It was necessary, not discretionary, 'a small and temporary deviation from the strict order of regular hereditary succession', and recognized at the time as such. As with all effective reforms, it was limited in scope and duration, and insulated from the rest of the body politic. Why? Because, as Burke memorably put it, 'A state without the means of some change is without the means of its conservation.' The true point of comparison for Burke is not the Glorious Revolution, but the Civil War of the 1640s, with all its disorder and bloodshed. The error of Dr Price and his friends was to follow the French doctrine of natural rights. This in turn led them to take the constitutional exception for the rule, and to support not gradual change but revolution. They preferred their own imaginings to the settled idea of the constitution handed down through time 'in our histories, in our records, in our Acts of Parliament . . . and not in . . . sermons, or the after-dinner toasts of the Revolution Society'.

Individual foolishness thus supplanted shared wisdom. But such a supplanting, such a rejection, was in effect a rejection of society itself, and of social institutions: 'We are afraid to put men to live and trade each on his own private stock of reason; because we suspect that this stock in each man is small, and that the individuals would do better to avail themselves of the general bank and capital of nations, and of ages.' Society was the product not principally of reason but of affection, built up from below: 'To be attached to the subdivision, to love the little platoon we belong to in society, is . . . the first link in the series by which we proceed towards a love to our country and to mankind.' And its domain, its sphere of moral concern, was not a person, or a group or class, or even a generation, but the social order itself, persisting over time. Society was 'a partnership not only between those who are living, but between those who are living, those who are dead, and those who are to be born'.

But the *Reflections* is a work not merely of thought but of polemic and anger. Most famous is Burke's piteous description of Marie Antoinette herself. Recalling his earlier visit, he said:

> It is now sixteen or seventeen years since I saw the Queen of France . . . at Versailles; and surely never lighted on this orb, which she hardly seemed to touch, a more delightful vision . . . little did I dream that I should have lived to see such disasters fallen upon her in a nation of gallant men, in a nation of men of honour and cavaliers. I thought ten thousand swords must have leaped from their scabbards to avenge even a look that threatened her with insult. But the age of chivalry is gone. That of sophisters, economists and calculators has succeeded; and the glory of Europe is extinguished forever.

Though it would also be used against him, Burke's tableau is masterly propaganda. But it also contains a deep philosophical point, as we shall see.

At five shillings and 356 pages, the *Reflections* was more than three times the price and three times the length of a typical political pamphlet. But it sold 9,000 copies within the month, and 17,500 by the end of the year. It was quickly reviewed, important passages were widely reprinted, and the whole had been translated into French, with further huge success, by mid-1791. Its wider impact was still greater, however. In *Smelling out a Rat* (see overleaf), James Gillray depicts the clash of opposing forces: Dr Price is caught in the act of seditious propagandizing itself by a monstrous Burke of nose and glasses, bearing the emblems of Church and state. But, monstrous or no, the book had clearly tapped into a deep seam of counter-revolutionary emotion across Europe.

Closer to home, the book finally redeemed Burke in the eyes of old friends and admirers like Fanny Burney, the society hostess Elizabeth Montagu, and Edmund Gibbon, who drolly described

Pub.d Dec.r 3. 1790 by H. Humphrey No. 18 Old Bond Street.

Smelling out a Rat, — or — The Atheistical-Revolutionist disturbed in his Midnight "Calculations".

Vide A tract on " ——
——ditions "

the book as Burke's 'most admirable medicine against the French disease'. It also won him a new reputation among his former adversaries, including supporters of Hastings and the previously dismissive Horace Walpole. The most notable of these new adherents was none other than George III, who set aside three decades of criticism and Burke's support for a regency to receive him at a levée, declaring that 'there is no man who calls himself a gentleman, who must not think himself obliged to you, for you have supported the cause of the gentlemen'.

Not surprisingly, the book elicited a massive counter-attack from the radicals, who responded immediately with a volley of publications denouncing Burke on every conceivable ground, leading to a pamphlet war that became known as the Revolution Controversy. In particular, they fastened on Burke's lament that in the face of the revolution 'learning will be cast into the mire, and trodden down under the hoofs of a swinish multitude', deliberately misreading this as an attack on multitudes, and so the people, as such. The most famous of the radical publications is Thomas Paine's *Rights of Man*, issued in two parts, which used the *Reflections* as a cue to set out Paine's own brand of republican politics, praising the events in France, reviling the established order in Britain and calling for a complete overhaul of the existing constitutional arrangements from first principles. Paine's pamphlet far eclipsed even Burke's sales; together, both parts may have sold as many as 100,000 copies in their first two years.

But an equally interesting early response came in *A Vindication of the Rights of Men* by Mary Wollstonecraft. Wollstonecraft was a woman of fiercely independent temper, later to influence and be much influenced by Richard Price and by the philosopher William Godwin, whom she married. Less well known than its later companion piece, *A Vindication of the Rights of Woman*, her diffuse and indignant pamphlet did not merely make the case for individual reason and republicanism. It directly attacked Burke's insistence on the importance of tradition and institutions, arguing that they perpetuated injustice; and it attributed to Burke a patronizing and offensive view of women in particular, tracing this back to the discussion of beauty in the *Enquiry*. Above all, it cleverly aped the discursive and highly rhetorical style of the *Reflections*, as though to establish by direct comparison an equality of intellect and voice between the two authors. It was widely admired, and made Wollstonecraft's name.

Some radicals, notably Catharine Macaulay, had long regarded Burke as an apologist for the establishment. But others had seen him – the defender of the rights of the American colonists and of Catholics in Ireland, supporter of free trade, harsh critic of the depredations of the East India Company – as a sympathetic voice in Parliament. For them, the *Reflections* was provocative and enraging. It was not merely wrong, but a work of betrayal and apostasy: the friend of progressive thought had become its enemy. They found themselves unable, or deeply unwilling, to understand how a set of ideas evolved by Burke over many years could consistently encompass their pet causes, yet now reject the one cause they had come to cherish above all else.

Meanwhile Whig opinion in Parliament was split. The old grandees broadly welcomed the *Reflections*, while worrying that it was too extreme in language and thought, and fearing for party unity. Earl Fitzwilliam, Burke's principal patron, offered 'his most decided approbation of all and every part', but declined to make a public declaration in its favour. As for Fox himself, in truth his long friendship with Burke had started to fray some years before, perhaps as early as 1783–4. His leadership remained as unsteady as ever: brilliant in the House and inspiring of deep affection in others, he was also lazy, opportunistic and highly ambitious for power, all qualities which Burke deprecated as unworthy of a statesman. His leadership in forming the Coalition with North and in ostentatiously backing a regency had been questionable, to say the least; but Burke had been closely involved throughout, at some cost to his own reputation.

Most recently, Fox had sought to drop the Hastings trial, much to Burke's displeasure. Now the revolution in France was pushing the two men apart politically, philosophically and personally; indeed, part of the point of the *Reflections* was precisely to warn of the dangers of a 'new republican Frenchified Whiggism' in Britain itself. The Duchess of Devonshire remarked that the relationship between Fox and Burke was 'perfectly Irish, for they are now on worse terms than ever'. The two men's estrangement was encouraged by Sheridan, who increasingly saw himself as Burke's rival and the unofficial leader of the radical Whigs. As for the two Irishmen, as one contemporary noted, 'Charles Fox says, that when Burke had fairly got the start in absurdity, it proves very superior parts in Sheridan to have recovered the lost ground, and made it a near race.'

The first public clash between Fox and Burke came while the *Reflections* was still in gestation, over the army 'estimates' or budget in February 1790. Linking the issue rather tendentiously to the events in France, Burke proclaimed the revolutionaries to be 'a lawless and sanguinary mob', which had 'committed every sort of excess, marked their footsteps with blood, singled out every man of rank . . . for vengeance'. This directly controverted Fox's known views, but Fox was emollient in reply. Not so Sheridan, who hotly defended the revolution and implied that Burke was preparing to defect to Pitt. Burke instantly rose to announce that henceforth he and Sheridan would be 'separated in politics'.

In March came a second clash, in a debate on repeal of the Test and Corporation Acts, which for centuries had required all those holding public office to be communing members of the Church of England. Burke intensely disliked the test, but given his wider fears he now argued against a full repeal, which might expose the institutions of government to infiltration from revolutionaries and republicans. This time Fox was publicly dismissive, accusing Burke of apostasy, indeed 'dereliction', proclaiming an easy mind on the French revolution and quoting back to Burke material from one of Burke's own speeches on the American war. Burke did not respond, but these wounding remarks would be remembered.

The final breach began to open more than a year later on 15 April 1791, in a debate on Russia. The proposed French constitution contemplated a constitutional monarchy subject to the overriding sovereignty of the people. Now, accused by Pitt of being a closet republican, Fox extravagantly described it as 'the most stupendous and glorious edifice of liberty which had been erected on the foundation of human integrity in any time or country'. Visibly moved, Burke wanted to reply, but was unable to do so before the vote was called. Fox then visited him privately a few days later in an attempt to procure his silence, before characteristically leaving for the races at Newmarket. His attempt was unavailing. The scene was now set for a climactic showdown between the two men.

On 6 May Burke used a debate on the governance of Quebec to discourse again on the evils of the new French constitution. Heckled on all sides by young Foxite MPs, he retained the presence of mind to quote *King Lear*, to perfect effect: 'The little dogs and all, Tray, Blanche and Sweetheart, see they bark at me!' Fox then rose, rebuked Burke for the irrelevance of his remarks to Quebec, and repeated his praise of the revolution. According to the *Parliamentary History*, Burke then replied that 'a personal attack had been made upon him from a quarter he never could have expected, after a friendship and intimacy of more than twenty-two years'. He had been publicly accused of inconsistency not merely on the basis of public words and writings, he said, but of confidential conversations. There had been previous matters on which the two men had disagreed, but without destroying their friendship. The *History* continues:

> Mr Fox here whispered that 'there was no loss of friends.' Burke said there was a loss of friends . . . he had done his duty at the price of his friend. Mr Fox rose to reply; but his mind was so much agitated and his mind so much affected by what had fallen from Mr Burke that it was some minutes before he could proceed.

Tears trickled down his cheeks, and he strove in vain to give utterance.

It is a heartbreaking moment – and a brief one, since Fox quickly returned to the attack.

And not merely a moment of personal importance. For 6 May 1791 marks the beginning of the end of the first genuine proto-political party. Created by Rockingham in 1765–6, intellectually and organizationally shaped by Burke, led latterly by Fox, the Rockingham Whigs stood for constitutional monarchy but within the settlement of 1688; for the Church of England, but with toleration for dissenters and Catholics; for economical reform and restraint on patronage and waste; for just, effective and accountable administration of the colonies; and for personal liberty but not individual licence. With no national administration, no campaigning arm and no manifesto they lacked the apparatus of the modern political party. But the core idea – of party not faction, of a political group sustaining itself on principle and policy for long periods out of office, then implementing that policy on its return – this idea originates in practical terms with them. Burke now felt himself an outcast from a party which he had done more than anyone then living to create. In reality, that party was ceasing to exist at all.

His anger expressed itself as it had always done, in writing and action. Already by April 1791 he had published, originally in Paris, his *Letter to a Member of the National Assembly*. In it he analysed the effects of the revolution on the social and political culture of France. The sweeping away of the existing order had left the people biddable and lacking in direction, he said, and easy prey for impostors posing as idealists. Young people in particular had become deeply corrupted by revolutionary ideas. They had fallen under the malign influence of Rousseau, 'the insane Socrates of the National Assembly', a philosopher whose person and thought were dedicated to an 'ethics of vanity', which exalted the self and ignored values of honour, duty, humility and personal virtue.

France was in the grip of a tyranny, and those in power would never willingly abandon it. They had become 'a college of armed fanatics, for the propagation of the principles of assassination, robbery, rebellion, fraud, faction, oppression and impiety'. Government, far from restraining disorder, had become its accomplice. The result, Burke predicted, would be nothing less than regicide: 'In spite of their solemn declarations, their soothing addresses, and the multiplied oaths which they have taken and forced others to take, they will assassinate the King when his name will no longer be necessary to their designs.' And the canker would spread to other nations. To stop this, for the first time Burke now scouted the idea of external intervention in support of counter-revolution. It was a theme he would sound with increasing stridency in the years ahead.

In August Burke returned to the domestic fray. Now in a minority of one, exiled from his own party, he felt the fire of self-justification burn more fiercely than ever. But still more important was the issue of principle: casting the issue in a Manichean spirit of good vs. evil, he feared that Fox was leading his followers towards Jacobinism – the word used to describe the most famous of the French revolutionary clubs, by then a byword for revolutionary zeal. Jacobinism of any description in British politics would, Burke was certain, be a ruinous development for the country; at all costs it must be averted. He knew the views of the *Reflections* were shared among many Whigs, in particular the crucial figures of the Duke of Portland and Earl Fitzwilliam, the heir to Rockingham. These men must be recalled to their duty, indeed forced to choose publicly between him and Fox, even if the result was to split the party.

The result was *An Appeal from the New to the Old Whigs*. Again, this is a work teeming with ideas, which can only be briefly summarized. On the surface, it is a legal appeal written by an anonymous third party to show how the views of 'Mr Burke' spring directly from the founding Old Whig principles of the 1688 revolution, while those of Fox and his New Whig acolytes are dangerous innovations based on French revolutionary ideas. Burke is thus a New Whig in chronology, but an Old Whig in spirit. That minor source of confusion apart, this is Burke assuming an independent and authoritative persona in order to settle a grudge, extend the arguments of the *Reflections* and *Letter*, drive a political wedge between Fox and his more moderate supporters, and force the moderates to declare themselves.

The *Appeal* opens with a highly personal *exordium* or introduction defending 'Mr Burke' against charges of inconsistency or bad faith, and expounding the content of his missing speech in the Quebec debate. It then moves to a relatively spare and forensic analysis of Old Whig principles, before opening out in characteristic fashion into an expansive statement of political philosophy. The revolution in France is *sui generis*, Burke insists. The new constitution is 'a tyranny far beyond any example that can be found in the civilised European world of our age . . . not a transient evil . . . but . . . only the means of producing future and (if that were possible) worse evils . . . it is so fundamentally wrong as to be utterly incapable of correcting itself by any length of time'. Far from creating peace among nations, the revolutionaries have been bent on destroying it: 'these common enemies to mankind . . . meditated war against all other governments, and proposed systematically to excite in them all the very worst kind of sedition, in order to lead to their common destruction'.

In England these sentiments were being unconsciously advanced by the New Whigs under Fox. Their gospel it was that the people are sovereign and so:

> may set up any new fashion of government for themselves, or continue without any government, at their pleasure; that the people are essentially their own rule, and their will the measure of their

conduct . . . and that, if a contract *de facto* is made with them in
one age, allowing that it binds at all, it only binds those who are
immediately concerned in it, but does not pass to posterity.

But this is both a mistake, Burke insists, and wildly divergent from
founding Old Whig principles. No one denies that sovereignty
originated from the people; but the genius of the British constitution is precisely that it creates a mixed polity, in which monarchy,
Lords and Commons divide power between them, and set bound-
aries to each other. The popular will is not unfettered, therefore:
the constitution binds the people just as surely as it binds the other
estates of the realm. The wisdom of the whole comes through the
whole, and only through the whole. Individuals possess not merely
the rights conferred by the social order; they are also bound by its
duties, whether they like them or no.

Burke ends the *Appeal* with a hymn of praise to the British
constitution:

> This British Constitution has not been struck out at an heat by a
> set of presumptuous men, like the Assembly of pettifoggers run
> mad in Paris . . . It is the result of the thoughts of many minds
> in many ages. It is no simple, no superficial thing, nor to be esti-
> mated by superficial understandings. An ignorant man, who is
> not fool enough to meddle with his clock, is, however, sufficiently
> confident to think he can safely take to pieces and put together,
> at his pleasure, a moral machine of another guise, importance and
> complexity, composed of far other wheels and springs and balances
> and counteracting and co-operating powers. Men little think how
> immorally they act in rashly meddling with what they do not
> understand. Their delusive good intention is no sort of excuse for
> their presumption.

The *Appeal* did not merely advance Burke's wider argument. It was
also a very conscious political move. Moderate Whigs largely agreed

with its sentiments, but they reacted badly to having the group's dirty linen, and specifically the growing hostilities between Burke and Fox, aired in public. In this they were no different from political parties of every stripe ever since. Political parties are coalitions based on loyalty, whose effectiveness depends on maintaining the capacity for collective action. Internal discipline is therefore at a premium. Yet here was Burke not merely advertising his dissent, but deliberately seeking to foment a split among the Whigs. Fitzwilliam thus maintained his silence, while Portland moved a judicious distance away and, with some misgivings, kept up his support for Fox. The younger Foxites continued to accuse Burke of apostasy, their allegations fed by rumours of the King's admiration for the *Appeal* and of Burke's treating with the very Friends of the King that he had denounced in his *Thoughts on the Cause of the Present Discontents*. Pitt and Dundas meanwhile rejoiced at Fox's discomfiture.

But what of Fox himself? He undoubtedly felt the loss of Burke's friendship. But he had carelessly dismissed the *Reflections*, admitting in May 1791 that he had not even read the book. Intellectually, Fox was trapped in the arguments of the 1780s: he insisted on seeing the French revolution as a re-run of 1688, with Louis XVI as James II. For him, in France as with George III, the issue was one of monarchical power run amok. It was the duty of the Whigs to support the transition to a new and stable constitutional order.

In practical terms, Fox remained the Whigs' undisputed leader, a position bolstered by displays of political moderation through which he sought to place himself between Burke on the one hand and the radicals on the other. But there was little doubt about where his true sympathies lay – if a man who lived so much in the present could be said to have had true sympathies outside the turf, the card table and the bedchamber. As often happens, political pressures and public opinion had a centrifugal effect, pushing him towards radicalism. And beneath the surface his party was in increasing disarray, as its members pondered the questions raised by the *Appeal*: was Fox's identification with the principles of the French revolution good politics? Was it wise? Was it even consonant with Whig principles at all? These questions particularly resonated in the minds of the Whig grandees, on whom Fox relied for funds and political influence.

Fox's position was made still more uncomfortable by external events in 1790–2. Spurred on by the pamphlet war, radical clubs were springing up across the country proclaiming and disseminating the principles of Paine's *Rights of Man*. Many were new; some, like the Society for Constitutional Information, had existed for more than a decade. As a counterweight, and to solidify their party against Burke, the Foxites had formed the more moderate Association of the Friends of the People. But even this required delicate handling by Fox. To make matters worse, rumours started to circulate that the King was growing disenchanted with Pitt. In that event, Fox mistakenly believed, he himself might be invited to form an administration. For him at least, this was an outcome still fervently to be desired.

It was events in France that decided the matter. On the night of 21 June 1791 Louis XVI, Marie Antoinette and their family attempted to flee Paris in disguise for the royalist stronghold of Montmédy in north-eastern France. The King was dressed as a butler, but he was recognized and the family detained en route in Varennes. They were returned to Paris under guard and still in disguise, where they were received by the mob in enforced silence and confined in the Tuileries. The flight to Varennes further stoked the fires of republicanism in France, and pushed thousands of loyalist troops into the hands of the émigrés on its borders. But it also provoked a wider international crisis. The humiliation of the once-magnificent Bourbon Court struck horror into the ruling houses of Europe, and brought the Holy Roman Emperor and the King of Prussia into a declaration at Pillnitz Castle near Dresden. In it, they vowed to oppose the French revolution and called on other European powers to intervene if Louis were threatened.

In April 1792 France declared war on Austria, and attempted to invade the Austrian Netherlands (roughly, present-day Belgium and Luxembourg). Prussia in turn declared war on France, and the Duke of Brunswick assembled a large invasion force, crossing the border in August. After some initial successes including the capture of Verdun, the Prussians were badly beaten by the French cannonade at Valmy on 20 September. To the utter dismay of monarchists and counter-revolutionaries across Europe, the Duke then negotiated a ceasefire with the French general Dumouriez and began an orderly retreat before the end of the campaigning season. Dumouriez, however, felt no such scruple. Possessed of a large army with highly effective artillery, he promptly reinvaded the Austrian Netherlands, taking Brussels on 14 November and menacing the Dutch Republic, an important British ally. Another French army annexed Savoy.

Paris had been engulfed by war fever over the summer, and the new constitution was swept away in a tide of revolutionary radicalism. All available troops had been despatched to the front, leaving a mob of armed urban demonstrators, or sans-culottes – so called for their refusal to wear aristocratic breeches – in control. In August the sans-culottes of the new Paris Commune attacked the Tuileries, cut down some 800 Swiss Guards who defended it, took the King into custody, suspended the monarchy and called a Convention to draw up a republican constitution. After news of the fall of Verdun reached the city in early September, and with the way to the capital seemingly clear for the Prussians, the general alarm was sounded and panic seized the mob. Five days of uncontrolled violence ensued. Kangaroo courts were set up and as many as 1,400 prisoners or half the prison population executed, including common criminals, royalists and priests who refused to swear allegiance to the constitution. The new guillotines busily plied their abominable trade.

In his budget speech of February 1792, Pitt had remarked that 'unquestionably there never was a time in the history of this country, when from the situation of Europe, we might more reasonably

expect fifteen years of peace, than we may at the present moment'.
Events were to show that this was a monumental political misjudgement. But as the situation deteriorated in France the British government was far from idle. It encouraged loyalist associations to
convene in opposition to the radicals, called out the militia and
announced an Aliens Bill to control the movements of foreigners.
Paine, who had fled to France, was tried and convicted of seditious
libel *in absentia*.

Fox, however, remained supremely confident, continuing
throughout 1792 to insist privately that France posed no danger.
Retaining close links with many important figures there, notably
the revolutionary leader Lafayette, he simply could not accept the
imminent prospect of war. But, deny them though he might, the
facts could not be controverted. Matters finally came a head in
December. On the 4th of that month Fox spoke at the first meeting
of the new Whig Club and destroyed the last vestiges of Fitzwilliam
and Portland's faith in him with an incendiary statement of radical
belief and coded support for the revolutionaries. On the 13th, he
outraged moderate Whig opinion in the Commons by accusing
Pitt and the King – on whom events in France had bestowed a new
reputation as a 'Patriot King' – of using popular fear of revolution
to suppress democratic freedoms and seize power for the executive.
His amendment was lost by 290 votes to 50, an enormous majority.

On 15 December, Fox moved a motion in the Commons to
negotiate with France in an effort to avoid war. This was immediately denounced as treating with the enemy, and dismissed without
even a vote. Fox may have believed his actions were justified to
recall his followers to their duty, and keep them from Pitt. In reality,
they destroyed his political and intellectual authority, his capacity
for leadership, and his party. It was only a matter of time before
the Whigs formally broke up, as they did eighteen months later
when Portland led a large rump of the Whigs across the House to
join Pitt.

On that same day, 15 December 1792, France passed a decree that revolution would be instituted in all conquered territories. On 21 January 1793, Louis XVI was publicly beheaded by guillotine in what is now the Place de la Concorde. The act was greeted by the assembled multitude with a huge cry of 'Vive la Nation! Vive la République!' On 1 February, by unanimous vote of the Convention, France declared war on Great Britain, a state of affairs acknowledged by the King and Commons on the 12th. Sparked by conscription, loyalty to the Church and economic crisis, rebellions against revolutionary authority now broke out in the Vendée in the west, in Lyons and Marseilles and in other provincial cities. On 5 September the use of terror was officially adopted by the revolutionaries' new Committee of Public Safety, in these terms: 'It is time that equality bore its scythe above all heads. It is time to horrify all the conspirators. So legislators, place Terror on the order of the day! Let us be in revolution, because everywhere counter-revolution is being woven by our enemies. The blade of the law should hover over all the guilty.' One by one, Burke's hideous prophecies were coming to pass.

Yet his greatest prophecy still remained to be fulfilled. In the *Reflections*, Burke had written:

> In the weakness of one kind of authority, and in the fluctuation of all, the officers of an army will remain for some time mutinous and full of faction, until some popular general, who understands the art of conciliating the soldiery, and who possesses the true spirit of command, shall draw the eyes of all men upon himself. Armies will obey him on his personal account. There is no other way of securing military obedience in this state of things. But the moment in which that event shall happen, the person who really commands the army is your master; the master (that is little) of your king, the master of your Assembly, the master of your whole republic.

The King would be dead already. But otherwise this is a frighteningly exact description of the emergence of Napoleon Bonaparte.

In 1793 the young general was already making a name for himself with the siege and seizure of Toulon. In 1799 he staged a coup d'état, naming himself First Consul and moving into the Tuileries. By 1804 he would be Emperor of France. A year later, he would be master of continental Europe.

Edmund Burke was now moving into the twilight of his long political career. As the European situation declined, he continued to argue vehemently for Pitt to lead a counter-revolutionary war against France, to destroy the seditious canker at source before it could spread to other European countries, and to restore the monarchy and the *status quo ante*. Yet his pleas fell on deaf ears. Pitt was not anxious to take the offensive, and felt no great commitment to a Bourbon restoration. This view was reinforced after the French Directoire took executive power in 1795, and a period of comparative calm ensued.

Throughout the 1790s Burke had continued to work on the impeachment of Warren Hastings. It was a long and arduous process. Unlike the general election of 1784, that of 1790 had been more a collection of local contests than a single national one; it had slightly strengthened Pitt's position. As always, the dissolution of Parliament had terminated all parliamentary business, including the trial in Westminster Hall, and it was only with great difficulty that Burke was able to persuade Fox to renew the struggle. Public interest in the impeachment had evaporated, and each sitting was now attended by only a small rump of peers. In June 1794, after six years, at the end of a nine-day marathon sitting in which Burke spoke for just under twenty-seven hours, the case for the prosecution was finally completed. It was another year before the verdict came: as Burke had expected, Hastings was acquitted on all counts.

That epic 'Speech in Reply' was to be Burke's parliamentary swansong. It was then and remains now formally impossible for

MPs to resign their seats and retire voluntarily from Parliament. However, by a resolution of 1624, they are able to do so indirectly, by applying for an 'office of profit' under the Crown. Immediately after the Hastings prosecution had ended, Burke applied for such an office, known as the Chiltern Hundreds. At the age of sixty-four, after a career of nearly twenty-nine years in the House of Commons, a career which had made him one of the most famous politicians in Europe, he was now a free man. To his delight, out of respect for the older man and for his belief in the hereditary principle, Fitzwilliam very generously offered the seat at Malton to Burke's son Richard. Richard was duly elected on 18 July, and Burke declared that day to be the happiest of his life.

In the same month the Portland Whigs moved to join Pitt's ministry, with the Duke taking over the Home Office and Fitzwilliam becoming Lord President of the Council. The following February Fitzwilliam was sent to Ireland as Lord Lieutenant. Ireland was then in some turmoil. Henry Grattan – leading Irish MP, the architect of the Catholic Relief Act 1793 and a good friend of Burke's – was pressing for further concessions from London, and in particular the right of Catholic men of property to sit in the Irish Parliament. Grattan's was in fact a deliberately rather modest measure. But many at Westminster viewed Dublin as a likely back door to Jacobinism, while others saw the Protestant political hierarchy as stimulating republican sentiments by their own corruption and provocative actions. Pitt's intention was for Fitzwilliam to conciliate and calm tempers. But the idealistic and politically inexperienced Fitzwilliam did the opposite, quickly removing several key figures from the Irish government and strongly sympathizing with Grattan. There was a rapid backlash from London, and Fitzwilliam was recalled after just three months in Ireland. It was a humiliation for Fitzwilliam, a source of huge sadness for Burke and a severe setback for Ireland, which continued what would be a long slide into violence and chaos in 1798.

His son Richard's election apart, Burke had suffered a series of terrible political reverses. But to them was added personal affliction as well. In 1792 his dear friends Reynolds and Shackleton died, and they were followed in February 1794 by his brother Richard Burke Sr. Richard had tried his luck first in business and then fortune-hunting in India, and had failed. His public positions – joint Secretary to the Treasury on two occasions, and Recorder of Bristol – had come through Edmund. But Burke adored and respected his younger brother, and was distraught. By this time, moreover, Will Burke – Richard's co-venturer in India, and Edmund's close friend for nearly forty years – had returned from the subcontinent in broken health, bringing all his old money worries with him. He took up residence again at Gregories, where he suffered a series of strokes and was twice arrested for non-payment of debts. Desperately indebted himself, Edmund nevertheless assumed responsibility for Will's financial affairs.

But the cruellest blow of all was yet to fall. On 28 July, just ten days after his election to Parliament, Edmund's son Richard fell gravely ill and was moved from London to the fresher air of Kensington, then in the countryside. Four days later he died, apparently of tuberculosis. He had never been robust, but his sudden decline took Edmund and Jane completely by surprise. In his final moments Richard was distressed by his father's silence, and asked him to speak of religion or morality, or indeed anything at all. But Burke could not. The greatest orator of the day was silent, entirely overcome by emotion.

Richard had not had an especially easy life, loaded up with expectations on all sides as he was. He was ambitious, verbose and possessed of a brittle self-confidence which alienated others, who often struggled to see the brilliance that his father identified in him. But he was also a loving and dutiful son, who had discharged much on his father's behalf without demur. Homer says it is the worst of all evils when the child dies before the parent, and the agony must have been compounded by Richard's election, which promised to take him at last from out of his father's shadow and

Joshua Reynolds Esq.r Pinxit.

James Ward Sculp.t Painter to Engraver in Mezzotint
to his Royal Highness the Prince of Wales

RICHARD BURKE
OBIIT. AUG. 2. 1794. AT. 56.

As precious Gums are not for common fire,   As was he seen exhaled and vanish'd hence
They but perfume the Temple and expire.   A short sweet Odour at a Vast expence.

O DOLOR ATQUE DECUS

Pub.d July 4.1800 by MESS.rs WARDS & C.o N.o 1, Newman Street London.

into the limelight. Burke was utterly devastated, both by the loss
of his son and, since Richard had no heirs, by the extinction of his
family line. He bitterly reproached himself for relying too much
on the young man, and even seems to have contemplated suicide.

Among other things, Richard had been much involved in
managing the estate at Gregories, and his father's financial position.
That position was now exceedingly precarious, especially since
Burke's departure from Parliament had removed the cover of parliamentary privilege and so exposed him to legal proceedings from
his creditors. Nonetheless there were some grounds for optimism.
Specifically, Burke had been encouraged to believe that he might
be given a pension in recognition of his long public service to his
adopted country. The King had relaxed his hostility. Burke's friends
William Windham and Walker King pressed the case, and Pitt was
supportive, seeing the political attractions of further splitting the
Whigs and destabilizing Fox. Indeed at one point Pitt had mooted
a peerage for Burke, but this met with some opposition. After
Richard's death the idea was dropped; there could be no dynasty.

In the event Burke's pension was just one part of a larger financial settlement, and with official delays it was not until July 1795
that the matter was resolved. Burke was, in effect, the victim of his
own principles. Unlike many politicians of the time, he had not
used public office to enrich himself. Instead, he had fought a
constant battle to reconcile his aspirations with his ideals: to square
his desire for social status and public recognition with his insistence
on personal accountability and independence of mind and action.
As a result, for nearly thirty years his political life had been a hand-
to-mouth existence, forever sustained by credit and reliant on
grants, sporadic fees, forgiven debts and bequests. Even as late as
June 1795, with his creditors threatening to foreclose on a crucial
mortgage, Burke contemplated fleeing to America and Portugal to
escape them. A month later he could, at last, rest easy.

* * *

But of course he did not. Burke was incapable of resting easy, and his last two years were ones of undiminished intellectual vitality, almost to the end. He had poured forth ideas and arguments like a volcano throughout his life. Now in 1796, despite declining health, there came a final huge explosion of energy.

That energy was both practical and intellectual. Burke had become seized with the plight of the children of French refugees, especially royalists, and this led him to establish a school for some sixty boys in Penn, close to Beaconsfield. It was to be in part a military academy, with a special emphasis on mathematics and English. Unusually for him, he immersed himself in the practical details: raising the money, which came mainly from a government grant; defending the new school against the misguided ideas of the French émigré clergy; and addressing a host of smaller issues, from school uniforms to bills and supplies of drawing paper. The house at Gregories, never free of guests, became fuller still. The school continued until 1820, long after Burke's death.

Part of the point of the new school was to preserve what Burke took to be the chivalric values and culture of the French aristocracy in the face of revolution; and Pitt may have agreed to fund it precisely in order to keep Burke's mind from his next project. For the possibility that Britain might make peace with the French Directoire had continued to obsess him. Over the winter of 1795–6 he worked on a pamphlet that was published the following October, after some hiccups, as *Two Letters on the Prospect of a Regicide Peace*. This argued that a peace with France could have no principled basis, since it would mean an acknowledgement and acceptance of revolutionary values: 'The present case . . . is not a revolution in government. It is not the victory of party over party. It is a destruction and decomposition of the whole society . . . This pretended Republic is founded in crimes, and exists by wrong and robbery . . . To be at peace with robbery is to be an accomplice with it.'

Indeed, Burke maintained, regicide France was not in the true sense a nation at all:

We are in a war of a *peculiar* nature. It is not with an ordinary community ... not with a State which makes war through wantonness, and abandons it through lassitude. We are at war with a system, which, by its essence, is inimical to all other Governments, and which makes peace or war as peace and war may best contribute to their subversion. It is with an *armed doctrine* that we are at war. It has by its essence a faction of opinion, and of interest, and of enthusiasm, in every country. To us it is a Colossus which bestrides our channel. It has one foot on a foreign shore, the other upon the British soil.

A nation was a moral essence, not simply a set of geographical features.

Britain could not escape the invasion of this seditious doctrine; and it should not. For, like it or no, its own history was too intimately entwined with that of Europe. Both were parts of the wider body of Christendom. Indeed, Burke insisted,

> the great resource of Europe was in England. Not in a sort of England detached from the rest of the world, and amusing herself with the puppet show of a naval power ... but in that sort of England, who considered herself as embodied with Europe; in that sort of England, who, sympathetic with the adversity or the happiness of mankind, felt that nothing in human affairs was foreign to her.

Resolution and action were called for. But Burke was memorably scathing about the shallowness and short-termism of some of his former colleagues in the House. 'In truth, the tribe of vulgar politicians are the lowest of our species. There is no trade so vile and mechanical as government in their hands. Virtue is not their habit ... A large, liberal and prospective view of the interests of States passes with them for romance; and the principles that recommend it for the wanderings of a disordered imagination.' At a time of the utmost moral seriousness, they were surrounded by bad influences: 'The calculators compute them out of their senses. The jesters and buffoons shame them out of every thing grand and elevated. Littleness, in object and in means, to them appears soundness and sobriety. They think there is nothing worth pursuit, but that which they can handle; which they can measure with a two-foot rule; which they can tell upon ten fingers.' It would be nice to record that the House of Commons always heeded these words in the years that followed, or indeed today.

Nor, as Pitt had feared, did his government escape specific criticism. Instead of launching wild escapades in the West Indies – a large expedition sent there to strike at French colonies had started to fail in the face of sickness and defeat – it should prepare to wage a long war with France, Burke argued. 'This new system of robbery in France, cannot be rendered safe by any art ... it must be destroyed, or ... it will destroy all Europe.' Again, the words were prophetic. But the sheer emotion of the *Letters* rendered them suspect. James Sayers's caricature *Thoughts on a Regicide Peace* (see overleaf) counterpoints a calm and sleeping Burke with a wild and disordered bubble of imagination showing a British lion at bay over Shakespeare's famous words about 'this sceptred isle', while a French revolutionary bestrides Britain and Ireland, holding Louis XVI's head on a pikestaff and leading the Dutch Republic in submission. These were the fears of many. But they were no basis for policy.

But Burke's most brilliant late effusion came in February 1796. As with so many of his writings, *A Letter to a Noble Lord* mixed high principle and angry self-justification in equal measure. Burke had long been suspected by radicals and Foxites alike of moving towards Pitt from a desire for patronage. His attendance at the King's levées had been noted, and Thomas Paine had denounced him in the *Rights of Man* as one 'accustomed to kiss the aristocratical hand that hath purloined him from himself'. There seemed a yawning contradiction: for was not Burke renowned for a lifetime's opposition to the extension of Crown patronage, and for his wide-ranging proposals for economical reform in 1780–2?

Thoughts on a Regicide Peace

In this context, the award of a pension to him was certain to arouse controversy, and in November 1795 both pension and recipient were the victims of much mockery and derision in the House of Lords from two young Foxite aristocrats, the Duke of Bedford and the Earl of Lauderdale. The young bloods' offence was compounded by its inaccuracy – Burke had never opposed pensions for good service – and by its timing. Burke was then in the worst of spirits. The impeachment of Hastings had failed, Hastings later receiving a huge financial settlement from the East India Company; Burke himself had left the Commons; an inglorious peace was in prospect with France; his health was worsening; his brother, closest friends and son were now all dead.

The result is what Somerset Maugham called 'the finest piece of invective in the English language'. From his very first words, Burke sets out to put the upstart aristocrats in their place:

> My Lord, I could hardly flatter myself with the hope that so very early in the session I should have to acknowledge obligations to the Duke of Bedford and the Earl of Lauderdale . . . To be ill spoken of, in whatever language they speak, by the zealots of the new sect in philosophy and politics . . . is no matter of uneasiness and surprise . . . I have to thank [them] for having so faithfully and so fully acquitted to me whatever arrear of debt was left undischarged by the Priestleys and the Paines.

There follows a proud recapitulation and defence of his own career since 1780, as a *novus homo* serving his country. 'I have, through life, been willing to give everything to others; and to reserve nothing for myself . . . I do not say I saved my country; I am sure I did my country important service. There were few, indeed, that did not at that time acknowledge it . . . It was but one voice, that no man in the kingdom better deserved an honourable provision should be made for him.'

The contrast with the young Duke was manifest:

I was not, like his Grace of Bedford, swaddled and rocked and dandled into a legislator . . . I was not made for a minion or a tool . . . At every step of my progress in life . . . I was obliged to show my passport, and again and again to prove my sole title to the honour of being useful to my country, by a proof that I was not wholly unacquainted with its laws, and the whole system of its interests both abroad and at home.

Indeed, Burke scornfully notes, the Duke's colossal Russell family fortune was itself originally acquired not merely by grant, but by expropriation from the Church under Henry VIII:

The Duke of Bedford is the leviathan among all the creatures of the crown. He tumbles about his unwieldy bulk; he plays and frolics in the ocean of the royal bounty. Huge as he is . . . he is still a creature. His ribs, his fins, his whalebone, his blubber, the very spiracles through which he spouts a torrent of brine against his origin, and covers me all over with the spray, everything of him and about him is from the throne. Is it for him to question the dispensation of the royal favour?

Irony builds upon irony. For the revolution which the noble Duke celebrates will, Burke suggests, have the Duke himself among its early victims. Its scientists are already measuring his properties:

As [the geometricians] have an eye upon his Grace's lands, the chemists are not less taken with his buildings . . . They have calculated what quantity of matter convertible into [explosive] is to be found in Bedford House, in Woburn Abbey, and . . . in Covent Garden . . . the brave sans-culottes may make war on all the aristocracy of Europe for a twelvemonth, out of the rubbish of the Duke of Bedford's buildings.

Yet even here the philosopher-statesman shines through, for Burke insists that innovation is not reform. The French revolution is not a more extreme version of his own reforms of Crown patronage; it is completely different in character. Nor does he resile from his deep belief in property as the basic guarantor of the social order. The inadequacies of particular aristocrats like these young men do not undermine the case for a natural aristocracy of virtue. Indeed, considered as an institution, the Duke himself makes the case: 'The Duke of Bedford will stand as long as prescriptive law endures: as long as the great stable laws of property, common to us with all civilized nations, are kept in their integrity, and without the smallest inter-mixture of laws, maxims, principles, or precedents of the grand Revolution.'

He himself might have hoped to join that aristocracy, but out of virtue and not expropriation. As he turns to Richard, Burke's tone is deeply poignant and elegiac.

> Had it pleased God to continue to me the hopes of succession, I should have been . . . a sort of founder of a family: I should have left a son, who, in all the points in which personal merit can be viewed, in science, in erudition, in genius, in taste, in honour, in generosity, in humanity, in every liberal sentiment, and every liberal accomplishment, would not have shown himself inferior to the Duke of Bedford, or to any of those whom he traces in his line . . . I live in an inverted order. They who ought to have succeeded me are gone before me. They who should have been to me as posterity are in the place of ancestors.

As Burke stepped back from the public fray, his fears did not diminish. They were captured perfectly by James Gillray, whose print *Promised Horrors of the French Revolution* (see overleaf) showed their purport for Britain. St James's Palace is in flames, the revolutionaries are storming up St James's itself, there is slaughter and mayhem in the streets, Tories have been hanged by the neck

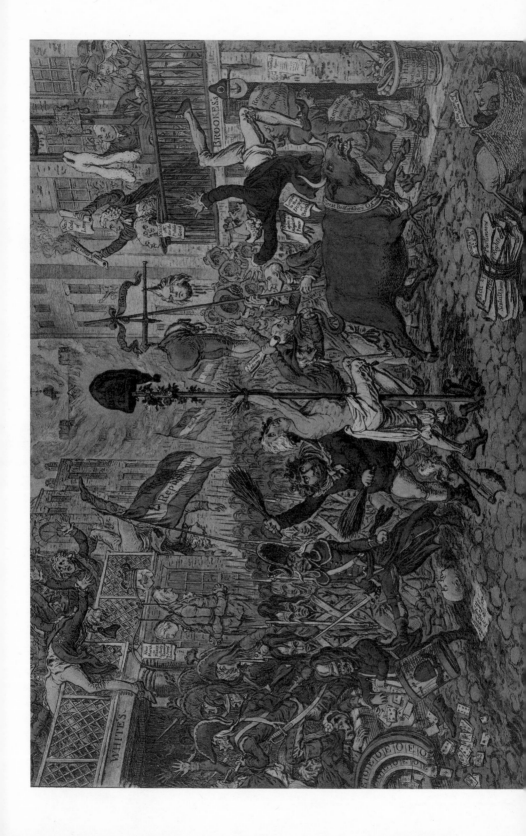

outside White's Club, while the Whigs operate a guillotine from the balcony of Brooks's. In the foreground a great Bedfordshire ox, signifying the Duke, is goring Burke. Even today it is a strangely disturbing image.

Physically, Burke had enjoyed robust good health, one or two episodes apart, for some sixty-five years. But over the next few months he grew frail from a gastric ailment diagnosed after his death, perhaps mistakenly, as stomach cancer. He went to London for a second medical opinion, and characteristically emerged with four; he took the waters at Bath with Jane; he tried opium in an unsuccessful attempt to relieve the pain. He maintained a wide correspondence, raging and despairing to the end as the world continued to go up in flames around him.

In April 1797 there was a serious mutiny on sixteen Royal Navy vessels moored at Spithead, near Portsmouth, followed by a lesser one in the Thames Estuary. Wracked by religious and political unrest, Ireland was on the brink of rebellion; and it had only narrowly avoided an invasion the previous December by a French army headed by Wolfe Tone, the leader of the United Irishmen. One of Burke's last letters shows the depths of his despair about his native country. In 'a reduced state of body and in [a] dejected state of mind', he says,

> There is no hope for the body of the people of Ireland, as long as those who are in power with you shall make it the great object of their policy . . . that the mass of their countrymen are not to be trusted by their government, and that the only hold which England has upon Ireland consists in preserving a certain very small number of gentlemen in full possession of a monopoly of that kingdom.

Edmund Burke never saw the Irish revolution which he had so long feared. He died soon after midnight on 9 July 1797. Afraid lest his body be discovered and defiled by Jacobins, he had earlier asked to be buried in an unmarked grave on the estate. But in the end he was buried next to his son and brother in Beaconsfield church. He had refused a visit from Charles James Fox, desiring no reconciliation at the deathbed, but his coffin was borne on the shoulders of his most distinguished friends and admirers, including the Dukes of Portland and Devonshire, the Earls Fitzwilliam and of Inchiquin, and the Speaker of the House of Commons. Burke's will left his estate in full to 'my entirely beloved, faithful . . . affectionate . . . and incomparable wife'. Jane lived on at Gregories until 1812 on a life interest, having sold the property and paid off the family's debts at last.

In the *Letter to a Noble Lord*, Burke had written, 'The storm has gone over me; and I lie like one of those old oaks which the late hurricane has scattered about me. I am stripped of all my honours; I am torn up by the roots, and lie prostrate on the earth!' Lacking in proper public honours Burke's life may have been. But his achievement is one of inextinguishable glory, as we shall see.

PART TWO

Thought

SIX

Reputation, Reason and the
Enlightenment Project

IN THE 200-ODD YEARS since his death Burke's reputation has
followed a great arc. It rose steadily throughout the nineteenth
century, reaching almost to apotheosis in the late Victorian era,
when he was admired on both sides of the Atlantic as much as a
master of English prose as a source of political wisdom. It remained
high in the first quarter of the twentieth century, when the 'Speech
on Conciliation' was regularly studied in American schools. Since
then, however, it has been in decline, apart from brief rediscoveries
during the Cold War and at the fall of the Iron Curtain. Academic
interest is greater than it has been for many years. But for the
public, with the partial exception of the *Reflections*, Burke's writings
and speeches lie idle on library shelves. Politics has passed him by.
His struggles, his style, his passion have come to seem irrelevant,
even quaint, to a world of post-modernist irony and mass culture.

In the chapters that follow, we turn from Burke's life to his
thought. We examine the social, political and intellectual context
of his ideas, their shifting impact over time, and his key influences

and adversaries. With luck, what will emerge is a sense both of Burke's power and coherence as a philosopher in action and of his remarkable relevance and importance today.

Two days after his death, however, *The Times* of London was in no doubt about its verdict: 'Mr Burke will live as long as strength of imagination and beauty of language shall be respected by the world.' Inevitably, however, this view was quickly contested, and Burke was denounced by radicals and Foxites alike in a continuation of the pamphlet war he had helped to start. But there followed a series of laudatory or even hagiographic biographies, most notably a *Memoir of Burke* by James Prior in 1824, which portrayed him as a statesman, free of *parti pris*, his eye firmly fixed on the national interest and the need to preserve Britain from revolution. This picture was assisted by the rapid if selective publication of his posthumous *Works*, including various writings, speeches and letters. These went through a number of different editions and achieved a wide circulation.

Politically, Burke cast a long shadow forward. He was followed by a younger generation of brilliant Irishmen entering English politics; these included the future Prime Minister George Canning and the leading minister in the Commons of Lord Liverpool's administration, Robert Stewart, later to become Lord Castlereagh. Canning had grown up under the influence of Fox and Sheridan, but was deeply impressed by the *Reflections* and became a follower of Pitt and a vigorous opponent of Jacobinism after 1793. Castlereagh was, characteristically, more equivocal: elected as a young and progressive reformer in County Down in 1790, he came to share Burke's analysis of the revolution, but was opposed to the idea of a counter-revolutionary war against France. In 1794 he too joined Pitt. As acting Chief Secretary for Ireland he was closely involved in suppressing the disastrous Irish rebellion of 1798, and then helped to engineer the Acts of Union between Great Britain and Ireland shortly thereafter. It was an extraordinary political journey.

William Pitt had cuttingly described the *Reflections* as 'rhapsodies in which there is much to admire, and nothing to agree with'. But he had perhaps been more influenced by Burke than he admitted on India, and also on Irish policy, through the Catholic Relief Act of 1793 and the highly controversial endowment of a seminary for Irish Catholic priests at Maynooth in 1795. After his death in 1806 Pitt was all but canonized as the saviour of the nation; and in the following decades he was specifically co-opted by sections of Tory opinion as a Christian constitutionalist, defender of the status quo against revolutionary foreign doctrines and opponent of Catholic emancipation. This ignored the inconvenient facts that Pitt's personal views about religion were unknown; that he had supported, not opposed, both parliamentary reform and Catholic emancipation; and that he had had little hesitation in suspending habeas corpus in 1794 – supported by Burke – and defying established constitutional principle for reasons of state in the struggle against Napoleon. Then as now, the propagandists did not let such trifles get in the way of a good story.

By contrast, Burke's Irish lineage and widely known sympathy to the Catholics prevented such easy assimilation. After the Catholic Relief Act of 1829, however, Pitt and Burke became increasingly joined in the public mind. The linkage was given a more specific political slant by Benjamin Disraeli in 1835. In his early *Vindication of the English Constitution in a Letter to a Noble and Learned Lord* – the rather Burkean title can hardly be accidental – Disraeli identified what he saw as a continuous Tory line of succession stretching back to the early eighteenth century and including Bolingbroke, Burke and the Younger Pitt.

Disraeli's evident desire was to be seen as a late flowering of the same tradition. But matters went horribly wrong when he was refused high office by the new Prime Minister, Sir Robert Peel, in 1841. It then became necessary for him to show that, far from following the true path, Pitt and his successors up to and including Peel had gone disastrously astray. Faithful to the principles of a lifetime, Disraeli therefore reversed himself completely, using his novels *Coningsby* and *Sybil* to denounce Peel as the offspring of a deviant 'Conservative' tradition, in contrast to Disraeli's own true Toryism. Neither the argument nor the reversal was persuasive.

On the Whig side, feelings about Burke followed a similar path from equivocation to assimilation. By mid-century, when the Liberal party emerged from the ashes of the Whigs after the Great Reform Act 1832, many Liberals disliked Burke's rejection of parliamentary reform and abhorred his criticisms of natural rights and of the French revolution. But they admired his support for the American colonists, his belief in religious toleration, his respect for the constitutional settlement of 1688, his hatred of undue monarchical influence and his campaigns against injustices in India and Ireland. William Ewart Gladstone, in many ways a political innovator, nevertheless regarded Burke as an 'idol', according to his colleague and distinguished biographer John Morley MP, who also wrote a notably successful short biography of Burke. As Morley recorded of Gladstone in 1885, 'Though ending his seventy-sixth year . . . he nearly every day reads Burke: – "December 18 – Read Burke; what a magazine of wisdom on Ireland and America. January 9 – made extracts from Burke – *sometimes almost divine.*"'

This bipartisan esteem, and specifically the ability of different politicians to quarry what they liked from Burke's writings, carried over to the United States as well. The hard-driving Theodore Roosevelt was a professed admirer of Burke, and in particular of his emphasis on political virtue and character, even as he tested the limits of the American constitution as President with drastic action at home and abroad. On the Democrat side, the scholarly Woodrow Wilson wrote acutely about Burke, acknowledging his hero's weaknesses but emphasizing the coherence of his thought and his capacity to blend telling generalizations with mastery of precise detail. For Wilson, Burke is a conservative first to last in spirit, and, above all, he is English: 'this man, this Irishman, speaks the best English thought upon politics . . . he remains the chief spokesman for England in the utterance of the fundamental ideals which have governed the actions of Englishmen in politics.' These were high recommendations indeed.

But admiration for Burke was not limited to politicians or political thought. Woodrow Wilson himself made the point eloquently: 'Burke is not literary because he takes from books but because he makes books, transmuting what he writes upon into literature . . . He is a master in the use of the great style. Every sentence, too, is steeped in the colours of an extraordinary imagination. The movement takes your breath and quickens your pulses. The glow and power of the matter rejuvenate your faculties.'

Exactly the same point had been made four generations earlier by the English essayist William Hazlitt:

> His stock of ideas did not consist of a few meagre facts . . . his mine of wealth was a profound understanding, inexhaustible as the human heart, and various as the sources of human nature. He therefore enriched every subject to which he applied himself, and new subjects were only the occasions of calling forth fresh powers of mind which had not been before exerted . . . Burke's was a union of untameable vigour and originality.

Hazlitt's own enormously fertile mind constantly returned to Burke, as inspiration and as adversary, at once seductive and yet dangerous, and irresistible to weaker spirits. In his essay 'On Reading Old Books', Hazlitt remarks of Burke, 'I did not care for his doctrines. I was then and am still, proof against their contagion.' But as for his style, 'If there are greater prose-writers than Burke, they either lie out of my course of study, or are beyond my sphere of comprehension.'

Like their contemporary Hazlitt, the early Romantic poets also acknowledged Burke's mastery of the English language. But, initially at least, they were repelled by his politics. Wordsworth had spent an ecstatic period in France during the early revolution, whose ideals he strongly supported. In the words of his masterpiece *The Prelude*, 'Bliss was it in that dawn to be alive / But to be young was

very heaven.' For their part, in the mid-1790s Coleridge and his
then brother-in-law Robert Southey planned to establish a 'panti-
socracy', or entirely egalitarian society, on the banks of the
Susquehanna in Pennsylvania. This utopian scheme came to
nothing and the two men drifted apart, Southey into Jacobinism
and Coleridge into rustic living, close association with Wordsworth
and the creation of the *Lyrical Ballads*.

But all three of the Lake poets fell increasingly under the influence of Burke's ideas. There are Burkean themes of habit and experience in Wordsworth even as early as his famous Preface to the
second edition of the *Lyrical Ballads* (1800), now widely seen as the
first manifesto for Romantic poetry. The same was true of Coleridge,
whose final book, *On the Constitution of Church and State*, can be
read as a highly idiosyncratic reworking of Burkean ideas with
British common law and Church traditions, and a heavy dose of
continental philosophy. It was also true of Southey, who by the 1820s
blended an orthodox Burkean defence of the constitution with
thoroughgoing opposition to Catholic emancipation, support for
Robert Owen's cooperative movement and an attack on the alienation and brutalizing effects of industrialization which mirrored the
thought of William Cobbett and, later, Thomas Carlyle.

Amid the ferment of early nineteenth-century social, economic
and political change, then, many different writers were able over
time to find ideas of enduring value within Burke. Wordsworth's
late revisions to *The Prelude* made his own feelings all too clear:

> Genius of Burke! Forgive the pen seduced
> By specious wonders . . .
> I see him old, but vigorous in age
> Stand like an oak whose stag-horn branches start
> Out of its leafy brow, the more to awe
> The younger brethren of the grove. But some –
> While he forewarns, denounces, launches forth
> Against all systems built on abstract rights,

Keen ridicule; the majesty proclaims
Of Institutes and Laws, hallowed by time;
Declares the vital power of social ties
Endeared by Custom; and with high disdain
Exploding upstart Theory, insists
Upon the allegiance to which men are born.

As a recantation, it is both elegant and complete.

Burke's influence upon the historians was also marked. Macaulay described him as 'the greatest man since Milton', yet one in whom reason was yoked to passion: 'Mr. Burke, assuredly, possessed an understanding admirably fitted for the investigation of truth – an understanding stronger than that of any statesman, active or speculative, of the eighteenth century – stronger than every thing, except his own fierce and ungovernable sensibility. Hence, he generally chose his side like a fanatic, and defended it like philosopher.'

In his brilliant essay of 1841 on Warren Hastings, Macaulay highlighted the power of Burke's recreative and empathic imagination:

He had, in the highest degree, that noble faculty whereby man is able to live in the past and in the future, in the distant and in the unreal. India and its inhabitants were not to him, as to most Englishmen, mere names and abstractions, but a real country and a real people. The burning sun, the strange vegetation of the palm and the cocoa-tree, the rice-field . . . All India was present to the eye of his mind, from the hall where suitors laid gold and perfumes at the feet of sovereigns to the wild moor where the gipsy camp was pitched . . . Oppression in Bengal was to him the same thing as oppression in the streets of London.

For his part, the Irish historian W. E. H. Lecky in his *History of England in the Eighteenth Century* echoed Hazlitt: 'No other politician or writer has thrown the light of so penetrating a genius on the nature and working of the British Constitution . . . He had a

peculiar gift of introducing into transient party conflicts observations drawn from the most profound knowledge of human nature.'
And Lecky highlighted Burke's wisdom: 'there is perhaps no English
prose writer since Bacon whose works are so thickly starred with
thought. The time may come when they will be no longer read.
The time will never come in which men would not grow the wiser
by reading them.' The great historian Lord Acton concurred, despite
his own marked lack of political sympathy.

In the twentieth century, Burke has been pressed into service on
numerous occasions. In the 1950s and 1960s his anti-totalitarian
rhetoric was adopted by conservative American politicians and
thinkers in their fight against communism during the Cold War.
After the fall of the Berlin Wall in 1989, intellectuals and policymakers across eastern and central Europe drew once again on
Burke's positive theories of government in their own constitutional
reflections. There has been a persistent desire by some conservative
writers to relocate Burke away from a Lockean framework of natural
rights and find in him a specifically Christian, indeed Thomist,
doctrine of natural law.

But even from the outset Burke's memory was hardly uncon-
tested. The critics' familiar refrains of inconsistency, treachery and
reactionary defence of privilege were heard again, and further
themes added thereto. In his Life of Sheridan of 1824, Thomas
Moore went further, arguing that there were in fact two Burkes:
'His mind, indeed, lies parted asunder in his works, like some vast
continent severed by a convulsion of nature – each portion peopled
by its own giant race of peoples, differing altogether in features
and language, and committed in eternal hostility with each other.'

But perhaps the most consistently damaging attack purported
to explain Burke in terms not of split personality but of simple
self-interest. Here the prime mover was his bitter radical adversary
Thomas Paine. Burke had once remarked of Paine that 'we hunt
in pairs', but this overstates the matter; while Burke restricted
himself to a defence of the colonists' rights against the Crown,

Paine made a great success of his outspoken support for the American revolutionaries in his pamphlet *Common Sense*. Paine had visited Burke at Gregories on more than one occasion, and had hoped for Burke's support for the revolution in France. The *Reflections* was a profound disappointment to him, and fuelled an outpouring of words in which moral outrage and personal pique were equally blended.

In the first part of his *Rights of Man* of March 1791, it will be recalled, Paine had described Burke as 'accustomed to kiss the aristocratical hand that hath purloined him from himself'.

> He is not affected by the reality of distress touching his heart, but by the showy resemblance of it striking his imagination. He pities the plumage, but forgets the dying bird.

But Paine's critique went far beyond that; he also hinted darkly that Burke was the recipient of a 'masked' or secret pension. The hint was repeated in the second part of the same book, which came out the following year. Shortly afterwards Paine went still further, undertaking in a public letter to the British Attorney General to show that Burke had been 'a masked pensioner at £1,500 per annum for about ten years'. Further writings continued the attack. As far as we can tell, the allegation was entirely untrue, and relied on a series of deliberate misrepresentations about Burke's Civil List Act of 1782. Though Burke had long been supported financially by Rockingham and other Whig grandees, it was not in fact until July 1795 that he received any money from the Crown. Even so, Paine's campaign to discredit Burke personally had some effect, and the charge that Burke was simply the King's hireling gained currency from the start of the revolution controversy.

The charge did not go away. In his *Observations on the State of Ireland* (1818), J. C. Curwen described Burke as 'a Whig from interest, but a Tory from principle'. Half a century later Karl Marx said of Burke in *Das Kapital*:

This sycophant – who in the pay of the English oligarchy played the romantic *laudator temporis acti* against the French Revolution just as, in the pay of the North American colonies at the beginning of the American troubles, he had played the liberal against the English oligarchy – was an out-and-out vulgar bourgeois. 'The laws of commerce are the laws of Nature, and therefore the laws of God.' . . . No wonder that, true to the laws of God and Nature, he always sold himself in the best market.

In the twentieth century, the idea that Burke was merely a hireling received indirect reinforcement from a quite different quarter after 1929, when the historian Lewis Namier published *The Structure of Politics at the Accession of George III*. Namier argued that eighteenth-century politics was at root a matter not of grand parties and high principle but of personal self-interest expressed via an ever-shifting kaleidoscope of political factions. Working through detailed analysis of individual biographies and personal interrelationships, he was able to shed much new light on how patterns of patronage influenced such matters as elections, the behaviour of MPs, parliamentary process, the formation of different ministries and the workings of the Court. To the socially and often statistically minded historians that followed Namier, what mattered was the generality, the mean and median, not the exception. The standard texts divided eighteenth-century politicians into 'Whigs' and 'Tories', with big personalities locked in principled political debate; now these histories quickly came to seem outmoded, as did the statesmen they depicted. None more so than Burke.

By the 1950s Namier and the Namierite 'method' had become enormously influential among historians. Namier and his followers have been severely criticized by Burke's admirers, notably by his biographer the distinguished Irish politician Conor Cruise O'Brien, often somewhat unfairly. True, there are some notorious instances of animus quite at odds with the Namierite insistence on detailed mastery of the facts, as when the historian Richard Pares sneeringly remarks: 'If we regard his social origins, we can only classify as an Irish adventurer the great Edmund Burke, the theorist and high priest of snobbery.' But in relation to Burke, the Namierites' references were generally rather few.

And that is the point. For if they and Paine and Marx are right then their common criticism is the most damaging of all, for it cuts at the root not merely of Burke's achievement but of his moral authority. If politics is simply a matter of patronage and self-interest, not principle, if Burke is simply a paid propagandist, a lackey wearing the livery of others, someone driven by opportunity and expediency whose personal ambition lies in acting as a mouthpiece for a sectional or class interest, then for all his literary and intellectual brilliance he cannot be worthy of our respect. He is not an independent thinker, or indeed an independent person, at all. We may admire his technical facility, but we cannot respect him. He becomes, not a great man, but a little one.

At first glance, the problem becomes still worse when one considers Burke's *Thoughts on the Cause of the Present Discontents* of 1770. For this was designed to be as much a rallying cry and party manifesto as a work of deep political analysis. Its central thrust was to seek to limit the power of the monarch, which inevitably meant increasing the power of the Whig aristocrats; and these aristocrats were Burke's patrons, as we have seen. Financial support was nothing new, of course; it was more or less the only way at the time for a young man of talent to get on in politics. But it sharpens the question: was Burke little more than a stooge?

The issue has been debated for generations. In 2012, however, an important new piece of evidence emerged, with the ascription to Burke of an early essay on political parties, in a leading academic journal. This has been dated to 1757, during Burke's first flowering of work with the publisher Robert Dodsley, thirteen years before publication of the *Thoughts*. In the essay, Burke attributes early party conflict between Whigs and Tories to the religious arguments of the late seventeenth century, before suggesting that, far from

being sources of division, parties can be used within the constitution to promote political moderation and good government. Citing
a wide range of historical precedents, he then denounces factions
as 'cabals fomented by ambition swelled up by popular madness
and nothing more. Hence it is that party is always useful, faction
always pernicious, which has hardly been enough considered.'
Genuine political parties are capable of principled opposition, he
argues; indeed they are required by the need for balance within the
constitution. However:

> we have at the present no party properly so called among us . . .
> but . . . mere factions: without any design, without any principle,
> but only a junction of people intriguing for their own interest . . .
> there can be no body of people united by a bond strong enough
> to hold them together, or animated by a principle vigorous enough
> to give them activity . . . when they have not some general scheme
> and some fixed object.

The distinction between faction and party was hardly new, of course.
Nevertheless, this essay is a decisive rebuttal to Paine, Marx and
Namier. It shows clearly that at a very early stage, well before Burke
had even begun to make his way in politics – indeed eight years
or so before he had met Rockingham or entered Parliament – he
had already mastered a large body of historical thought and political reflection on factions and parties. He was already arguing the
case, not merely against factional politics but, what was far more
novel, in favour of parties as a source of good government – and
doing so in terms that strikingly anticipated the *Thoughts*. If we
take this with the evidence of Burke's letters and other activities,
we can see that, far from being merely his master's voice or just a
mouthpiece for the Whig aristocrats, by 1770 Burke was working
to turn the Rockingham Whigs into a vehicle for a constitutional
theory much of which he had developed over a decade earlier.

William Hazlitt said, 'It has always been with me a test of the sense and candour of any one belonging to the opposite party, whether he allowed Burke to be a great man.' We have seen that Burke is not a stooge, but can we allow him to be a great man? Should we? The answers are Yes and Yes. We can indeed recover a proper sense of Burke's greatness, and not merely as a politician and a writer, but as a thinker. But to do this we need to shift gear, and move from history and biography to analysis and argument. We need to analyse Burke's ideas, and see what light they can shed both on his own time and on ours.

What we will discover is unexpected, and extraordinary. In the first place, Burke becomes the hinge or pivot of political modernity, the thinker on whose shoulders much of the Anglo-American tradition of representative government still rests. But he is also the earliest post-modern political thinker, the first and greatest critic of the modern age, and of what has been called liberal individualism: a set of basic assumptions about human nature and human well-being that arose in the nineteenth century, long after Burke's death, in reflection on the Enlightenment, and that govern the lives of millions, nay billions, of people today.

The great paradox is that, thus understood, Burke the anti-radical becomes a far more radical thinker even than Karl Marx himself. But to see why this is so we need to turn back to the eighteenth century, to the Enlightenment itself – and to Jean-Jacques Rousseau. It is against Rousseau that Burke most sharply defines himself; and here too his critique begins almost a decade before he entered Parliament.

Almost every aspect of what we still call 'the Enlightenment' has been disputed by scholars. But there is no doubt that something extraordinary took place in European thought in the seventeenth and eighteenth centuries. By the year 1600 the old certainties of Aristotle and his followers were breaking down. The Aristotelians had taught that the sublunary world was imperfect, the celestial

world divine; that the circle was the perfect form in nature; and
that science should be concerned with the search for basic causes
and first principles. But Copernicus and Kepler had undermined
the traditional view of the solar system, with their arguments for
heliocentrism and elliptical planetary orbits. Tycho Brahe and
Francis Bacon had highlighted the value of precise observation,
both of the heavens and of the everyday. Galileo had used the new
telescope to discover unexpected imperfections in the surface of
the Moon, and showed how mathematics could be employed to
explain physical forces and natural phenomena.

Most deeply of all, the mathematician and philosopher René
Descartes had dismissed Aristotle's basic categories altogether.
Descartes deliberately started from a position of extreme doubt,
about his own existence and that of the world around him. What
emerged from his reflections was the idea that the physical universe
is not made up of an indefinite array of different kinds of thing,
each *sui generis* and unique in its own way; it simply consists of
objects extended in space. Because objects are extended, they and
their relations and interactions can be measured, ranked and counted.
Body is thus separated from mind and from God, and astronomy
and physics can be studied in isolation from theology. Nature
becomes quantifiable.

This was a revolution in thought, whose effects continue to
reverberate today. It was given stupendous influence and prestige
by the publication in 1687 of Isaac Newton's masterpiece, *Philosophiae
Naturalis Principia Mathematica*. As the name implies, this was
designed to show that, in the words of Galileo, 'The book of Nature
is written in the language of mathematics.' It did so in the most
dramatic way possible, by laying down a set of 'axioms' and 'postulates' – basic laws and assumptions – in the manner of the ancient
Greek geometer Euclid, from which a dazzling array of explanations
and predictions could be derived about the stars and planets. It is
only a slight exaggeration to say that *Principia Mathematica* demonstrated a means by which Newton – or in principle any suitably

trained mathematician – could give the exact position of every large body in the universe at any time in the past, present or future. True, Newton's version of the calculus (which he had also invented, independently of his great German contemporary Leibniz) was so difficult that for many years few others could master it; but this only added to his mystique. So it was little wonder that Alexander Pope wrote his famous epitaph for Newton thus: 'Nature and nature's laws lay hid in night; / God said "Let Newton be" and all was light.'

Newton's achievement caught the imagination of all Europe. Building as well on the work of scientists such as Robert Boyle, new physical laws were discovered, were tested in an array of increasingly sophisticated experiments, and slowly started to find their way into technological applications. Channelled through the Royal Society, through the printing press and through vigorous correspondence, the spirit of discovery radiated outwards into other experimental sciences such as chemistry, which underwent its own mathematical revolution in the hands of Antoine Lavoisier, a French contemporary of Burke's who was guillotined by the revolutionaries in 1794. The influence of science reached into ancient disciplines such as history, and shaped new ones, as it did after Adam Smith distilled and greatly extended early thinking on economics into *The Wealth of Nations*.

Yet if anything the scientific revolution had still greater impact in the arts, in culture, in society. To many people it seemed as though the key had been found to unlock nature herself, and that her mysteries now lay for the first time accessible to human thought. Darkness had been dispelled, reason was triumphant, and opinion and prejudice had yielded to rational inquiry. Man had been the measure of all things, and by measuring had tamed them.

But if this were really true, then what about tradition, authority and faith? If science was now the true canon of inquiry, then tradition started to look irrelevant, for what evidential weight could tradition ever have? If nature and human history were to be judged by individual reason alone, then surely scriptural, ecclesiastical and political authority must also be judged by reason alone, and yield to individual rights? If Cartesian doubt was the order of the day, then what role could there be for God and faith? Aristocratic privilege? Monarchy? Across all Europe, from Spinoza to Montesquieu to Bayle to the *philosophes* Voltaire, d'Alembert and Diderot, to David Hume and Adam Ferguson and Edward Gibbon, different thinkers began to explore the possibilities.

These were highly unsettling developments. In Britain the official reaction was in many ways a relatively calm one, for in the early eighteenth century Britain was becoming a beacon of tolerance and openness to the rest of Europe. Voltaire's *Philosophical Letters* of 1733, written after a two-year period of exile in Britain, celebrated the British constitution, which had imposed limits on monarchical power and given the people a share of government. The British were often rather coarse and vulgar, but Britain was a place where property could not be seized without due process, and private individuals enjoyed wide freedoms of thought and expression. The contrast with the autocratic and personal monarchy of the Bourbons, the intolerance of the Church hierarchy and the political weakness of the Parlement was evident, and Voltaire's book unleashed a wave of 'Anglomania' in France.

But Britain's openness to new ideas was not shared elsewhere in Europe. Across the continent ruling dynasties looked with horror and alarm at the spread of Enlightenment ideas, with their emphasis on individual rationality, economic materialism, democratic rights, moral equality and scientific advance. It was one thing to establish learned institutions for the promulgation of knowledge, on the model of the Royal Society, quite another to tolerate atheism, religious dissent and radical reform. That way led, surely, to upheaval, perhaps even – the scientific word now used in a social sense – to revolution.

Where, then, did this leave Edmund Burke? He was, in many ways, an Enlightenment figure: highly educated, making his way in London amid the hubbub of new ideas, conversing with men of the genius of Hume, Smith and Johnson. Through the *Annual Register*, he had read and reviewed some of the greatest thinkers of the period, including Smith, Rousseau and Montesquieu, while the papers published as his *Notebook* include a highly critical early note on Voltaire. In writing the *Account* with Will Burke, and his own unfinished *Essay*, he had been much influenced by Enlightenment thinking on history and historiography. And in his own life, he had worked unceasingly to promote reforms consistent with Enlightenment ideals. He had argued for religious tolerance in Ireland and for humane treatment of slaves as a preliminary to abolition of the slave trade; he had defended the rights of American colonists, and pressed for the East India Company to be held to public account; he had practised scientific agriculture on the farm at Gregories.

However, Burke's first instinct is always to protect and enhance human society. In his view genuine reforms do not overturn or undermine society; on the contrary, over time they strengthen it by addressing social needs and reducing grievances. Enlightenment beliefs in all-conquering reason and universal individual rights were quite different, he thought, precisely because they had the potential to threaten the basis of society itself, by providing a justification for revolution.

Burke's thought provides a deep critique of the legacy of the Enlightenment in contemporary Western politics and society, as we shall see. But his own preoccupation was with the Enlightenment as a spur to revolution in his own time. In particular, he singles out for attack the malign influence of Jean-Jacques Rousseau. Rousseau had become a cult figure to the Jacobins, and his remains were ceremonially reinterred in the Pantheon in 1794, a mark of the highest honour that revolutionary France could bestow. Burke had published respectful reviews of Rousseau's *Letter to d'Alembert* and *Emile* for the *Annual Register* in 1759, and some have seen his denunciations of Rousseau in the *Reflections* and the *Letter to a*

Member of the National Assembly as the product of a late turn
against him and an embittered retirement. This is a mistake. In
general Burke's thought is remarkably stable and consistent, even
as it develops throughout his life. The same is true of his devastating
critique of Rousseau's ideas, which begins as early as 1756 and *A
Vindication of Natural Society*.

Fêted by the political left, reviled by the right, Jean-Jacques Rousseau
is one of the most colourful figures of a colourful age. Born into
a middling family in Protestant Geneva, the home of Calvinism,
in 1712 he lost his mother soon after childbirth and later quarrelled
with his father. He became an itinerant tutor and secretary, relying
emotionally, sexually and financially on his older patron Madame
de Warens, before moving to Paris. In Paris he met the *philosophe*
Denis Diderot, wrote for the great Enlightenment digest of knowledge, the French *Encyclopédie*, and started to make his name through
a succession of works including the *Discourses*, the *Social Contract*,
Emile and the *Confessions*. While in Paris, in 1745 Rousseau met
Thérèse Levasseur, an illiterate laundry maid by whom he had five
children, all of whom were given up at his insistence not to various
aristocratic women who had offered to take them, but to almost
certain death at a foundling hospital. He married Thérèse in 1768
and died, after a long period of physical decline, ten years later.

For Rousseau, in thought as in life, man is first and foremost a
creature of nature, a solitary and self-sufficient individual. As such
he has absolute freedom, and with freedom comes the capacity to
exercise rational choice and so to be morally autonomous. These
features are not incidental to his humanity; rather, they are what
make him a human being at all: as Rousseau says in the *Social
Contract*, 'To renounce liberty is to renounce being a man.' It follows
for Rousseau, then, that any abridgement of man's freedom is an
abridgement of his humanity, which pushes the individual towards
the status of a slave, or even of an inanimate object.

The counterpart of this for Rousseau is that in any but an ideal society most people will be in a state of dependence or slavery on others: in his famous words, 'Man is born free, but is everywhere in chains.' Society itself, and specifically the unequal institution of private property, is thus a source of corruption, which privileges the few and enslaves the many. In society, men's natural desire for self-preservation is transformed into self-love or pride. The arts and sciences are not great human achievements or marks of civilized society, but merely expressions of that pride and corruption. Material progress becomes a means by which governments are enabled to suppress individual liberty and self-expression. That corruption can be avoided either in a state of nature or in what he terms a civil society, in which man is redeemed by the use of human reason, allowing man's natural compassion for others to flow.

How can redemption come through civil society? In particular, if there must be some sovereign power in a state, how can Rousseau square this with man's essential freedom? After all, he believes that any derogation from freedom is an intolerable act of enslavement. The answer is supposed to lie in his idea of a general will: when man is thinking rationally, has been relieved of inequality and is able to deliberate freely, he will understand that his desires are completely congruent with the general will of the people as a whole. As he identifies his will with the general will, his will is realized without any submission to the wills of others. Thanks to the perfect congruity of his will with the sovereign power, he remains free, and so morally autonomous. In giving himself to all, he gives himself to no one. A civil society is thus one in which people achieve their full rights and freedoms as citizens, by a social contract through which they create their own laws and so avoid enslavement and dependency on others.

Rousseau thus takes Enlightenment ideas of the supremacy of reason, social equality and the rights of man, and turns them against society itself. The individual and nature are exalted, while society is seen as intrinsically corrupt and capable of redemption only by means of a utopian project of wholesale reconstruction through which it and its individual members can be identified in the general will. With their shared emphasis on nature and the will, it is easy to see how Romanticism has roots in Rousseau's thought; so also do much Marxist, communist and fascist ideology, such is the way his arguments cut across later political categories. And it is easy to see why Rousseau's ideas were so enthusiastically taken up by the Jacobins during the French revolution. Was not the *ancien régime* a perfect example of the luxury and idleness, arrogance and pride of 'civilized' society? What were the assemblies, if not institutions whose purpose was to disclose the general will? What were the opposition, if not corrupted aristocrats and reactionaries, indeed subhuman animals consumed by self-love and incapable of understanding their own true needs through the general will? Was not the revolution itself the perfect expression of man's inalienable rights and liberties?

For Burke, as we shall see, these questions are themselves the result of a deep social pathology, one created out of Enlightenment ideas by the perverse and paradoxical genius of Rousseau himself. We can see this even at the very outset of his public thought. In the *Vindication* of 1756, his very first published work, he had mocked the suggestion that civilized society was a social evil responsible for war and oppression, and that man should return to a state of nature unmediated by social institutions.

Officially at least, the satire is an attack on Lord Bolingbroke's 'natural religion'; it does not mention Rousseau's name at all. But Rousseau's *Discourse on Inequality* had been published in France in 1755 and reviewed by Adam Smith in the same year, and many similar arguments were the fashionable talk of the day in London. There are, moreover, significant overlaps of structure and thought between the *Discourse* and the *Vindication*. It is hard, then, to read Burke's essay without seeing it also as an attack on Rousseau. This impression is strengthened by Burke's publication of a rather mixed 1759 review of the *Letter to d'Alembert*, which decried 'a tendency to paradox, which is always the bane of solid learning, and which threatens now to destroy it, a splenetic disposition carried to misanthropy, and an austere virtue pursued now to an unsociable fierceness'. And the same line of thought was repeated three years later in a review of *Emile*, also published by Burke in the *Annual Register*, which identified 'very considerable parts that are impracticable, others that are chimerical; and not a few highly blameable, and dangerous both to piety and morals'.

In other words, even as early as the 1750s – ten years before he entered politics – Burke is intellectually very sure of his ground, and able to identify and attack a line of thought with which he would only fully clash some four decades later. In the 1790s, his central political and intellectual project became the need to prevent the destruction of European society and preserve its institutions against the spread of revolutionary ideas, many of them derived from Rousseau. Far from great inconsistency and incoherence, then, there is evidence here that Burke's thought is in fact remarkably coherent over time. Far from being the productions to order of a paid lackey, his ideas put down their roots a full decade before he became a public figure.

Between the 1750s and the 1790s Burke argued for a new conception of representative government in Britain, and fought injustice and oppression over Ireland, over the American colonies and over India. In the following chapters we will see how these campaigns sprang from a single and extraordinarily powerful body of ideas. But to understand Burke better, we must grapple with his thought directly and in its own terms. To this we now turn.

SEVEN

The Social Self

IN THE PROVOST'S HOUSE at Trinity College Dublin there is a superb portrait of Edmund Burke by James Barry, his brilliant but rather quarrelsome protégé (see opposite). We see Burke from around his left shoulder. He is at his desk, several great volumes stacked behind, an open book in front of him, his quill held up from the paper, his head turned half towards us. He is not frowning, but his lips are set and the look is purposeful and dignified. The standard reproductions are too bleached: in the painting itself Burke's head and hand are highlighted against a much darker background, as though his mind is shining its light directly upon the paper. The brushwork is very fine; the effect abrupt, photographic and intimate. This is man of action caught in a moment of deep thought.

But was Burke really a deep thinker? Over the past two centuries his supporters and critics have clashed over innumerable aspects of his life and legacy. But on one point they have been united: that his thought is adventitious not orderly, a patchwork rather than a system. On this view Burke is a politician. He gives us ideas, he gives us rhetoric, but he does not give us a body of thought as

such, still less a philosophy. He is too clever to be entirely persuasive, too passionate and partisan to be entirely honest. His friend
Oliver Goldsmith once said of him: 'Who born for the Universe,
narrow'd his mind / And to party gave up, what was meant for
mankind. / Tho' fraught with all learning, kept straining his throat
/ To persuade Tommy Townshend to lend him a vote.' This has
been read as suggesting that Burke was no philosopher precisely
because he was a party hack.

Even those who have sought to portray Burke as a philosopher
have done so in relatively narrow terms, and appear at a loss to
find the definition of terms, the first principles, the chains of
reasoning, the thought experiments or the discussion of cases seen
as characteristic of the discipline. For some, a certain intellectual
disorder is even an advantage: as one scholar rather hopefully puts
it, 'We should emphasize the *absence* of system in Burke's political
ideas and underline his characteristic lapses into inconsistency.
Only through understanding the flexibility of his thought can we
appreciate its richness, its variety and its humanity.'

In this judgement such writers have claimed a surprising ally:
Burke himself. Burke is invariably rude about abstract theorizing
and 'metaphysicians'. In the *Reflections* he says, 'There are people
who have split and anatomised the doctrine of free government,
as if it were an abstract question . . . they have disputed whether
liberty be a positive or a negative idea . . . Others [are] corrupting
religion as these have perverted philosophy . . .' In his *Letter to the
Sheriffs of Bristol* he asks, 'What is the use of discussing a man's
abstract right to food or medicine? The question is upon the method
of procuring them and administering them . . . I shall always advise
to call in aid of the farmer and the physician, rather than the
professor of metaphysics.' In his *Letter to Sir Hercules Langrishe* he
says, 'I think you the most remote that can be conceived from the
metaphysicians of our times, who are the most foolish of men, and
who, dealing in universals and essences, see no difference between
more and less.'

Nevertheless, there is good reason to think that this conventional picture of Burke is largely wrong. Of course it is true that Burke is not, and would hardly have wished to be, the creator of a great philosophical system in the style of Spinoza or Kant. He does not have the distinctively questioning temperament of a Hume, or the mystical flashes of a Wittgenstein. Nevertheless Burke has a rich and distinctive worldview of his own. It is not built up *a priori* from axioms by the application of logical principles but springs, unsurprisingly, from instinct, law and history: it is assembled from different compositions of thought and then reflectively extended to new contexts. It is not intended to be a closed and completed body of doctrine; indeed it is anti-ideological in spirit. Yet it is full of philosophical insights, and its coherence and power suggest that it bears a more than contingent relationship to the facts of human existence.

Indeed, on closer examination Burke is not even quite as dismissive of abstract thought as these and other passages suggest. His position is not that of the bluff English squire or man of business, who dismisses philosophy as so much airy-fairy theorizing. Rather, he is effectively making a series of rather sophisticated and challenging philosophical points: that absolute consistency, however desirable in mathematics and logic, is neither available nor desirable in the conduct of human affairs; that universal principles are never sufficient in themselves to guide practical deliberation; and that it is a deep error to seek to apply concepts from the exact sciences willy-nilly to the messy business of life. On the contrary: 'Circumstances (which with some gentlemen pass for nothing) give in reality to every political principle its distinguishing colour and discriminating effect. The circumstances are what render every civil and political scheme beneficial or noxious to mankind.'

As between science and life, speculation and action, his own choice is clear: 'It is the business of the speculative philosopher to mark the proper ends of government. It is the business of the politician, who is the philosopher in action, to find out proper means towards those ends, and to employ them with effect.' Coming from *Thoughts on the Cause of the Present Discontents*, his great manifesto for principled party politics, this is surely autobiographical. Provocatively, Burke identifies the politician with the philosopher in action. Far from despising philosophy, he claims the status of philosopher, as well as that of politician, for himself.

In approaching Burke's philosophy, we need to start with his two great predecessors, Thomas Hobbes and John Locke.

Hobbes was born in 1588, and lived through ninety-one of the most interesting years in British history. His youth was spent in the time of Shakespeare, Jonson and Donne; his middle age during the constitutional crises of the 1630s, from which he fled to Paris in 1640 just in time to escape the English Civil War; and his old age in the midst of the scientific revolution. In his book *Leviathan*, published in 1651, Hobbes addressed one of the most fundamental of all political questions: what is the basis of legitimate government? He argued that government owed its existence to a contract between all members of society, by which they voluntarily traded a measure of autonomy for security. In the absence of government people would live in a state of nature or maximal distrust, a 'war of all against all', in which all were constantly at risk and constantly afraid of violent death; a state in which people's lives were, in his famous phrase, 'solitary, poor, nasty, brutish and short'. To escape this fate, individuals cede some freedoms on a once-and-for-all basis to a single sovereign authority which maintains order and so gives them the legal and physical protection to associate freely with each other.

According to Hobbes it is this act of empowerment, this 'social contract', that makes society possible. The sovereign may in principle be a monarchy, an oligarchy or a democracy. But it and it alone is the source of legitimate power, and its legitimacy derives from being freely given by all. The sovereign can properly pass legislation because we, the people, have authorized it to do so; and according to Hobbes we are under a moral and not merely a legal obligation to obey its laws for the same reason.

The idea of a social contract was taken up and subtly reshaped by John Locke in the second of his *Two Treatises of Government*. Locke's earlier work saw human beings as God's creation, but it insisted on what he took to be a far more realistic account of human psychology. People were not born with innate ideas, he suggested, but learned to live through sensation and experience of the world; the human imagination was not creative, but only able to recombine what it had already sensed or experienced; and human identity derived from consciousness, not from some soul or other immaterial substance. In keeping with this down-to-earth picture, in the *Second Treatise* Locke places the emphasis on government as arbitrating between competing claims, and establishing a framework within which man can exercise his ownership of life, liberty and property. This generates an important difference with Hobbes: since political authority rests for Locke not on a one-time pooling of sovereignty but on the continuing consent of the governed, the people retain their rights under government, and in particular retain the right to revolt against their rulers. Government thus operates within a framework of trust, not merely one of authority. Coming just forty years after the execution of Charles I, the point was not lost on his readers.

Hobbes's account of the social contract is extremely familiar, and many people today seem to possess an instinctively Hobbesian conception of political authority, grounding it in rational self-protection, rather than in any divine bequest. But a simple but devastating objection to it has often been attributed to David Hume: how can individuals have promised to obey a social contract, unless the institution of promising already existed beforehand? But if the institution of promising already existed, then how can the individuals have genuinely been in a state of nature at all?

It is not in fact clear that Hume was the source of this objection. But it is interesting that Burke hints at a related argument indirectly

in the *Vindication*, his satire on Lord Bolingbroke, by raising a
question about what the idea of humanity in a pure state of nature
is or could ever amount to. Nearly forty years later, he made a
similar point in the *Appeal* in relation to the revolution in France:

> In a state of rude nature there is no such thing as a people. A
> number of men in themselves have no collective capacity. The
> idea of a people is the idea of a corporation . . . When men,
> therefore, break up the original compact or agreement which gives
> its corporate form and capacity to a state, they are no longer a
> people . . . they have no longer a legal coactive force to bind within,
> nor a claim to be recognised abroad.

What matters is not the individual as an atom, but the collective
capacity created by individuals considered as a people or society.
Following Aristotle, then, for Burke man is a social animal, a *poli-*
tikon zoon, an animal whose nature is to be in society. Indeed, there
is little or no sense to be attached to the idea of man as an atom,
wholly cut off from human society. The human self is a social self.
This is an idea with vast and often still unrecognized implications,
some of which we will explore below.

Unlike Hobbes, Locke and Rousseau, then, Burke begins not
with a state of nature, but with what is given – that is, with the
fact of human society itself. Human beings grow up within human
society, and this is what much of their humanity consists in.
Different societies may in fact differ in various ways – rich or poor,
open or closed, centralized or dispersed, warlike or peaceable. But
each has a social order, which links people together in an enormous
and ever-shifting web of institutions, customs, traditions, habits
and expectations built up by innumerable interactions over many
years. Thus in eighteenth-century England the social order would
include the great estates of the realm: the monarchy, the aristocracy
and the commons; the 'establishments', such as the Church of
England and the universities; the City of London, the guilds and

trading companies; the institutions of local government; the navy and army; the legal system and judiciary, and so on. But by extension it would also include the institutions surrounding marriage, birth and death; church attendance and prayer; the tavern and the theatre; the arts and culture; booksellers and the press; gambling, drinking and the mob; and patterns of education, self-enrichment and social mobility.

These institutions are ultimately grounded in feeling and emotion, which guide and direct man's reason. They are bound together by affection, identity and interest. They matter for three reasons. First, they constrain each other, competing and cooperating as required to survive, diffusing power across communities, and providing a social challenge to state power. Secondly, they give shape and meaning to people's lives, as work or play, setting rhythms to the day or year, creating overlapping identities and personal loyalties. Revisiting Burke's famous words in the *Reflections*: 'To be attached to the subdivision, to love the little platoon we belong to in society, is . . . the first link in the series by which we proceed towards a love to our country and to mankind.' Finally, institutions trap and store knowledge. Composed of a myriad private interactions, traditions and practices as it is, the social order becomes a repository of shared knowledge and inherited wisdom.

Among these institutions is that of the market, itself the object of increasing thought and study in the late eighteenth century, most notably by Adam Smith in *The Wealth of Nations*. Smith once remarked that 'Burke is the only man I ever knew who thinks on economic subjects exactly as I do, without any previous communications having passed between us,' and in *Thoughts and Details on Scarcity*, a paper assembled from some of Burke's writings after his death, we can see the congruence of his thought with Smith's. The paper has often been criticized for its apparently callous attitude towards the very poorest in society, whom Burke insists should be supported by private charity and not by public intervention. But this is arguably rather unfair. The principal memorandum (now lost) behind it was presented privately to William Pitt the Younger and others in 1795, amid famine conditions and in response to public concern about grain supplies. It was not so much a weighty statement of principles as a specific response to crisis.

Burke's main point was that grain prices were governed by economic laws which gave the producers a fair profit and indirectly secured private property, and that government interventions to manage either prices or wages were likely to be damaging to employment or supplies. Government had a proper power to regulate, but should not become an economic actor in its own right. Burke did not use the phrase 'invisible hand' – contrary to popular impression, the phrase hardly appears in Smith's work either – but the line of thought is very close to that of *The Wealth of Nations*. And just as Smith embeds the idea of a market in a broader moral context of human sympathy in his *Theory of Moral Sentiments*, so Burke sees markets and other institutions as operating within, drawing from and contributing to a broader moral community. Neither is, in the modern sense, an out-and-out free trader.

The social order is not, then, the result of any overall design. It is not the outcome of any specific plan or project. It evolves slowly over time. Different social orders may evolve in different ways, and some may be more effective and successful than others. Each is *sui generis*, a largely incidental and historically contingent human achievement. It therefore makes an enormous difference how exactly each has evolved, and how it functions. Any practical or theoretical reflection on such a human artefact – and this applies to any institution, large or small, peoples and nations as much as words or ideas – must therefore begin with history and experience. How did it first arise? How did it evolve, and according to what principles? Was its evolution continuous or in stages, was it fast or slow? What were its effects and what did it actually mean to those involved? For Burke, nothing human can be adequately understood without answering these or similar questions. All inquiry into human affairs, and all practical deliberation and action, thus begin with history.

For Burke the social order is, in the language of the *Enquiry*, sublime: it far outstrips human understanding, triggering the instinct for self-preservation, and so feelings of awe and humility, in those who seek to grasp it. It is an inheritance, which imposes on each generation the obligation to preserve and if possible enhance it, before passing it on to the next generation. And there is no opt-out. In the words of the *Reflections*:

> Society is indeed a contract . . . but the state ought not . . . to be dissolved by the fancy of the parties. It is to be looked on with other reverence . . . It is a partnership in all science, in all art, a partnership in every virtue and in all perfection. As the ends of such a partnership cannot be obtained in many generations, it becomes a partnership not only between those who are living, but between those who are living, those who are dead, and those who are to be born.

There is, then, a social contract for Burke. But it is of a very different kind to the social contracts of Hobbes, Locke and Rousseau. For Hobbes, the social contract is the minimal basis required to secure the right of a sovereign to govern. For Locke, it is a pragmatic means by which man can protect and enjoy his rights to life and property, and the sovereignty it creates can properly be overthrown by revolution. For Rousseau, as we saw in the last chapter, it is the first part of a mechanism by which the individual will and the collective will are made one. But Burke, in effect, rejects all of these conceptions: the first, because it covertly assumes a collective identity whose existence it is supposed to justify; the second, because it allows a right of revolution, which no social order can provide, although it may be necessary in extreme circumstances; and the third, because, as he saw it, it seeks to privilege the transient urges of the mob over and above the social order itself. For Burke, there can be no such thing as a state of nature, and appeals to one are a recipe for anarchy.

Moreover, all three purported social contracts of Hobbes, Locke and Rousseau are idealizations. Burke, on the other hand, does not see himself as arguing for an idealized compact between the generations, as though it were a good idea. He takes himself to be simply pointing out a contract that exists, and explaining how that contract confers benefits and imposes obligations on those who fall under it. He does not introduce his conception of the social contract in the *Reflections* with any fanfares. But this should not allow us to ignore what is an extraordinarily interesting and powerful idea, which appears to be original to Burke himself.

The social order is not a fixed and unchanging construct, and the rigidity and hierarchy of eighteenth-century France was a standing reminder that some societies could be far more closed and repressive than others. As we have seen, Burke is often taken to be a reactionary who defends wealth, privilege and inequality as such, and opposes threats to them such as parliamentary reform. It is true that he did not support parliamentary reforms, such as shorter parliaments and extension of the franchise, and his concerns appear overblown in hindsight. But Burke was no reactionary in his own life: growing up in Ireland had made him far from blind to poverty and want, and his whole life evinces a deep concern for those in need. Nor was he afraid to question the status quo far in advance of public opinion, as his opposition to slavery – no small matter in a slave port like Bristol – well demonstrates.

Burke's thought, too, is not reactionary. The point for him as for Locke is simply that when a society or social order is functioning well it gives to individuals the priceless gift of liberty secured by legal rights, and in particular the right to own property. In principle, it provides a public context in which individuals can legally acquire and maintain property without expropriation or theft, wherever they are in society. Far from choking off individual energy and aspiration, then, it makes social and economic advancement possible. It is a colossal collective achievement, which must be treated with the utmost respect by would-be reformers.

A successful social order thus affords rights and liberty to individuals, as well as imposing duties on them. Burke is often thought
to be unremittingly hostile to natural rights. But in fact this is not
true; indeed rights are an essential component of his worldview.
What he rejects are universal claims divorced from an actual social
context, or based on man's rights in a purported state of nature.
For Burke there is a core of natural rights (given by God, the author
of nature) which is developed and reinforced within human society
by process of law. In his 'Speech on Fox's East India Bill', he puts
the point thus:

> The rights of men, that is to say, the natural rights of mankind,
> are indeed sacred things; and if any public measure is proved
> mischievously to affect them, the objection ought to be fatal to
> that measure . . . If these natural rights are further affirmed and
> declared by express covenants . . . they are in a still better condi-
> tion . . . The things secured by these instruments may, without
> any deceitful ambiguity, be very fitly called the chartered rights of
> men.

What matters, then, is that natural rights are filtered through and
grounded within society by process of law.

In addition to legal rights, Burke also recognizes rights afforded
by usage or 'prescription' because they have been known and established over long periods of time. Like common-law rights these
are, in effect, summaries of human experience. They are settled,
they are well understood, and they have been elaborated, nuanced
and defined across many different contexts through countless legal
judgements. In the *Reflections* he says:

> Far am I from denying in theory; full as far is my heart from
> withholding in practice . . . the *real* rights of men . . . If civil society
> be made for the advantage of man, all the advantages for which
> it is made become his right . . . Whatever each man can separately

do, without trespassing upon others, he has a right to do for himself; and he has a right to a fair portion of all which society, with all its combinations of skill and force, can do in his favour.

Such rights are very different from the 'universal rights of man' promoted by the revolutionaries in France. These are the 'natural rights' of Rousseau (and, arguably, of Locke), rights which mankind is somehow deemed to have enjoyed in an original state of nature. They are not legitimate, because they have been divorced from any context of law, custom or tradition. Rather, they are slogans, uncertain in their full meaning and potentially revolutionary in their effects.

For Burke, the social order is in the broadest sense what constitutes a nation. In the *Abridgement* he had explored the ethnic roots of English nationhood; and it was a theme of eighteenth-century political discourse that that sense of nationhood, and of English and indeed British exceptionalism in civic institutions, derived from the longevity of Parliament and the constitutional settlement of 1688. But Burke has a more inclusive conception in mind. By the time of the French revolution this conception of nationhood as social order is perhaps one reason why Burke is instantly able to see France as a country which has, in effect, forgotten itself.

Yet the social order is itself sustained by a constitution more narrowly defined, and in Britain it is sustained by a set of legal documents, statutes, traditions and conventions that make up the British constitution. Again, these are ratified by usage and experience. They are not the product of one mind at any time, but of many minds operating over centuries. Underlying them is the English common law, the 'law of the land', and its rights or freedoms may be periodically codified or recorded in statute. This is to be welcomed when such a statute operates, in his words, on the principles of the common law.

The genius of the British constitution, for Burke (drawing on classical republican theory, Montesquieu and several centuries of

English political reflection), is that it has evolved in a way which balances the great interests that dominate the social order: the monarchy, the aristocracy and the commons. Because the constitution is balanced, it is flexible and can adapt to circumstances and new social demands; it has the means of its own correction. Three things follow from this. First, any serious attempt by a particular interest to step outside the limits of its proper powers must be resisted – we see here the basic source of Burke's opposition to the extension of Court influence. Secondly, the constitution itself must not be subject to drastic or radical change, for this destroys part of the inherited wisdom of the social order, and might also undermine its capacity for self-correction. Finally, when such change is unavoidable, reform must be limited and proportionate to the requirement of the moment.

Thus Burke is not opposed to change as such, only to radical or total change. On the contrary: for him acceptance of change is the indispensable corollary of commitment to a given social order, which will itself be continuously evolving. To recall the words of the *Reflections on the Revolution in France*, 'A state without the means of some change is without the means of its conservation.' Far from reviling the Glorious Revolution of 1688, Burke celebrates it in the *Reflections* and the *Appeal* as the necessary and limited change required to preserve the constitution. After all, the new monarch William III and his Stuart and Hanoverian successors – at least, Burke believed, until George III – had upheld the balance created by a constitutional monarchy. After 1688 sovereignty in Britain was not exercised as it had been in the traumatic years 1625–60, when the King, Parliament and the army had ruled in succession. Rather, it was exercised collectively by the King-in-Parliament, wherein Parliament constrains the will and actions of the monarch according to established convention and law. So it still is.

* * *

The balance of power in 1688 had been held by the great aristocrats, and in his own time Burke regarded the aristocracy as indispensable to the proper functioning of the constitution, and thus to the wider social order. Burke put the case in a rather florid letter to the 3rd Duke of Richmond in 1772:

> You people of great families and hereditary trusts and fortunes, are not like such as I am, who, whatever we may be, by the rapidity of our growth, and even by the fruit we bear, flatter ourselves that, while we creep on the ground, we belly into melons that are exquisite for size and flavour, yet still are but annual plants, that perish with our season, and leave no sort of traces behind us. You, if you are what you ought to be, are in my eye the great oaks that shade a country, and perpetuate your benefits from generation to generation.

This is sometimes read as a piece of mere obsequiousness, but as so often with Burke much of the meaning lies below the surface – note the characteristically Burkean caveat: 'if you are what you ought to be'. His point was not that 'perennial' aristocrats were innately superior to 'annual' men of ambition, but that the landed estates uniquely shaped the ecosystem within which society flourished as a whole. For their part, enlightened Whig aristocrats were quite conscious of the need to bring new talent and energy into the political system, and specifically the House of Commons, in part to validate and legitimate the settlement of 1688.

For Burke, inequality of wealth and power was an unavoidable aspect of human life. It was right, he believed, for individuals to do what they could to help themselves and their families to succeed, and to help others in need. But the great fortunes of the aristocrats were among the fundamental guarantees of the social order itself. Their capital was landed, permanent and embedded in particular communities, not temporary and moveable like financial capital. Periodically a person and a family might prove sufficiently distinguished to be raised to a peerage. But the desire to create equality through a levelling attempt to requisition private property was impractical, an outrageous infringement of individual liberty, and a threat to the social order itself: 'It is true, that the Peers have a great influence in the kingdom, and in every part of the public concerns. While they are men of property, it is impossible to prevent it, except by such means as must prevent all property from its natural operation: an event not easily to be compassed, while property is power; nor by any means to be wished.'

Landed private property was, then, both inevitable and valuable to society as a whole. But as with all forms of power, its privileged status conferred duties as well as benefits. For Burke all power brings responsibility, and so the landed families had obligations to be virtuous in their public conduct and independent-minded in their political opinions. Prescriptive right brings with it prescriptive virtue – that is, a high public expectation of virtue on people of property and influence, which arises from their wealth and station. There is an implicit contrast with liquid financial wealth, seen as less public, less permanent, less demanding of care and virtue on the part of its owner, and more prone to be used for consumption; and in his *Thoughts on French Affairs* of 1791 Burke specifically argued that the revolution in France had arisen in part from instability and corruption due to an increase in financial wealth, since the republicans had deliberately destroyed the landed estates.

Burke applied his own Ciceronian standard of public virtue in his personal transactions with the great and the good, even of his own party. In his letters he frequently criticizes them for their sloppiness, laziness, selfishness and lack of responsibility, and he constantly seeks to recall them to their duty, in polite but direct terms. And when the young Duke of Bedford breaches this public standard of prescriptive virtue, Burke is unsparing in his criticism: 'It would not be gross adulation, but uncivil irony, to say, that he has any public merit of his own to keep alive the idea of the services, by which his vast landed pensions were obtained. My merits, whatever they are, are original and personal; his are derivative.' This is ornate, but deadly: for Burke the Duke is a man of no personal ability or consequence, unworthy of a great family and sustained only by accident of birth and the social importance of private property.

Thus Burke defended aristocratic power and duty as an anchor of the social order during his own time, alongside a mixed constitution that balanced the interests of the few and the many. His own belief, however, is ultimately in an aristocracy not of presumed but of actual virtue and achievement. As he says, 'I am no friend to aristocracy, in the sense at least in which that word is commonly understood'; without constitutional restraint, aristocracy threatens an 'austere and insolent domination'. But to adapt the language of his letter to the Duke of Richmond, the purpose of the oaks is to shade and support the growth of new men and new fortunes, some of which may put down roots of their own – as he himself had hoped to do through his son Richard. Here too, then, Burke is rather more of a meritocrat than is commonly recognized; and he holds that when the social order is properly underpinned by a constitution binding monarchy, aristocracy and commons together, it too is fundamentally meritocratic.

But the social order does not merely rest upon the virtue of those in positions of power; more fundamentally, it rests upon the habits and behaviour or 'manners' of those in all walks of life. Man is a social animal; people naturally imitate each other; they cooperate and compete; and they establish practices, habits, rules and codes of behaviour which make this cooperation and competition possible. Individually, good habits become internalized into virtues; collectively, they create institutions, and the result is what would now be called social capital or trust. For Burke, perhaps influenced by the Scottish historian William Robertson, this trust was built up in Britain through two specific historical developments: the emergence in the early Middle Ages of codes of chivalry among the nobility, by which a warrior ethos was transmuted into one of courtesy, courtliness and public responsibility, especially towards women; and the literacy, learning and charitable ethos of the clergy. 'Nothing is more certain than that our manners, our civilization . . . depended for ages upon two principles, and were indeed the result of both combined: I mean the spirit of a gentleman, and the spirit of religion.' Chivalry 'obliged sovereigns to submit to the soft collar of social esteem . . . and gave a domination, vanquisher of laws, to be subdued by manners'. Commerce and business have promoted the growth of manners; but ultimately both commerce and politics rely on manners – that is, on the trust engendered by the social order. Manners are what make the British both a polite and a commercial people.

Even morality and law themselves depend on manners, according to Burke, for manners affect society, the basis of all law, directly. 'Manners are of more importance than laws. Upon them, in a great measure, the laws depend. The law touches us but here and there . . . Manners are what vex or soothe, corrupt or purify . . . barbarize or refine us . . . they give their whole form and colour to our lives. According to their quality, they aid morals, they supply them, or they totally destroy them.' Manners too are the product not of reason, but of unreflective individual habit and social wisdom. This, not racial or religious or political bias, is what Burke means by 'prejudice'. Of course some prejudice may be ugly, as with slavery or religious intolerance. But in Burke's usage 'prejudice' refers to a person's composite experience or intuition, which works prior to reasoning or the weighing of evidence and is often a source of wisdom. It is a small extension of Burke's thought to note that it is then prejudice that allows a man to act quickly and rightly, when a more reasoned self-interest might push him towards dishonesty.

Liberty, then, is the result of a well-ordered society; it is the product of the complex constraints and possibilities imposed by the habits, traditions, institutions and manners that make up a given society. Burke thus draws on a traditional distinction between liberty and 'licence'. Licence is the imagined freedom to do anything one wants, regardless of circumstance. It emerges from a view that values, not the well-being of society as such, but the sanctity of the individual will. On this view social benefit is a by-product of individual action, and for it to be fully realized the individual will must be unfettered. For Burke, however, this view is deeply mistaken, both in ignoring man's fundamentally social nature and the true sources of individual well-being and in its utopian claim that man can and should somehow transcend society. Not only that: it corrupts and undermines the social order itself, which alone makes liberty possible.

By contrast for Burke, as for Hobbes, it is written in the law of nature that no man shall be judge in his own cause. Thus no part of society is free to do just what it pleases. How so? Recall that Burke argues that the social order is a trust, and all those who hold public office have a public duty to uphold that trust on behalf of the people. Indeed, he says in the *Thoughts*, they are representatives of the people: 'The king is the representative of the people; so are the lords; so are the judges. They all are trustees for the people, as well as the Commons; because no power is given for the sole sake of the holder; and although government certainly is an institution of Divine authority, yet its forms, and the persons who administer it, all originate from the people.' But as with monarchy and aristocracy, so the people's will is and must be constrained.

The fundamental constitutional principle in Britain is thus one not of popular sovereignty, but of *parliamentary* sovereignty. For it is Parliament that represents, distils, debates, constrains and ultimately balances the different views and interests in society. Statutes, laws, are not directives handed down from the sovereign power to the people; they are agreements, negotiated between monarch, Lords and Commons – that is, created by the nation for itself. By contrast, Burke thinks of democracy as the direct and unbounded expression of the popular will; and in this sense he is no democrat. But he is insistent that power must be accountable, and that it must be publicly exercised at all levels on behalf of the people. These are strikingly modern, indeed democratic, thoughts.

Though Burke does not mention it as such, the economic value of social constraints had been perfectly demonstrated by events after 1688. Before then, British monarchs who needed revenue – as they regularly did to fund their own courts and to fight wars – were reluctant to do so through taxation, since this meant calling a parliament, which inevitably sought new rights and privileges from the Crown. Accordingly, they had long raised funds by selling off titles and Crown estates, by creating and selling the rights to artificial monopolies such as in tobacco, and by 'forced loans' from nobles and London bankers. Each had serious drawbacks: titles became devalued; selling off estates meant the Crown had a smaller and smaller revenue base, which merely compounded the original problem; artificial monopolies pushed prices up and inhibited trade; and forced loans were a form of gentlemanly extortion and were rarely repaid.

All this changed with the accession of William III. Under the new constitutional order, sovereignty now lay not with the King, but with the King-in-Parliament. The King was enabled to hold executive power, especially in matters of defence, but only as constrained by Parliament. The effect of this was to discipline the public finances. Because the new monarch had less power, he was more trustworthy. Parliament would not allow William to default, and so his promises to repay loans suddenly became credible. The result was that Crown indebtedness rose from £1 million in 1688 to almost £17 million in 1697. Interest rates fell to reflect the new security of the loans, from 14 per cent in the early 1690s to 6–8 per cent before 1700, and only 3 per cent by the 1720s. Much of the money was spent on the War of the Spanish Succession, in which the Duke of Marlborough won his great victories in the first decade of the new century.

By contrast, France had long been the great continental superpower under Louis XIV. But its autocratic and personal monarchy, rigid administration and inert parliament created a weak system of government. It lacked the openness, trust and free institutions to generate a large entrepreneur class and, above all, it lacked credit, since the government defaulted repeatedly on its debts. It was this specific lack of public credit that precipitated the calling of the Estates General in 1789 and, as Burke was well aware, it played a major role in hastening the revolution that followed.

We can now understand better the full force of Burke's critique of Rousseau. In fact, in some ways the two men had more in common than either might have cared to admit. Both disliked the domination of scientific ways of thought; both believed in the wisdom of ordinary people and personal experience, as against officially certified expertise; and both accepted the idea of a distinctively human nature, founded not merely in reason but in the emotions.

Thereafter, however, their thinking sharply diverges. Apart from the tacit critique of the *Vindication* and his publication of some rather mixed book reviews, Burke had paid no great attention to Rousseau during his lifetime, or indeed for more than a decade after his death in 1778. However, the decision in 1790 of the French National Assembly to erect a statue in Rousseau's honour – and the revolutionaries' subsequent decision to reinter his remains in the Pantheon – triggered an outpouring of invective from Burke in his later writings. Much of this is highly personal: Rousseau is 'the insane Socrates of the National Assembly', and a 'philosophic instructor of the ethics of vanity': 'He melts with tenderness for those only who touch him by the remotest relation, and then, without one natural pang, casts away, as a sort of offal and excrement, the spawn of his disgusting amours, and sends his children to the hospital of foundlings.'

But the true core of Burke's criticism is not personal abuse but argument. For Burke, Rousseau's thought is an exaltation of the individual and individual reason, to the dire cost of society itself. It works by ignoring the facts and circumstances that, as we saw, 'give in reality to every political principle its distinguishing colour and discriminating effect'. In particular, it prises principles and rights away from the legal and social context that alone can give them meaning. Thus abstract nouns like 'liberty', 'equality' and 'fraternity' become mere vehicles for the emotions, to be used and abused by revolutionaries as they please. Reason gives to these words a 'delusive geometrical accuracy in moral arguments', although 'nothing universal can be rationally affirmed on any moral or . . . political subject . . . The lines of morality are not like the ideal lines of mathematics . . . They admit of exceptions, they demand modifications. These exceptions and modifications are not made by the process of logic but by the rules of prudence.'

Thus the drive for absolute consistency has impelled the Jacobins in their quest for an ideal society. It has made men turn to their own limited knowledge and unchecked imagination, instead of looking to history, experience and social wisdom for guidance, and Rousseau has taught the French revolutionaries to overturn the social order in the name of the abstract rights of man. The enabling constraints of established institutions have been discarded, and encouragement given thereby to individual savagery and cruelty. In place of collective understanding has come individual barbarism. Liberty has been replaced by licence.

The results are not merely hypocritical and self-contradictory, but disastrous. Under Rousseau's influence the revolutionaries have launched a project for the moral regeneration of man which has cast aside morals, law and manners in pursuit of an unattainable and utopian ideal. Individual well-being has been destroyed in an orgy of slaughter conducted in the name of individual well-being. Religious belief has been displaced by fanatical atheism and wickedness. Far from lessening the domination of man by man, it has increased that domination, for 'power will survive the shock in which manners and opinions perish'. This is an 'ethics of vanity', because it privileges the individual as a godlike will even while it corrupts that will itself. Rousseau himself exemplifies such an ethics, because rather than nurture his own children, at the insistence of his own reason he has defied common decency, 'prejudice' and his own principles in condemning them to death. He claims to offer himself naked and undisguised to his readers in the *Confessions*, but this too is an assertion of vanity and self-regard.

But the wider truth is that, despite some overlaps, Burke's whole philosophy stands as a reproof to the revolutionary rationalism inspired by Rousseau. Indeed, while it draws on the Enlightenment, it is a counterblast to much Enlightenment thought. For it insists that reason is guided by the emotions; that power is a trust; that the social order is a priceless inheritance; that there are no new moral principles, or principles of government; and that the proper attitude of those who aspire to power is humility, modesty and a sense of public duty.

We shall see in the next chapter how Burke uses these principles to set out his own profound and distinctive conception of government and political leadership.

EIGHT

Forging Modern Politics

AFTER A FIRST HALF OF FAIRLY mind-boggling complexity, Act II of Gilbert and Sullivan's comic opera *Iolanthe* (1882) opens on a moonlit night in Palace Yard, near the Houses of Parliament, now rebuilt after the great fire of 1834. To the left is the Clock Tower and Big Ben, to the right Westminster Hall, scene of Burke's great impeachment of Warren Hastings, while behind lies the House of Commons. In the centre of the stage, and bored to death of sentry duty, stands Private Willis.

Private Willis is just an ordinary soldier, albeit one whose unfathomable destiny later in the opera will be to marry the Queen of the Fairies. But being, as he informs the audience, 'an intellectual chap', he has been turning his mind to the mysteries of the British political system, and in particular to Britain's two political parties. As he sings, 'I often think it's comical / How Nature always does contrive / That every boy and every gal / That's born into the world alive / Is either a little Liberal / Or else a little Conservative!'

With only the Liberal and Conservative parties then on offer, the poor voters have very limited powers of choice, according to Private Willis. But so too do their Members of Parliament, who must 'divide' or vote as required by their parties: 'When in that House MPs divide / If they've a brain and cerebellum, too / They've got to leave that brain outside / And vote just as their leaders tell 'em to.' What, then, is the point of MPs if they are just to behave like political sheep, to be penned and counted in the voting lobbies? Simply that, as Private Willis acutely observes, the alternative is even worse: 'But then the prospect of a lot / Of dull MPs in close proximity / All thinking for themselves, is what / No man can face with equanimity.'

Many thoughtful people have uttered similarly despairing thoughts about the British political system over some 200 years. Surely, surely it must be possible to design a more intelligent system than one which offers voters just a few political parties, which forces people of goodwill to join political parties if they are to be elected, and which then subordinates their individual views to the party line?

The 'whipping' system, which is designed to ensure that political parties vote collectively, has come in for particular public condemnation. The whips are regularly castigated as evil enforcers trampling over politicians' individual consciences. Politicians who vote with the whip are denounced as craven lickspittles determined to grease their way up the political pole; those who defy the whip are regularly abominated as traitors and wreckers intent on putting their own egos ahead of loyalty to their colleagues. American politics has had weaker whipping; but in many ways it is held in even lower popular regard, with its embedded preference for a two-party system and constitutional vulnerability to interest-group politics and the 'money power'.

No human institution is perfect, of course, and many political parties are highly imperfect institutions. But the extraordinary fact is that properly functioning political parties have long been recognized in political theory as the very essence of mature democracy. Through them, ideologies clash. Different political opinions and concerns are stimulated, debated and gathered into manifestos or programmes of government. Policy ideas are developed in opposition and presented at elections. Individuals are recruited, educated in the craft and traditions of politics and taught to campaign. Power passes peacefully from one party to another. It is only through political parties and the whipping system or its equivalents that politicians are reliably able to carry into law policies on which they have been given a democratic mandate at elections. The cure for those who hate political parties is to visit countries in which there are no such parties, or only one.

In Britain a recognizable system of representative political parties emerged in the second quarter of the nineteenth century; the Conservative party is generally reckoned as the first modern political party, and traditionally traces its origins to the formation of the Carlton Club, before the Great Reform Act of 1832, and to Sir Robert Peel's 'Tamworth manifesto' of 1834. In the United States, party politics was initiated by Thomas Jefferson and James Madison through the Democratic Republicans in the 1790s; but it was Martin van Buren who made the full case for 'party' as against 'faction', and who built up the first fully functioning state party machine for the Democrats in the 1820s in New York.

Edmund Burke was not, then, the founder of a particular political party, or the founder of the two-party system as such. He never seems to have contemplated the idea of parties as mass-membership organizations campaigning across a nation; and their nearest eighteenth-century equivalents, the regional petitioning movements, often filled him with concern, if not alarm. The ideas of a single party whose own MPs must command a majority in the House of Commons for it to govern; of the leader of that party *ipso facto* becoming Prime Minister; and of the Prime Minister selecting Cabinet members without reference to the monarch, are many decades away.

Nevertheless, as we shall see, it is Burke who first sets out and argues for a modern conception of a political party, as 'a body of men united for promoting by their joint endeavours the national interest, upon some particular principle in which they are all agreed'. It is Burke who was the main architect of the first proto-political party, the Rockingham Whigs. It is Burke above all who articulated and pressed over more than two decades for his party's leading principles of restraint on Court influence and patronage, financial reform and accountability in government. And it is Burke who shows how even party politics must give way in the face of a common enemy, the Jacobinism of revolutionary France.

In Burke's words, party divisions are 'things inseparable from free government'. In a looser sense, political parties are as old as politics itself, for the simple reason that political questions invite disagreement and so partisanship.

But not all political parties, or all kinds of party politics, are the same. The origin of the names 'Whig' and 'Tory' lies in the Exclusion Crisis of 1678–81, and Burke's own analysis of party politics begins from that time. Charles II had been restored to the throne in 1660. But he was ageing, and had no legitimate sons by his wife Catherine of Braganza. The rules of succession therefore made Charles's brother James, Duke of York the heir to the throne. However, James refused to take the oath imposed by the Test Act in 1673, which required the swearer to renounce various Catholic doctrines and practices and to take communion within the Church of England, and it became apparent that he was a Roman Catholic. This view was then publicly confirmed by James's second marriage, to the Catholic princess Mary of Modena.

To a people raised on folk tales of the struggle of Henry VIII and Elizabeth to uphold Protestant values and the Church of England, for whom a civil war fought in part on religious grounds was a recent memory, and who associated Catholicism with bloodshed, absolutism and foreign influence, the prospect of James as king was highly unwelcome. Still more so since he had no surviving sons by his first marriage, so that a son by Mary would be his heir, raising the possibility of a Roman Catholic dynasty. Anti-Catholic feelings were heightened by allegations in the spring of 1678 of a Popish Plot to kill Charles and put James on the throne, which implicated Mary and pointed to secret links with Louis XIV.

The crisis broke in December 1678 when it was discovered that Charles himself had been in receipt of large payments from Louis in return for British neutrality in France's continental wars. Marshalled by the Earl of Shaftesbury (among other things the patron of John Locke), a group of MPs presented a Bill in the Commons calling for James to be excluded from the succession. To prevent this, Charles dissolved Parliament and the issue was repeatedly fought over in elections, 'Tories' – named after an abusive term for Irish rebels – supporting the King's (and so James's) prerogative rights, 'Whigs' – a Scottish term for Presbyterian rebels – against them. There were petitions, and mass demonstrations in London, including a procession with floats showing Jesuits and cardinals, and nuns disporting themselves like prostitutes, after which a huge effigy of the Pope was burned.

In the words of Macaulay, 'Never before had political clubs existed with so elaborate an organisation or so formidable an influence.' These clubs were not composed of men simply forced to take sides, but nor were they purely political; they were what Burke calls 'great' parties. But they were united only on the religious issue, were not intended to last beyond its resolution, and did not. Parties were seen as strictly temporary combinations called into being to meet an emergency.

After three parliaments in three years, the King fought his way through the Exclusion Crisis by the simple expedient of never summoning another parliament. But the Tories lost the wider war, with James II's flight into exile in 1688 and the exclusion of Catholics from the royal succession in the following year, a position reinforced in the Act of Settlement 1701. Thereafter the terms Whig and Tory were still in common use. But they gradually lost their original

meaning during the eighteenth century, as professedly Whig politicians predominated in politics under Georges I and II, and as
religious toleration spread. In the words of Horace Walpole, 'In
truth all the sensible Tories I ever knew were either Jacobites or
became Whigs; those that remained Tories remained fools.' The
failure of Bonnie Prince Charlie and the second Jacobite rebellion
in 1745 removed the last vestige of any dynastic threat from
Catholicism. On his accession in 1760, then, George III did not
merely rule a country in triumph over its victories in what would
be called the Seven Years War; he was the first Hanoverian to reign
secure from the threat of religious rebellion.

Politically, however, the new King did not like what he saw.
Feuding between monarch and heir was a Hanoverian speciality,
and George III greatly disliked his grandfather George II. He was
particularly critical of what he regarded as the complaisance of
both previous Georges in acceding on so many issues to the politicians of the day, such as Walpole and the Pelhams. George II had
failed repeatedly in public to exercise that most important of royal
prerogatives, the right of a king to choose his own ministers. His
son Frederick, Prince of Wales had been a thoroughly ineffective
source of political opposition, before an early death at the age of
forty-four. George III himself had been hemmed in by a class of
self-regarding politicians for a decade before his accession. Little
wonder, then, that he now sought to spread his wings and settle
old scores.

The constitutional settlement of 1688 had made clear what the
King could not do, but his positive powers were far less well defined.
The right to choose his ministers, the right to control Crown
patronage and create peers, the right to dissolve a ministry – these
were accepted prerogative powers, and George guarded them jealously. But the late eighteenth century saw a ceaseless battle between
the King and a succession of politicians over exactly how far and
in what areas monarchical power would, or could properly, extend.
The specific issues were large and small, and the battle went in

both directions. In 1765–6, for example, Rockingham had sought to ensure that the King's supporters would vote to repeal the Stamp Act – they did not. Mindful of this, when the Rockinghamites took office in 1782 they were careful to insist on their right to remove an unprecedented number of the existing junior office-holders. On the other side, many believed that the King had gone too far in actively fomenting the destruction of the Fox–North Coalition in 1783. But even then the King could argue that he had been prevented by Fox and North's parliamentary manoeuvring from appointing Shelburne, as he had wished.

Over several decades the powers of the King were gradually curtailed, in ways that prefigure the emergence of Britain's constitutional monarchy in its modern form. But Burke's fears of escalating royal influence and executive power were hardly misplaced; so much was made clear by the events of 1783, and by John Dunning's famous motion of 1780 – passed by the narrow margin of 233 votes to 215 in the Commons – that 'the influence of the Crown has increased, is increasing, and ought to be diminished'. Even so, opposition was a tricky matter, and not simply because George III was very powerful, highly active and indeed the central political player in his own right. There was a longstanding hatred in all quarters of 'faction', and a particular dislike for 'formed opposition'. It was one thing for a politician to disagree with the monarch on a specific matter of personal importance, quite another to attempt to enlist others to his cause. That was seen as a confession that the case could not be made on its own intrinsic merits; and more, as an attempt to challenge royal authority itself.

For Burke a hereditary monarchy was a vital component of a mixed constitution. Yet there were three recent ways in which royal influence had manifested itself in government, all of which he deemed highly defective. One was in Bolingbroke's old idea of a Patriot King, on which George III had been brought up: a monarch acting in the national interest on rational principles, superseding all factions and parties, purging corrupt politicians and governing through men of principle and ability. The second was rule by Court favourite, in the form of the Earl of Bute, whom George had made a minister in 1760 although he was a member of neither the Lords nor the Commons, and who partly in consequence had proven a dismal failure. The third was in sporadic support for a Great Man, latterly in the form of the Elder Pitt, who sought to rule by personal influence, national reputation and oratory in the Commons. Burke's verdict was trenchant and definitive: 'No man, who is not inflamed by vainglory into enthusiasm, can flatter himself that his single, unsupported, desultory, unsystematic endeavours, are of power to defeat the subtle designs and united cabals of ambitious citizens. When bad men combine, the good must associate; else they will fall, one by one, an unpitied sacrifice in a contemptible struggle.'

But, as his recently attributed essay of 1757 demonstrates, even before George's accession, and less than fifteen years after the second Jacobite rebellion, Burke was looking to make the case for responsible party politics. Politics, then as now, was an inexact and occasionally bruising business, and Burke was not starry-eyed about political parties: 'I do not wonder that the behaviour of many parties should have made persons of tender and scrupulous virtue somewhat out of humour with all connection in politics.' 'Connections' had risks, but were not always a bad thing: 'Connections in politics [are] essentially necessary to the full performance of our public duty, accidentally liable to degenerate into faction.' But as religious tempers cooled, so the way was open not for great parties but for 'small' ones, which could give legitimacy to principled or 'loyal' opposition and make it into a respectable or even honourable calling. Britain's mixed constitution since 1689 had created a balance of powers between King, Lords and Commons, and this recognized – indeed, it derived from the fact – that there might be disagreement and conflict between them. The question was how small political parties might translate this conflict into good government.

Burke's answer comes, effectively, in six parts. First and foremost, parties bring stability to politics. Recall that Burke defines a political party as 'a body of men united for promoting by their joint endeavours the national interest, upon some particular principle in which they are all agreed'. Parties allow the consistency of voting required to take forward difficult or complex legislation – or to oppose it. This was no small matter, given the significant practical difficulty of actually gathering MPs together and getting them to vote, difficulty which was experienced on all sides of Parliament throughout the eighteenth century. Moreover, unlike factions, parties do not disintegrate when they lose power. They remain united around a core of principles, and continue to make the case for those principles – and, we would add today, for policies and programmes based on those principles – even when out of office. This stability allows power to pass properly and peacefully from one party to another. Parties are thus an institutional corrective to personal, arbitrary or capricious government.

Second, parties bring openness and a focus on the national interest. Collective principles cannot be kept secret. The need to agree those principles within the parties, and the need to defend them in Parliament and in the public domain, create greater honesty in debate. Moreover, these principles will generally be framed in the national interest, for if they serve a mere group or section of society then that will be plain for all to see. Burke contrasts this commitment to public principles with Court intrigues: 'The discretionary powers which are necessarily vested in a monarch . . . should all be exercised upon public principles and national grounds, and not on the likings or prejudices . . . of a court.'

Third, parties moderate and control government. They compete for support from the people, and are thus enabled to exercise a check on the executive: 'It had always, until of late, been held the first duty of Parliament to refuse to support government, until power was in the hands of persons acceptable to the people, or while factions predominated in the court in which the nation had no confidence.' Parties require government to prove its continuing value by avoiding trouble and addressing public concerns. In addressing and resolving issues through Parliament, they also thereby channel popular discontents, removing the need for them to be expressed through other outlets.

Fourth, parties remove the need for statesmen in normal politics. Burke is scathing about the tendency of that time – as of this – to despise politicians great and small: 'It is . . . an effect of vulgar and puerile malignity to imagine that every statesman is of course corrupt; and that his opinion . . . is solely formed upon some sinister interest.' But parties do not require statesmen: they allow people of normal decency and ability to play a part in government. As collective institutions, they are able to trap and retain wisdom and experience over time, and to share information rapidly and effectively. The result is that 'the most inconsiderable man, by adding to the weight of the whole, has his value'. Indeed, parties make politicians more virtuous, because they unite them around shared public principles and not merely personal or factional interests.

Fifth, parties act as valuable gathering and testing grounds for politicians. They are not compulsory, but if a man 'does not concur in [the] general principles on which the party is founded . . . he ought from the beginning to have chosen some other, more conformable to his opinions'. Party members must prove their worth by demonstrating their experience and building relationships with colleagues. Burke is emphatic about both aspects: 'That man who before he comes into power has no friends . . . whose whole importance has begun with his office and is sure to end with it, is a person who ought never to be suffered by a controlling Parliament to continue in . . . the lead and direction of our public affairs; because such a man has no connection with the interest of the people.' 'The Romans . . . believed . . . that he who, in the common intercourse of life, showed he regarded somebody besides himself, when he came to act in a public situation, might probably consult some other interest than his own.' As with all institutions, but more than many, parties are rooted in 'manners', in personal friendship, in shared values and identity, and in the social impulse.

But there is, sixth, an important caveat. As Burke put it in his 1774 'Speech to the Electors of Bristol', 'Parliament is not a congress of ambassadors from different and hostile interests . . . Parliament is a deliberative assembly of one nation, with one interest, that of the whole . . .' Parties are thus groupings of the people's representatives, not of political delegates acting under instructions from their constituents, who are prevented by distance and numbers from taking part in the deliberations of Parliament. But, equally, parties should not be composed of Westminster politicians whose job is simply to spread the party line in the constituencies, for the Commons is not 'a control *upon* the people but . . . a control *for* the people'. An MP's 'unbiased opinion, his mature judgement, his enlightened conscience' he should not sacrifice to his constituents. But nor should he do so to his party: 'A rule of indiscriminate support for ministers . . . destroys the very end of Parliament as a control and is a general . . . sanction for misgovernment.'

Burke thus strikes a subtle balance: political parties must be strong and disciplined enough to hold government to account, and to provide the stability and openness on which a successful political system relies. But they must not be made so partisan that they lose sight of the public interest and undermine the deliberative function of Parliament: its capacity to debate the issues of the day and to scrutinize legislation. And they must not be so regimented that they prevent MPs from generally acting as representatives, and exercising their own mature judgement. Party politics should not mean invariably ignoring one's own conscience on important matters or, in modern terms, slavishly following the whips. Far from being just a party hack, then, Burke is in fact acutely aware of what happens when political parties fail to reconcile collective discipline with individual creativity and independent thought.

It is interesting to compare Burke's ideas about party with those of Thomas Jefferson and James Madison in the USA. Jefferson has the distinction of being the first man to found, organize and lead a new political party to electoral victory. He is regarded with reverence today as the primary author of the Declaration of Independence, and for his remarkably successful presidency. Fewer people remember the ugly side of Jefferson as party politician: it is astonishing to record that as Secretary of State he took active steps to undermine publicly his own President, George Washington; and then as Vice President to destroy the reputation of John Adams, his closest friend. He did this by establishing, funding (in part via a federal stipend) and feeding with information a muckraking journalist named Philip Freneau in Philadelphia, who set up the *National Gazette* to make the case for Jefferson personally and for his ideas, and to discredit Washington, Adams and other Federalists.

Jefferson was an Enlightenment rationalist. He believed that political parties should be the direct expression of the popular will, receiving instructions from the people which would be ratified and authorized through elections. On this view, parties are the instruments of majority rule, working strictly through the terms and procedures of the constitution. Burke would have disagreed at every point. For him, elected politicians are representatives, not delegates; they act not upon instructions, but upon their own judgement; popular majority rule is arbitrary rule, because it is unconstrained and breaches the fundamental principle that no person or group shall be judge in their own cause; and effective government cannot be merely according to law, but must take into account the temper of the people, and the great interests that make up society and the body politic.

As between the two, Jefferson's is simpler, clearer and founded in the common-sense politics of eighteenth-century radicalism. But Burke's view is more subtle, more enlightened and closer to the realities of government, as Jefferson's own presidency – which tested the limits of the constitution at several points – later underlined. And it has a further important consequence: parties start to move away from being merely private institutions or associations, and to play, at first informally, a public role within the constitution itself.

In essence Burke is extending within political practice a recognition of two vital countervailing principles within the British constitution. The first is what we would now call a democratic principle: that political control ultimately derives from the consent of the governed, as renewed at general elections. The second is a constitutional principle: that the popular will should be moderated through institutions which are not tied to the electoral cycle, but which reflect other views, other interests and other values, and which permit and encourage collective vision and a long-term perspective. As Burke puts it, 'No legislator, at any period of the world, has willingly placed the seat of active power in the hands of the multitude. The people are the natural control on authority; but to exercise and to control together is contradictory and impossible.' Sovereignty in Britain thus resides not in the people, but in Parliament.

It is sometimes forgotten, and Jefferson himself sometimes appears to forget, that the US constitution contains a parallel attempt to restrain the direct expression of the popular will and inhibit partisanship. The genius of the American founders, and above all of Jefferson's Virginian colleague James Madison, was to take a similarly institutional perspective, and amend and generalize it: to engineer a constitution that deliberately constrained and fragmented the power of government between state and federal levels; between executive, legislature and judiciary; and between House of Representatives and Senate. Each was thereby placed as a check and balance to another, forcing all into debate both on the issues of the day, and on the proper scope and limits of government itself.

This is a check not merely on government but on popular sovereignty as such. It creates what John Adams called a 'government of laws, not of men', making it all but impossible for any group of people or political party to take overall control of American government. For the founders as for Burke, then, the role of the constitution is not merely to exercise power, but to inhibit and channel its exercise. In both the UK and the US, democracy itself requires institutional constraints on the popular will. This remains the basic insight behind representative democracy today.

Let us briefly sum up. In the roughly two decades between the 1757 essay and his 1774 election speech in Bristol, Edmund Burke developed what is still the fundamental conception of a representative political party. The political context was quite different from that of today, of course, and there are many aspects of modern parties that he did not anticipate. But his thought was not merely the distillation of the conventional wisdom, or of the work of others. It was in large part an original act of creation and reflection by Burke himself, which he developed before and in the *Thoughts* and simultaneously sought to put into action through and with the Rockingham Whigs. Over time, these ideas and practices were more widely adopted, and became absorbed into the British constitution, and many of them, by a parallel process, into US political statecraft. As Britain's influence and prestige grew in the nineteenth century, so too did the influence of its system of representative political parties. Today such parties are widely recognized as the very touchstone of modern democracy. Truly, then, Burke can be said to be the hinge of Anglo-American, and indeed the world's, political modernity.

But Burke's thought is not restricted to reflection on political parties. It extends yet more widely and deeply, to the nature of politics itself, political change, political leadership, and political character and virtue.

It is important to remind ourselves that government in the late eighteenth century was very different from what it is today. Broadly, it consisted of maintaining public order, managing foreign affairs and trade, and waging war. The Poor Law apart, there was no national social safety net or welfare state, and so no

great spending programmes on healthcare, social security, education or pensions of the kind seen in most modern political economies. British public spending after the American Revolutionary
War returned to its peacetime average of below 10 per cent, a
level it would maintain until the 1870s–80s. In part for this reason,
vastly fewer areas of national life were subject to political decision-
making.

Even so, Burke's conception of politics was shaped as much by
his wider views on the nature of society as by circumstance. In his
view, perfection is not given to man, and so politics is an intrinsically messy business, in which any large decision risks doing damage
to the innumerable private arrangements and understandings that
make up the social fabric. People naturally aspire to support themselves and their families, to exercise their personal freedoms and
capacities, and to acquire property and status. The function of
politics, then, is primarily one of reconciliation and enablement:
to provide a forum and a framework of law and practice within
which individual differences and grievances can be redressed, individual freedom can be reconciled with the demands of the social
order, and public deliberation extended via man's inherent capacity
for self-government.

The corollary of this emphasis on custom and practice is a highly
distinctive conception of political leadership. For Burke government
is not merely about passing laws or aggressive law enforcement, for
'nations are not primarily ruled by laws: less by violence . . . Nations
are governed by the same methods . . . by which an individual
without authority is often able to govern . . . his equals and his
superiors; by a knowledge of their temper, and by a judicious
management of it.' Again and again, Burke returns in his writings
and speeches to the idea of governing 'with the temper of the
people', insisting that 'The temper of the people amongst whom
he presides ought . . . to be the first study of a statesman.'

This is a thought utterly foreign to contemporary notions of
political leadership, which focus on forward planning, motivating

ideology, great programmes of legislation, decisive action and the vigour of a leader's personal will. What, then, does Burke mean?

Recall that, for Burke, the point of politics is to preserve and enhance the social order, in the national interest. A social order is invariably distinctive and *sui generis*: a unique and unfathomably complex set of interlocking institutions, habits and shared practices. But it is not merely a set of relationships and interests; it is also a set of embedded values and changing opinions. As with individuals, then, every nation and every people has its national character. Political leaders must start with history and what would now be called sociology; they must take pains to understand how their specific social order evolved as it did, and where people's feelings really lie. Opinion polling was not available in Burke's day, of course; but it is clear that he has in mind a much deeper understanding of the basic drivers of popular sentiment, and how they react to different kinds of change, than that offered by even the most sophisticated pollsters today.

Political leadership thus begins with respect for the social order, which is sublime – that is, it begins in modesty. The same is true of political change itself. The political leader knows in advance that all change, however well intentioned, will disrupt the social fabric, with unforeseeable and potentially serious negative consequences. Still more is this true of sweeping, radical change – what Burke calls 'innovation' – which abolishes whole tracts of settled human understanding and social wisdom. For radical change to be genuinely worthwhile, it must bring overwhelming social benefit, or be the product of the most extreme necessity. Contrary to some views, then, Burke is not innately hostile to change as such, or even to radical change, as we shall see. But he argues that extreme measures of any kind, let alone revolution, are in practice almost never the path of good government. Rather, as he said in a 1789 letter to his young French friend Depont, 'moderation is a virtue not only amiable but powerful. It is a disposing, arranging, conciliating, cementing virtue.'

Instead, good political leadership must focus on 'reform'. Burke's comments on the nature of effective reform are scattered, but we can identify seven key characteristics. It should be early, anticipating the emergence of a problem before its full effects are felt. It should be proportionate to the evil to be addressed, to limit collateral effects. It should build on existing arrangements and previous reforms, so that it can draw on any lessons learned from them. It should be measured, so that those making the change and those affected by it can adjust their behaviour appropriately. It should be consensual, so that the process of reform can avoid unnecessary conflict and outlast the leader's own period in office. It should be cool in spirit, to maintain consensus throughout the process of change. And finally, each step must be practical and achievable in itself.

But political leadership is never simply about reform, or laws, or policy: it is also about the virtue and character of leaders themselves. In his own time Burke was dismissive of Chatham's pet phrase 'not men, but measures', regarding it as a kind of self-regarding cant designed to disguise Chatham's own insistence on personal pre-eminence and control. What really mattered, he thought, was how ministers exercised their powers, and this was overwhelmingly a matter not of 'measures' but of personal character. For Burke, as we have seen, the prerequisites for an effective politician include wide personal experience, a deep connection with 'the interest of the people', and the ability to build relationships with colleagues.

But true leadership demands more. The modesty of a leader must extend not simply to respect for the social order but to the limits of his own powers, 'his own private stock of reason', which is so very much smaller than 'the general bank and capital of nations, and of ages'. With experience and shared wisdom comes judgement – that is, the capacity to fit political action to political circumstances. Moreover, since individuals' reason is limited, effective leaders will seek to have other people of high ability and experience around them, whom they can trust. And they will seek to develop their own virtues, for virtue is the result of good habit: 'It is therefore our business carefully to cultivate in our own minds, to rear to the most perfect vigour and maturity, every sort of generous and honest feeling that belongs to our nature.'

Above all, a political leader must be committed body and soul to public service. All power brings accountability, and for Burke the supreme duty is that of the political leader towards the preservation of society itself. That society is the nation, and nation is a moral essence, and not a merely civic, ethnic or geographical expression. It can survive despite the loss of any specific individual or group. But it can also be damaged, broken or destroyed. The ultimate test of political leadership thus lies in preservation of the nation.

Burke's conception of political leadership is thus one not merely for normal times, but also for crisis, war and revolution. As he acknowledges in his thought and practice, in the face of a grave national threat there will be an overwhelming need for politicians to put their differences aside and come together in a supreme collective effort to repel and destroy the enemy. This may mean the temporary suspension of crucial parts of the constitution, as Pitt suspended habeas corpus in 1794. It may even mean the temporary abolition of party politics in favour of an emergency coalition, as Burke and later the Portland Whigs acknowledged when they crossed to join Pitt. It will certainly mean vigorous and decisive action. But for Burke the essentials of political leadership remain the same: modesty, restraint, attention to history, judgement in fitting the action to the need, trust, consensus, coolness, a wholehearted commitment to public service and the preservation of the nation. Indeed, extreme political pressures and the exigencies of the moment may make these qualities more important, not less.

* * *

Burke's political philosophy, and specifically his views on parties, political leadership and political change, thus spring naturally from his deeper reflections on the nature of society and human well-being, explored in the last chapter. But they were also shaped, of course, by direct personal experience.

In particular, they shed a pitiless light by implication on the crisis in the American colonies. From a Burkean perspective, this provides a case study in inept political leadership. The dispute arose over a radical change in policy, the imposition of taxes for the first time on trade with America. The new policy was implemented quickly, without consensus-building at home or consultation with those affected. It was not measured, proportionate or cool in spirit. As Burke highlights in the 'Speech on Conciliation', it reflected no genuine understanding of the temper of the American colonists, either as Englishmen overseas or as the tough, highly independent-minded and legally grounded people which their own developing customs and ideas had made them. There was no continuity either in the policy or in British government itself, even after the advent of Lord North in 1770; and when there was such continuity, the administration continued to misread colonial feeling. Opportunities to prevent the war or to end it early were missed; and such was the domestic reaction in Britain that the eventual peace terms were almost certainly more generous than required. A heavy share of the blame for this debacle must go to George III.

Yet Burke's thought is not merely a generalization from personal experience; it is itself a timeless source of political wisdom and understanding. We can see this by moving forward a century or so into the future: to the early 1860s, the American Civil War and Abraham Lincoln. For Lincoln is himself the very model of a Burkean political leader.

At first sight this claim may seem absurd. There is virtually no evidence that Burke's writings exercised any influence on Lincoln, and what little there is, is negative. Indeed, Lincoln read and much admired Burke's radical adversary Thomas Paine. Burke had had an elementary, school and university education, as well as studying at the Inns of Court; Lincoln grew up near the frontier, had very little formal education at all and learned much of the law from painstaking immersion in the *Commentaries* of Blackstone. Unlike Burke, Lincoln was not regarded as a great orator or prose stylist. He had to be, perforce, a managerial politician in a way that would have been barely comprehensible a century earlier. And under no circumstances would Lincoln ever have made the case, as Burke did, for a system of government which included aristocracy and monarchy. He was to his fingertips, and saw himself as, a democrat and a believer in 'government of the people, for the people, by the people'.

Yet, grounded as Lincoln was in Blackstone and in the Whig beliefs of his hero Henry Clay, his leadership is Burkean through and through. Lincoln was a great student of history, who sought to master the detail of an issue before committing himself. His political persona was modest and mild almost to a fault, so much so that he was regularly criticized for not being more publicly assertive, and for being too lenient with mischievous or incompetent subordinates. He did not trade solely 'on his own stock of reason', but famously reached out to build a 'team of rivals' from the defeated candidates in the 1860 election. He was adept at building personal relationships both within the fledgling Republican party and across parties and states, using his extraordinary frontier experiences and unending fund of stories and off-colour anecdotes to break down barriers. He was assiduous in seeking to cultivate his own personal virtues, hiding his melancholy and taking huge personal and familial setbacks with outward equanimity. Indeed he wrote his so-called 'hot letters' in private and then destroyed them, to manage his own feelings of rage and despair at the poor progress of the Civil War. He avoided confrontation unless absolutely required to achieve his goals, arguing for conciliation in his first Inaugural Address and refusing to fire first on those who were illegally besieging Fort Sumter in Charleston Harbor, South Carolina.

Like Burke, Lincoln insisted on reform over innovation. His Cooper Union address of 1860 contains a simple and powerful statement of belief: 'What I do say is, that if we would supplant the opinions and policy of our fathers in any case, we should do so on evidence so conclusive, and argument so clear, that even their great authority, fairly considered and weighed, cannot stand.' To the despair of abolitionists, despite his strong personal feelings Lincoln was initially rather measured in his public condemnation of slavery. He supported Henry Clay's efforts to resettle slaves in Liberia in the 1830s, and confined himself to opposition to the extension of slavery in the new states through the Kansas–Nebraska Act in 1854. He voted to accept slavery in states where it already existed and counter-manded General Frémont's proclamation in Missouri in 1861 freeing the slaves of those who had abetted the confederacy. He rejected regional attempts at emancipation, canvassing alternatives and renewing efforts to settle freed slaves overseas. Even after drafting the Emancipation Proclamation in the summer of 1862, he waited for the military success which finally came at the battle of Antietam before publishing it. This provided the basis in turn for the 13th Amendment, outlawing the institution of slavery itself.

Lincoln's highest priority was that of Burke himself: to preserve and sustain his nation – that is, to save the Union. Lincoln is less prone than Burke to moralize, and far more willing to reach out and energize the mass of the people; but the two men share a conception of leadership which fundamentally demands the projec-tion of moral character and virtue. Neither patronizes his audience. Rather, both invariably make the case, seeking to bring others along by personal example, by evidence, by argument and on occasion by some of the most beautiful and moving words in the English language. Lincoln's extraordinary leadership during the American Civil War came three or four generations after Burke hammered out his own ideas of representative party politics and of political leadership. But in celebrating Lincoln's leadership we are celebrating an ideal of the statesman given canonical expression by Burke.

But Burke's wisdom is not confined to the politics of the eighteenth and nineteenth centuries. He is not merely the forgemaster of our political modernity; he is also, as we have noted, the first post-modern political thinker. As we shall see in the chapters that follow, he challenges, even more than Marx himself, the assumptions underlying present-day Western politics, society and economics, in ways from which we still have much to learn.

NINE

The Rise of Liberal Individualism

> When I awakened, it was just daylight. I attempted to rise,
> but was not able to stir: for, as I happened to lie on my
> back, I found my arms and legs were strongly fastened on
> each side to the ground; and my hair, which was long and
> thick, tied down in the same manner. I likewise felt several
> slender ligatures across my body, from my armpits to my
> thighs. I could only look upwards.

WASHED ASHORE ON A MYSTERIOUS ISLAND, Lemuel Gulliver
finds himself tethered and bound by the tiny Lilliputians. Such was
the genius of Jonathan Swift that *Gulliver's Travels* is at once an
adventure story, a travel diary, a novel, a political tract, a satire and
a parable, and there are few more arresting images in literature
than that of Gulliver staked out helpless on the ground. Ever since
the book's first publication in 1726, that image has symbolized the
soul and the self of man as an individual, brought to consciousness
in a society of which he is not the author and for which he bears
no responsibility, and shackled by other people's rules, social
conventions and religious dogma.

Gulliver longs to be able to throw off the tethers of the Lilliputians and stand tall. And to many people, through many histories, in many classrooms, on many editorial pages, this is the simple lesson of the past three centuries. Man, born free but everywhere in chains, has become self-conscious, risen up and thrown off his shackles. Prejudice has been replaced by tolerance; social convention by diversity; religious authority by freethinking; anecdote and dogma by science; guilds and tariffs and mercantilism by free markets; political control by free speech, universal suffrage and human rights. Reactive government has been replaced by active, expert government, which steers national economies and improves social welfare. This is the distinctive contribution of Enlightenment ideas in Britain and western Europe, spreading out to North America and now around the world – and it is the gold standard of civilization.

Not only has this happened, the conventional story goes; it must happen. The argument is over, socialism is dead and we have reached the end of history. The world has become flat, competition is global and the consumer is king. Only by massive programmes of social and economic liberalization can more traditional societies around the world become truly modern; only so can developing countries achieve the levels of wealth and prosperity that exist in the West. Compare the massive prosperity of the Western democracies with the sluggish growth of their communist counterparts after 1945. Or take Korea. In 1983, thirty years after the Korean War, GDP per capita in capitalist South Korea was five times that of communist North Korea; in 2009 it was sixteen times greater. China's economic growth only began to accelerate in the 1980s, when it opened up special economic zones and started to implement market-oriented reforms. Trade, not aid, is pulling Africa out of poverty after decades of stagnation.

But there is a problem. The happiest countries around the world, such as Denmark and Norway, are in many ways highly traditional, while the most successful developing countries today, such as Korea and China, are in many ways rather protectionist. Meanwhile, the conventional wisdom has failed to prevent – and some have blamed it for – a succession of recent disasters. Market liberalization and a new hard-currency regime were supposed to lead to stability and growth in Russia in the 1990s; instead they led to what may be the largest appropriation of publicly owned assets in history, as a relatively small number of private individuals exploited the lack of established property rights to make themselves extraordinarily rich. The invasion of Iraq after 2003 was supposed to lead to the establishment of a Western-style free-market democracy; instead it led to a religious and ethnic civil war, as different groups fought for power in the absence of both the Baath regime and an effective new government. The deregulation of global financial markets was supposed to lead to lower borrowing costs for industry and increased economic growth; instead it led to the greatest economic crisis the West has suffered since the Depression.

And there are also signs of a deeper unease: a kind of moral panic about Western society itself. This can be seen in worry about social indicators such as levels of drug abuse, loneliness, suicide, divorce, single motherhood and teenage pregnancy, and in fears of a loss of local or national identity. It can be seen in concern about falling social mobility and the emergence of entrenched and self-selecting elites, in the growing distrust of political authority, and in suspicion that those in power are distant, unaccountable and incapable of leadership. And it can be seen in the spreading belief that basic values of respect, hard work and public service are being lost in celebrity worship, consumerism and the money culture.

Such unease was aptly summarized in 2012 in a newspaper article by the British writer and broadcaster Matthew Parris:

> We have been living beyond our means. We have been paying ourselves more than our efforts were earning. We sought political leaders who would assure us that the good times would never end and that the centuries of boom and bust were over; and we voted

for those who offered that assurance. We sought credit for which we had no security and we gave our business to the banks that advertised it. We wanted higher exam grades for our children and were rewarded with politicians prepared to supply them by lowering exam standards. We wanted free and better health care and demanded Chancellors who paid for it without putting up our taxes. We wanted salacious stories in our newspapers and bought the papers that broke the rules to provide them. And now we whimper and snarl at MPs, bankers and journalists. Fair enough, my friends, but you know we really are all in this together.

Edmund Burke would have welcomed much of the history of the past 200-odd years. In general, he would have celebrated the growth of free markets, of religious toleration, of responsible and open government, and of personal liberty and the rule of law. We have so far seen him as a powerful advocate of these ideas during his own life, and as the great theorist and early practitioner of representative party politics – the hinge of our political modernity. But it is also his extraordinary achievement to be the first and greatest critic of many aspects of modernity itself. It is Burke now, more than two centuries after his death, who offers the most radical and compelling analysis of what has gone wrong, and who points the way to sources of possible recovery.

We saw earlier how developments in thought during the early Enlightenment emphasized two key themes: first, the primacy of reason, and specifically of science as a model of rational thought, able in principle to offer a comprehensive account of the workings of nature; and second, the moral value of the individual. During the past two centuries these ideas have been developed into a body of thought which has proven to be extraordinarily influential, indeed almost a modern orthodoxy today. It is not a single theory – more a collection of assumptions and theories that come together into a worldview. We can think of it under the broad heading of 'liberal individualism'. ('Liberal' here is used in its British sense of 'valuing freedom or liberty', not to mean 'left-wing' or 'progressive' as in the US.)

To understand liberal individualism, we need to go back briefly to first principles. The word 'individual' originally means 'what cannot be divided without ceasing to be itself'. Within the sciences, individuals are atoms: that is, independent and autonomous entities which form the fundamental basis for any reasoning, explanation or prediction. Within this worldview, then, the human individual is the basic unit of account in morals, in politics and in economics. Individuals do not merely have moral value; they have moral priority over society itself, and their interests are to be generally preferred over the constraints imposed by society. Indeed, the whole notion of society becomes questionable; for what, it is often asked, is society over and above the individuals that compose it? And if society is nothing more, then how can any claims be made on behalf of 'society' and against a specific individual or group of individuals?

If the individual is morally fundamental, the thought continues, then individual freedoms are socially, economically and politically paramount. Different people have different interests, needs or opinions; it is not for others – and specifically not for 'society' or the state – to decide what would make them happy, or to arbitrate between different conceptions of the good life. State and society must be, as the jargon has it, value neutral. The same is true in economics: individual freedoms should be respected, and the state should impose as little of the economic constraints of tax, subsidy, tariff or market intervention as possible. And again in politics: the individual freedom to vote, the franchise, is deemed to be fundamental. It should, then, be exercised as widely as possible, in preference to other methods of political decision-making. Liberal individualism thus emphasizes mutual tolerance, civil rights, competitive markets and popular sovereignty.

Finally, science enters the picture. Public decisions must command authority. In a context of free speech, that is, they must be rationally based and rationally defensible. Science offers the benchmark for rationality, and so on this view public decisions must be either directly based on science, or justifiable according to the standards, language and concepts of the sciences. The sciences are descriptive disciplines, not normative ones: they describe how the world is, not how it ought to be. They do not choose or promote one set of moral or cultural values over another. They too are thus value neutral.

This, then, is liberal individualism. Within politics, it has provided a unifying backdrop to many different parties and shades of opinion, from the social liberalism often associated with the left to the economic liberalism or libertarianism of the right. Its specific origins are many, varied and hard to pin down: we have seen several early ones already in the thought of Hobbes, Locke and Rousseau. Others lie in the radical tracts of the late eighteenth century, and specifically in the pamphlet war that followed the *Reflections*, and in Thomas Paine's rejoinder *The Rights of Man*. But a crucial influence was the work of Jeremy Bentham.

Bentham has a good claim to be the most prolific major writer on any subject in any language, producing an estimated 30,000,000 words over a lifetime of eighty-four years, on a bewildering range of topics including jurisprudence, ethics, penal theory, economics, psychology, politics and public administration, social policy and religion. He was moved to do so by his anger at what he saw as the obscurity, irrationality, unfairness and corruption of the systems of power and thought around him. In particular, he was gravely disappointed by the failure of his long-running scheme to build a Panopticon or scientifically inspired penitentiary in London, a failure which he attributed to the opposition of various aristocrats eager to protect their property holdings.

Bentham is best known as the founder of utilitarianism and his Greatest Happiness Principle that 'It is the greatest happiness of the greatest number that is the measure of right and wrong.' But this itself was only part of a far wider project, which was to found not merely morality but law, economics and politics itself on a scientific basis. For Bentham, the basic question was 'What is the point of that?' Every rule, practice or institution in society should, he thought, be subjected to an objective test as to its value or utility, in effect a cost-benefit analysis, and reformed or discarded if it failed the test. For Bentham, moreover, it was a simple fact of psychology that humans are governed by pain and pleasure, and he developed an elaborate 'hedonic calculus' by which different public or personal decisions could supposedly be evaluated in terms of their net effects on happiness. By this means he thought both morality and actual practice – what people should do and what they actually do – could be made objective, quantifiable and so scientific.

Bentham's ideas cast a long shadow. They inspired his admirer and one-time disciple James Mill to develop a utilitarian theory of politics, on which government is treated purely instrumentally, as a means to the end of the greatest happiness for the greatest number. And they inspired James Mill's son, John Stuart Mill, to develop his own version of utilitarianism, and to enunciate in *On Liberty* what would become a central tenet of liberal individualism, the so-called Harm Principle: 'The only purpose for which power can be rightfully exercised over any member of a civilized community, against his will, is to prevent harm to others. His own good, either physical or moral, is not a sufficient warrant.'

They also inspired a revolution in economics, reconceived now not in the broad terms of Adam Smith, but as the science of the individual pursuit of wealth. Recall that, according to liberal individualism, people are seen as indivisible and independent atoms. In the latter part of the nineteenth century, this assumption and the Benthamite drive to ground public policy on the sciences inspired a generation of economists to lay the foundations of modern economics. According to this theory, people should be

understood as individual economic agents. In the words of John
Stuart Mill himself, economics:

> does not treat of the whole of man's nature as modified by the
> social state, nor of the whole conduct of man in society. It is
> concerned with him solely as a being who desires to possess wealth,
> and who is capable of judging of the comparative efficacy of means
> for obtaining that end. It predicts only such of the phenomena of
> the social state as take place in consequence of the pursuit of
> wealth. It makes entire abstraction of every other human passion
> or motive.

Within the theory, then, the only things that matter are the individual, the desires or preferences of the individual for wealth, and
the marginal costs and benefits of satisfying those desires. This
became the intellectual basis for the rapid growth of economics as
a discipline in the twentieth century.

Specifically, much of modern economics still arises from three
basic simplifying assumptions about human nature: that individuals
are perfectly rational; that they maximize their utility, benefit or
profits; and that they act independently of each other, on the basis
of perfect information. These assumptions have allowed economists
to deploy a dazzlingly sophisticated array of mathematical techniques. As a result, economics today is full of formulae, data sets
and technical terminology, and – faithful to Mill's injunction to
'make entire abstraction of every other human passion or motive'
– it deliberately ignores much of the messy detail of individual or
collective human behaviour, which it has found impossible to model
in mathematical equations. Even so, the result has been a body of
theory which is an extraordinary technical achievement. In particular, economists have been able to show in a formal way and under
certain very specific conditions that a market economy is at once
maximally efficient and maximizes the benefit of the people in it.
In theory, then, socialism, indeed any derogation from perfect

competition in a market economy, not only creates inefficiency but also makes some people worse off. That's quite a result.

Modern neoclassical economics is thus an indirect offshoot of liberal individualism, emphasizing, like its parent, the primacy of the individual and the importance of scientific rigour in public policy. It influences human language, with its talk of incentives, agents, preferences, behaviour and utility. It is used in a wide array of other contexts, from analysing crime to marriage to religion. And it shapes politics, by applying economic principles to political matters such as voting, the working of special interest groups and the behaviour of politicians – often implying that much of politics is really economics in disguise and that, deep down, politicians and bureaucrats, far from following any vocation or devotion to public service as they often profess, are in fact purely self-interested.

More widely, it is easy to see that the influence of liberal individualism as a basic worldview is now pervasive across many different areas of human life in Western countries, including attitudes towards education, race, health, globalization, religion, women's rights, older people, international development and trade, the treatment of minorities and debates over immigration. Indeed, it has become partly constitutive of political modernity: nations, cultures or communities that do not share the basic assumptions of liberal individualism are often deemed to be 'primitive', 'traditional' or 'backward', whose only escape route lies through massive social and economic liberalization.

Yet those wishing to celebrate this apparently rosy picture should not do so prematurely. From a Burkean perspective, liberal individualism carries with it its own pathology, its own sources of weakness. Burke's thought does not address modern developments directly, of course; he died too early for that. But nevertheless it carries within it a devastating analysis and critique.

Start with the very idea of an individual as independent and indivisible, an atom. Both philosophically and legally, Burke acknowledges the status of individuals, as we have seen; and he recognizes the power of the individual will in history and politics, such as that of Oliver Cromwell, or of Chatham in his own time. But to Burke there is little meaning in the idea of an individual human being entirely cut off from others. Man is a social being, not merely in the sense that humans tend and have tended to congregate together and cooperate with each other, but in the much deeper sense that their emotions, allegiances and identity are intrinsically social and interdependent. The self is a social self. More than this: it is an active self, whose well-being lies in its interaction with others. It is not, then, the basically passive vehicle for utility or preferences assumed by much modern economics.

More generally, liberal individualism mistakes the true order of priority between the individual and society. Society is not just an added extra, a mere epiphenomenon, which comes along after a group of individuals have decided to live alongside each other; it is there from the outset. More than this, it is what makes those individuals into human beings at all. Growing up within a given society is not simply a process by which humans become civilized; it is a process by which they become human. Indeed, not just people's humanity, but their individual identities too are embedded in their history, and in the institutions – family, school, religion, work, play – within and through which they live. By the same token, for Burke there is no real sense to be attached to the idea of individual rights apart from a particular social context. Not that he is denying the importance of rights, as we have seen. Indeed he hints in the *Reflections* that in a free society the citizens have not merely wide personal freedoms, but the right to claim by talent and hard work a 'fair portion' of what society has to offer. This too is a right afforded by and within the social order.

But according to Burke there is a deeper mistake in seeing people as mere individual atoms. In effect it is a denial of their collective identities as participants in the social contract or trust between the generations: a denial of the covenantal nature of society itself. Like Gulliver with the Lilliputians, it seeks to assert the primacy of the individual will, and sees all social constraint as fetters to be thrown off. Liberty becomes licence: the absence of impediment to the will. The danger, then, is that liberal individualism makes people profoundly selfish; that they slip from 'enlightened' to 'unenlightened' self-interest, in the words of the great political theorist Alexis de Tocqueville; that it actively encourages them to adopt a purely egoistic perspective on their own and others' lives, asking simply 'How am I affected? What's in it for me?' Instead of grasping the intrinsically social nature of their own selves and their own well-being, they see themselves as apart from others, or from the institutions around them. It may be no coincidence that a recent in-depth study found that young people in America now have great difficulty in identifying or describing moral issues. Lacking relevant moral concepts or vocabulary, researchers found, they default to a typical position of liberal individualism: the view that moral decisions are simply a matter of personal taste.

This is the 'ethics of vanity', in Burke's pungent phrase. In similar spirit, he might well have viewed with great concern the fact that the ideas of Bentham, the utilitarians and indeed modern economics have themselves now become highly influential institutions in their own right, embedded in universities, business schools and corporations around the world. Since their basic tenet is often that humans are purely economic agents, seeking gain and shunning loss, the danger is that this creates further feedback loops, inculcating successive generations into an orthodoxy of self-interest and thereby making them more selfish. What starts with an economist's assumption ends up as a deep cultural pathology.

And not just for individuals. For there is a similar danger of collective egoism, according to Burke: a danger that whole generations may see themselves as no longer bound by the basic trust which unites past, present and future generations. They may

arrogantly assert the supremacy of their own interests over those
of their children and grandchildren, or of their own knowledge
over that of their parents. On a small scale, any such assertion
involves the loss of social wisdom, the loss of community and the
loss of identity. At its most extreme, it is a recipe for social collapse;
this is the lesson of the French revolution.

It is interesting to compare Burke again here with Thomas
Jefferson. In a letter to James Madison written from Paris on 6
September 1789 – two months after the fall of the Bastille – Jefferson
argued precisely the opposite case at length, saying 'I suppose [it]
to be self evident, "that the earth belongs in usufruct to the living;"
that the dead have neither powers nor rights over it.' The issue was
a particularly live one at that time. France had a huge burden of
inherited debt, the previous two months had seen the ransacking
of tax offices and toll gates, and tax evasion had massively increased,
leading to a rapid fall in revenues. The question was increasingly
asked as to whether the revolutionaries should not simply repudiate
France's debts, or nationalize the vast lands belonging to the Church.

As a convinced Enlightenment radical, Jefferson came down
firmly on the side of the revolutionaries. In his words:

> What is true of every member of the society individually, is true
> of them all collectively, since the rights of the whole can be no
> more than the sum of the rights of individuals . . . The earth
> belongs always to the living generation. They may manage it then,
> and what proceeds from it, as they please, during their usufruct.
> They are masters too of their own persons, and consequently may
> govern them as they please.

But from Burke's viewpoint this whole doctrine is profoundly
mistaken. Indeed it is madness. What is worse, it is the madness
of reason gone mad. It abolishes whole swathes of settled human
life in pursuit of a utopian project, according to a set of abstract
ideas divorced from any practical or social context that could give

them meaning. But again here Burke seems to have a deeper philosophical point in mind as well. Concepts from mathematics and the exact sciences can be given precise definitions, which are not tied in any way to a particular time or place: for example, a circle can be defined as a set of points an equal distance from a given point, and we do not doubt that this will hold now or 1,000 years hence, here or in a distant galaxy. Similarly, axioms or postulates and rules of inference can be precisely specified, such as in Newton's Second Law, that Force equals Mass multiplied by Acceleration. But the same is not true in relation to the conduct of human life and human affairs. Here the principles are imprecise, and their meaning heavily governed by context, and the 'distinguishing colour and discriminating effect' of circumstance.

According to Burke, moreover, it is a deep mistake in logic to seek to apply abstract principles out of context to human affairs: 'Aristotle, the great master of reasoning, cautions us, and with great weight and propriety, against this species of delusive geometrical accuracy in moral arguments, as the most fallacious of all sophistry.' Universal principles are thus never sufficient in themselves to guide practical deliberation. Their imposition always involves a degree of fallacy or logical error; in extreme cases that error may prove to be disastrous, leading to huge and often damaging unexpected consequences. When Burke talks of the age of 'sophisters, economists and calculators' in the *Reflections*, it is this error that he has in mind.

But, more than this, Burke suggests that absolute consistency is neither available nor desirable in the conduct of human affairs, since there will inevitably be conflicts between different principles and values, all of which are deeply and sincerely held. Political and other leaders must act; they must make choices, however incomplete the facts or theory. They must thus accept such conflicts, and the obligation those conflicts impose to think through the right course of action in concrete situations all things considered, rather than seek to create, or obey, a foolish and ideological consistency.

In effect, then, Burke identifies a cluster of further risks inherent in liberal individualism. The first is that the belief in the supremacy of individual reason may tip over into an ignorant arrogance among those in authority. Instead of attending to circumstance, working to reconcile the demands of conflicting interests and principles and governing modestly with the temper of the people, they may launch utopian and ultimately counterproductive schemes of their own. In Burke's words, 'It seems as if it were the prevalent opinion in Paris, that an unfeeling heart, and an undoubting confidence, are the sole qualifications for a perfect legislator. Far different are my ideas of high office. The true lawgiver ought to have a heart full of sensibility. He ought to love and respect his kind, and to fear himself.'

Secondly, the attempt to impose uniform and universally valid principles on to human nature and a given social order – what Kant referred to as the 'crooked timber of humanity' – is fraught with peril. It is in effect a modern version of the ancient Greek myth of Procrustes, who invited strangers on the road to Eleusis to spend the night on his bed, but insisted they fit it exactly, stretching those who were too short and cutting off the limbs of those too tall. Thus on this view Bentham's desire to subject every institution in society to a cost-benefit analysis is not a genuine move towards reform, but a move to eradicate many or all such institutions altogether. Social institutions are historical artefacts, which rarely if ever have a purely rational basis; and if they start on such a basis, they soon outgrow it. Individuals are creatures of habit as much as of economic incentive. Furthermore, Bentham and his successors illegitimately reverse the burden of proof. In a free society, without independent cause for concern, the burden should not be on institutions to justify themselves; it should be on those in power to make the case for their abolition or reform.

These are not superficial criticisms. On the contrary, the effect of this line of thought is to destroy the central intellectual project lying behind the idea of liberal individualism: the reduction of politics to science, and so the abolition of political choice in favour of expert technocratic government. The point is not simply that abstract principles such as Bentham's Greatest Happiness Principle and John Stuart Mill's Principle of Harm can never in fact be universally applied in a way which is at once exact, consistent and worthwhile. Nor is it that the attempt to apply such principles implies a radical divorce of ends and means, as though the ends or purposes of policy are brute and cannot be affected by the means available for their achievement.

No, the critique is still more fundamental: it is that if the attempt to apply mathematical and scientific concepts and principles to politics always involves logical error, as Burke implies, then Bentham's 'hedonic calculus' and its offshoots can never succeed even in principle. This raises the fascinating further possibility that the same may be true for modern economics as a whole: that the simplifying assumptions required to push economics towards the hard sciences, and to make economics into a mathematically tractable discipline, may themselves import logical error in the way identified by Burke and attributed by him to Aristotle.

What, then, when a given generation decides to take matters into its own hands? What about revolutions? Surely all revolutions are basically the same – an expression of the fundamental human desire for freedom and autonomy, a yearning to throw off the shackles of society? And if so, isn't Burke hopelessly inconsistent, in supporting the American colonists and bitterly opposing the Jacobins?

The answers are No and No. In fact, directly or indirectly, Burke accepted or supported not one but at least five separate uprisings against authority: the Glorious Revolution of 1688; the rights of the colonists in the American War of Independence; the Corsicans' struggle for freedom after Corsica was sold to the French in 1764; the War of the Bar Confederation, by which the Poles sought to eject the Russians from the Polish–Lithuanian Commonwealth after 1768; and several revolts against the East India Company under Warren Hastings in India. In each case, he is supporting the underdog; each is, broadly, a communal uprising against the imposition of some arbitrary and oppressive innovation, in the name of existing liberties and established custom. Each is seeking to preserve its social order and its way of life.

Thus, in Burke's eyes, the revolution in America came about in reaction to specific grievances, and specific claims of right, over taxation. It arose from a wrongful and arbitrary assertion of power by the British government, not by the revolutionaries. It was at root a conflict over a specific conception of English liberty; as he says in the 'Speech on Conciliation', 'The colonists [are] not only devoted to liberty, but to liberty according to English ideas, and on English principles. Abstract liberty, like other mere abstractions, is not to be found. Liberty inheres in some sensible object.' Thus, although it involved war and the overthrow of British rule and monarchical power, it did not involve the overthrow of much of British culture and values in America. Nor did it lead to the destruction of America's society or institutions; and, there being as yet no constitution or federal government, it would not have done so even if the British had been successful in suppressing it. And it took place 3,000 miles away. To Burke, then, the American conflict is an uprising against an illegitimate imposition of authority – a partial revolution and not a total one.

However, the conflict in France was very different. It did not seek the redress of specific grievances as such. It involved what Burke saw as a wrongful and arbitrary assertion of power by the revolutionaries, through long periods of mob disorder and violence. It was an uprising conducted not to defend an existing way of life but in the name of abstract universal rights, slogans whose true meaning was unclear and uncertain. It led from the outset to a wholesale destruction of existing French institutions, including the monarchy, much of the aristocracy and much private property

– although property rights were specifically defended as natural and imprescriptible in Article 2 of the Declaration of the Rights of Man. It expropriated and nationalized the lands of the Church. And it took place just 22 miles away, posing by its force and example a grave threat to Britain itself. It was a true and total revolution.

John Locke had taught that civil government depends on the consent of the governed, and that the governed had a right of revolution against tyranny or the abuse of power. Burke accepts the Lockean distinction between legitimate and illegitimate authority. But for him there is a further distinction to be drawn between partial revolution against political authority (which Burke sometimes condones), and total social revolution; and far from being wholly inconsistent, this underlines the fundamental coherence of his thought. But Burke does much more than this: he invents the modern idea of revolution itself. For Aristotle, a revolution is a partial or total change of constitution. The pre-modern conception was a literal one derived from cosmology, science and the seasons: a revolution was a turning of the wheel of life, which restored what existed before and allowed new growth. This is the language of the Glorious Revolution of 1688. But Burke's idea is very different: it is one of a rapid and violent upheaval that succeeds in engulfing not merely politicians and constitution but the whole of society, and which obliterates what was there before. This is the sense in which we think of revolution today.

For Burke what matters is the preservation and improvement of the social order. In cases of extreme necessity rebellion may be necessary in order to preserve what matters in a social order or a way of life. But there can never be a right to revolution. Rights are largely derived from society; but revolution threatens the destruction of society itself.

Where, then, does this leave us? Burke's ideas suggest that liberal individualism, despite its many attractions and achievements, also has some deep intrinsic flaws. It underplays or ignores the basic nature of man as a social being; it wrongly asserts the priority of the individual over society; and it threatens to undermine the habits and institutions that give meaning to people's lives. And this is not all, for it also carries with it inherent risks: a risk of encouraging selfishness in society, at both the individual and generational level; a risk of encouraging ill-informed and arrogant decisions by politicians and officials; at the limit, a risk of stimulating revolution, with potentially ruinous consequences.

But, as we have seen, Burke also attacks, indeed destroys, the Enlightenment dream of founding all public decision-making and all government on science. Politics and political choices, then, are inevitable; they cannot be reduced to economics or expert decision-making, and economics itself can never become a hard science. There can never be a wholly rational orthodoxy about politics – including the orthodoxy of liberal individualism.

This may strike many people as a rather sad result, given the present dire levels of trust in our elected representatives, and the public desire for certainty and official reassurance in difficult times. But actually, to all but the most committed anarchists or science-fetishists, Burke's critique should be good news, for three reasons. First, because it shows that there is and must always be a wide scope for the debate, exchange of views and trading off of different priorities that is the very essence of politics. Should you build this road or save this wilderness? Should you fund low-cost housing or put extra money into support for disadvantaged children? Should you cut taxes or spend more on the armed forces? These trade-offs cannot be abolished by relying on official expertise. Moreover, there can and must be debate even about the nature and limits of democracy, social liberalism and free markets, however obviously good these may seem to be.

Secondly, the Burkean critique reminds us that politicians are not economic automata, and that there is genuine scope for them to be moved not merely by self-interest but by ideas of duty and

public service. It implies that politicians should be amateurs, in
the best sense: highly professional in their actions, of course; ideally,
expert in certain areas of policy or national life, but not wholly
captured by a given profession or body of thought. We should see
them as the ancient Greeks saw them, as citizens first and foremost,
in whom a temporary, limited and qualified trust has been placed
to exercise public power on our behalf. As soon as they adopt a
particular professional viewpoint – be it that of the businessman,
the environmentalist, the doctor, the social worker, the soldier or
the economist – it becomes more difficult for them to strike the
right balance. Expertise can only get you part of the way. More
valuable by far are experience, wisdom, independent judgement
– and common sense.

Thirdly, Burke's analysis implies that the desire to see humans
as mere atoms, indivisible and cut off from others, is vain. In
effect, Burke fills up the empty space between the state and the
individual. He suggests there is a third category – that of institution, and specifically of society itself. We are social animals. Society
is relational and networked. It is not a mere composition of
individuals, but includes their institutions, customs, habits and
practices in it. It is not another thing – it is an arrangement of
things. To use a modern analogy, it is like a molecule in chemistry.
You cannot look at its different atoms individually in advance and
always say exactly what the final shape of the molecule will prove
to be – that depends on how the atoms link together. But on the
molecule's final shape and composition depends much if not all
of its power and effect.

Moreover, because we are social animals, we can never even in
principle step outside our skins and ask – as great thinkers from
Immanuel Kant to John Rawls have demanded – what we would
do if we were not ourselves. Liberal individualism may aspire to
be value neutral, but it is not value free, and its values bring problems of their own. More deeply, a value-free description of morality
or politics can never be achieved; indeed, a world free of values is

not a world we should ever want to inhabit. Human reason is a wonderful thing, but Burke insists we are above all creatures of sentiment, emotion, passion and allegiance, for good or ill. What matters and should matter to us is not abstract liberties, but the liberty to live our lives well alongside others and in our communities. Ultimately, it is not merely in his hatred of arbitrary power, but in his rejection of rationalism itself, that W. B. Yeats's Great Melody is to be found in Burke.

Now this is all fine and good, and it is a powerful and stimulating critique of the basic aspects of liberal individualism, which seems to be current orthodoxy in many parts of the world. However, it faces a key question: is it true? Is Burke right to insist with Aristotle that man is a social animal, with all that that implies?

In the next chapter, we will look at this issue in more detail. But there's a hint of the answer in *Gulliver's Travels* itself. For Gulliver does not in fact cast off his shackles and rise up a free man. He is initiated into the culture of the Lilliputians, and learns their language and customs. His shackles are removed by mutual agreement, and replaced by social ties. As a result, Gulliver enjoys all the benefits of a free life in Lilliput, at least for a period. Even in 1726, then, it looks as though Swift, like Burke, is rejecting liberal individualism in advance.

TEN

The Recovery of Value

PUBLISHED IN 2000 TO great acclaim, Robert Putnam's book *Bowling Alone* devotes more than 500 pages and 200,000 words to the idea of 'social capital'. It examines the reasons for success or failure of a wide array of independent organizations, ranging from parent–teacher associations to the boy scouts to freemasons and unions. The result is a passionate argument for the importance of family and friends, personal ties and institutional networks as social resources worthy to be ranked alongside a nation's financial capital and economic strength.

It is a telling fact that Putnam's book does not mention the name of Edmund Burke at all. Yet many of these ideas are Burkean to their marrow. Burke would have disliked the financial metaphor in the idea of social capital. He would probably have treated with extreme caution the claim that ideas grounded in history, in philosophy and in human experience could in any sense be validated by research in the social sciences. But the extent to which the modern world is now rediscovering some of the wisdom of Burke through the social sciences is very striking. In so doing, it is overturning the individualistic picture developed in the last chapter, substituting a vastly more subtle and interesting account of human motivation and social well-being.

Current anthropology, sociology and psychology may seem very far removed from Burke's thought, and we will have to travel some distance in this chapter to show the connections. But again and again recent research seems to support his central themes: that humans have a distinctive social nature of their own; that the emotions are what guide human reason; that reason itself is limited and fallible; that allegiance and identity are grounded in institutions; that institutions are the source of human well-being; that absolute freedom or 'licence' is disastrous both for individuals and for the social order; that moderate religions are a source of huge social value; and that what matters most of all is for humans to live together according to shared rules and norms in a moral community. And, as we shall see, it also offers fascinating hints of the forces that have pushed many Western countries, including the UK and the USA, into seeing themselves in an excessively individualistic way.

Let us start by looking at one of the standard benchmarks of human visual perception, the well-known Müller-Lyer test:

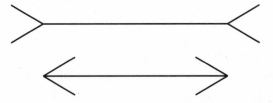

Take a long look at the horizontal line in each of the two figures: which seems to be longer? In fact, of course, the two lines are of the same length. But what's so interesting about this test is that even when you get out a ruler and measure the lines, it is still not enough to overcome the illusion that the top line is longer. This is an experimental finding that has been confirmed in the lab with thousands of subjects, over several decades. It is a basic fact about the way we see lines and objects.

Except that it isn't. If you're one of the San foragers of the Kalahari, immortalized in the writings of Sir Laurens van der Post, you do not see the illusion at all. The lines look like what they are: the same length. Moreover, for a whole range of different non-Western groups, the illusion either barely exists or has far less effect. It seems that the more you live in a built environment, a 'carpentered world' with sharp edges and corners, the more likely you are to be fooled. Inevitably, perhaps, the most easily fooled are American undergraduates, for whom the top line has to be 20 per cent longer than the bottom to appear the same length. The basic fact with which we started was, then, nothing of the kind. Even humans' visual perception appears to be partly culturally determined. People from other cultures literally see things differently.

In other words, *culture matters*. Human cultures arise from a complex, only partly understood and still disputed interplay between a host of social and genetic factors. But at their core and across all cultures, it increasingly appears, are two central truths: that man is a deeply social animal, and that 'social capital' is a vital source of human well-being. Both are distinctively Burkean themes. These claims have been contested at various points over the past two centuries. Yet a large body of new evidence is emerging to support them.

How we see the Müller-Lyer figure is culturally specific. But there are many other areas in which human behaviour is not, but where there is a basic core of human nature, which is stable across all cultures, no matter how different they may otherwise be. All humans have fundamentally the same facial expressions for anger, fear, disgust, contempt, sadness and shame. All divide time into past, present and future. All have a primal fear of strangers and snakes. All appear to have a language instinct, which allows them as children to acquire natural language at an extraordinarily rapid rate.

Something similar is true for numbers: human infants just twenty weeks old can correctly compute the answers to very simple addition and subtraction tasks. At the group level, all human societies have taboos against rape and murder. All distinguish between members and non-members, and their members rank each other for prestige in different ways. All produce art, enjoy story-telling and worship a god or gods.

What about reason and the emotions? Is reason the master of the emotions, is it their servant, or is there a more subtle relation between the two? Plato and the *philosophes* of the French Enlightenment had taught that reason was the master. But in his *Treatise of Human Nature* (1739–40) David Hume denied this, saying in a typically lapidary pronouncement that 'reason is, and ought only to be the slave of the passions, and can never attend to any other office than to serve and obey them'. Burke's view appears to be less categorical: that the senses can guide human action before the reason is engaged; that 'sentiment' or feeling is the original source of allegiance and identity; that reason provides justification for human beliefs, and often for human institutions; but that an unchained reason can also move people, as it moved the French revolutionary leaders, by exciting their emotions.

An increasing body of recent research appears to point towards the Hume–Burke side of the argument. For example, numerous studies have shown how people's everyday reactions can be affected by 'priming' their emotions first. Thus French music encourages people to buy French food in supermarkets. Telling someone a story of great achievement before a test generally raises their performance, while negative stereotypes worsen it. In one Newcastle University experiment led by Melissa Bateson, contributions to an 'honesty box' for tea and coffee went up in every week that different images of staring eyes were displayed alongside, and down for images of flowers. These studies show a wide range of contexts in which it appears that human reason is being unconsciously primed or guided by instinct and the emotions.

Money is an especially interesting, and disturbing, prime. In a remarkable series of experiments the psychologist Kathleen Vohs and others primed subjects with the idea of money in different ways. In general, money-primed participants were shown to be more independent, and less willing to seek or accept help on difficult tasks, than those without the trigger. They were also more selfish: when an experimenter accidentally dropped a box of pencils on the ground, they picked up fewer pencils; given the opportunity to contribute to a student fund, they gave less. And they were more inclined to be separate: when asked to set up two chairs for a get-acquainted conversation with another participant, they chose to locate their chair much further away than did their non-money-primed peers. In a later series of experiments, Eugene Caruso, Kathleen Vohs and colleagues showed that exposure to money primes encouraged test participants in their belief in free-market capitalism, in the fundamental justness of the world and in the inevitability of social inequality.

The implications of these experiments are extraordinary. They suggest that people who grow up surrounded by the images, language and culture of money – as they do overwhelmingly in highly developed economies around the world – may have their behaviour and attitudes unconsciously shaped by these primes, and that if so the effect is to make them more greedy, more selfish and more individualistic, and more accepting of social and economic inequality.

How might such a feedback loop work? One way is through the social sciences themselves. In 2010 the anthropologist-economist Joe Henrich and his colleagues showed how vast tracts of social science research are, in their provocative term, WEIRD – that is, based on samples drawn from Western, Educated, Industrialized, Rich and Democratic societies. Not only that: there is a specific focus on American undergraduates, who are routinely tapped as experimental subjects by their universities.

Yet, as Henrich and his colleagues point out, Westerners,

specifically Americans, and in particular American college students, are very different from the rest of the world, even to other Americans. They tend to be more egoistic in how they perceive the world, more independent in how they see themselves, more confident of their own views, more analytic or rule-based and less holistic or situation-based in their reasoning, and more selfish in how they bargain. They are the evidential source of most recent research in the social sciences, and they are probably the most individualistic people on Earth.

This suggests that the social sciences themselves may have given massive cultural reinforcement in recent decades for what was described in the last chapter as liberal individualism. For science itself has apparently spoken, with all its authoritative panoply of evidence, formulae and statistics. And it seems science has shown that people are generally like Western, and specifically American, undergraduates – but only by generalizing from the values and experiences of Western, and specifically American, undergraduates. As a result, we may be systematically misunderstanding both our own and other cultures, and using 'science' to ratify what is a specifically Western viewpoint. Not only that: we may be misunderstanding our own past, by retrofitting a specific set of current Western values on to it as supposedly basic facts about human nature.

Even with this caveat, it is striking how much evidence has emerged in recent years for the basically social nature of humans. For example, work in behavioural economics has undermined the standard picture of man as *Homo economicus* inherited from Bentham and the utilitarians. People systematically behave quite differently, and more interestingly, than the standard model suggests. Thus there is strong evidence that people are biased towards the present and the status quo; that they are far more averse to loss than keen on gain; and that they place a higher value on objects they own than on new ones. How people take decisions is heavily influenced by the way those decisions are framed: they choose one option when a given choice is framed positively ('exploring for energy') and another when it is framed negatively ('drilling for oil').

As social animals, humans need the society of others in order to flourish. In the earliest years, this means having a strong and secure attachment to others, and in particular to their parents. Thus securely attached children do better at school, withstand stress better, are more successful in life and are better able to form relationships with others. In his book *The Social Animal*, the writer David Brooks tells the story of René Spitz, an Austrian physician who visited an American orphanage in 1945. The orphanage was spotless, fully staffed and the babies well fed. But it had a policy of leaving the babies alone all day, and not touching them, in order to reduce the risk of infection. Sheets were hung between the cots to prevent the movement of germs, preventing further eye contact and stimulus. The result? Nearly 40 per cent of the babies perished before reaching the age of two. They were dying of lack of contact and empathy.

In adult life, social relationships are strongly correlated with happiness and well-being. Those in long-term marriages are generally much happier than those who are not. The daily activities most correlated with happiness are social (like seeing friends after work), while those that are worst for happiness (like commuting) tend to be solitary. The value of relationships is particularly marked for those who are actively engaged in their communities. Thus people who regularly give money, time or support to others enjoy better physical and mental health, have lower levels of depression and suicide and have increased longevity, compared to those who do not. People who donate to charity report higher levels of happiness than others. People who volunteer have lower mortality rates and lower rates of depression later in life than those who do not volunteer, especially if they spend more than 100 hours per year in volunteering, and if it involves repeated personal contact in helping strangers. People who are lonely and depressed are three to ten times more likely to die prematurely than those connected to others and to their communities.

The human need for sociability is deeply rooted in the subconscious. When people meet for any length of time, they unconsciously start to coordinate their behaviour. They mimic each other's breathing, conversational patterns and body language; and women who live together for some time find their menstrual cycles coincide. People do not quite literally feel each other's emotions, but they feel echoes of them. Research by Jean Decety and others suggests that there is a neural basis for compassion or empathy in the human brain. People who observe others in pain, especially their partners, seem to process this recognition in part through the pain centres in their own brains. People who consider the emotional reactions of others do so through their own emotional neural systems.

At a group level, people tend to absorb the norms and standards of groups or institutions with which they identify. They become colonized by each other: by their feelings, by their language and by their thoughts. Notably, they do so via language, and language acquisition is highly dependent on context. In their remarkable 1995 book *Meaningful Differences in the Everyday Experience of Young American Children*, Betty Hart and Todd Risley showed that the average American child has had some eight million words of practice in expressing themselves by the age of three. Children in the most talkative families have had twelve million words on average, as against only four million in the least talkative families.

The level of talk varies with socioeconomic differences between the parents; and in statistical terms talkativeness, far more than social class or income or race, predicts the child's future intellectual achievements. As Risley puts it:

> Parents may be taciturn or talkative . . . Of course they pass along their biological temperament to their children through their genes. But it is through their family micro-culture that they pass on to their children – while their children are still babies – the habits

THE RECOVERY OF VALUE

of talking a lot or a little, of what things to talk about, and of talking for pleasure or only for business. And, it is through this family experience that parents pass along their family culture to the next generation: a culture of family life full of words and social dance – or empty.

In other words, linguistic customs and practice transmit human culture through institutions (families), and that culture is what allows individuals to succeed and to live rich and fulfilling lives. Loving families matter. It is a very Burkean picture.

And it is one in which the emotions are absolutely fundamental, in two ways. First, because the emotions underlie the vital processes of attachment, linking, social engagement and the absorption of norms and culture by which human beings become human. And secondly, because the emotions endow objects and decisions with value and meaning. A world without the emotions is a world without value, and a world without value is one in which humans cannot survive.

The point is well made by the work of the neuroscientist Antonio Damasio. Damasio noticed that a group of patients with damage to a specific part of the pre-frontal cortex (above and behind the eyes) seemed to find it impossible to experience emotion. They could look at horrific photographs, or even recount tragedies in their own lives, without any apparent feelings of horror or sadness. They knew they were expected to have certain feelings, but they were simply incapable of having them. More than this, they could not make decisions or choices about even the smallest things, like agreeing to meet on a given date. Unable to make choices, they could only live foolish lives or, in the worst cases, sociopathic ones. For them, every option was as good as every other, because no option had any emotional value.

*   *   *

If this is right, then we need to think of man as a social animal, with a specifically human nature. The emotions guide our reason and underwrite our allegiances. We become human by immersing ourselves from earliest consciousness in human institutions of language and love. But institutions are not merely good for their members; they are good for society itself. This is the second great Burkean theme of this chapter.

People often think of institutions as huge organizations or great buildings: as the Church of England, say, or the Library of Congress. But it would be more accurate to say that they come in every imaginable size or kind, concrete and abstract. According to the evolutionary biologist Mark Pagel, the number of languages now spoken on Earth may be as high as 7,000; that is '7,000 mutually unintelligible systems of communication in one species, marking out at least 7,000 distinct societies. This is more different systems of communication in a single mammal species . . . than there are mammal species.' However you define them, that is an extraordinary profusion of different macro-cultures. And however you define the idea of an institution – and, at root, the idea is one of a set of rules or practices by which individuals coordinate their behaviour – the number of human societies is in turn vastly smaller than the number of different institutions that make them up.

Institutions are grounded in the human desire for connection with others, and in economic and social exchange and reciprocity. In the words of the immortal Yogi Berra, 'If you don't go to some-body's funeral, they won't come to yours.' There is now a wealth of evidence that highly connected societies and communities are more successful than their less connected counterparts. Social capital has also been used as a predictor of such things as crime rates, school drop-out rates and academic performance, juvenile delinquency, and immigrant and ethnic business success. In the words of Robert Putnam, 'where levels of social capital are higher, children grow up healthier, safer and better educated, people live longer, happier lives, and democracy and the economy work better'.

These communities benefit their members by embedding them in networks of information and influence, which help them to get jobs and improve their income, among other things. But they also have what economists call positive externalities: they help bystanders as well. Even free-riders who do not participate in the life of a close-knit community can benefit from its low crime levels, for example – provided there are not so many that the community's own norms and practices are undermined. Conversely, children who are taken away from their communities by multiple family moves suffer, because they are unable to put down roots and build networks. Communities which lose social capital also fare badly: for example, in a 1989 study Loïc Wacquant and William Julius Wilson charted how the loss of industrial employment and middle-class families from the south and west sides of Chicago destroyed social capital in those areas, leading to very high unemployment and welfare dependency.

However, it is often forgotten that social capital is not always positive for everyone. The sociologist Alejandro Portes has highlighted negative consequences including barriers to access for outsiders, business-sapping demands from free-riders, pressure for social conformity that can stifle innovation and enterprise, and alienation of certain groups from the establishment mainstream. Thus the very strong social networks that enabled Jewish merchants to dominate the New York diamond trade in the nineteenth century did so in large part by barring outsiders from entering; seventeenth- and eighteenth-century Puritan entrepreneurs cultivated an ethos of self-reliance that deterred claims for help from idle relatives; young people have left the countryside for city life in many countries for generations; and a 1995 study highlighted how Puerto Rican crack dealers used hostility to 'white' accents and values to reinforce a code of solidarity within their own networks. There are many other well-documented examples.

Social capital is not, then, an unmixed blessing; and it can create losers as well as winners. But in general its effect appears to be

overwhelmingly positive. People need human contact and relationships with each other, then, in order to flourish. But do they need
more? Are one-to-one links with other individuals in a community
enough? Emile Durkheim, one of the nineteenth-century founders
of sociology, thought not. He believed that people need to feel
themselves bound into a moral community as such, identifying
themselves with it and sharing its norms and values. In his
pioneering study of suicide, he argued that suicide rates in European
countries varied negatively with the level of social integration.
Specifically, he found that factors such as having large families,
being Catholic or Jewish and living in a nation at war increased
integration and reduced the suicide rate; factors such as wealth or
education or being Protestant reduced integration and raised self-
sufficiency, and so increased the suicide rate.

At the limit would be a society with few if any binding norms
or standards to hold it together, and so no moral community with
which individuals could identify themselves. Lacking any external
constraints, individuals would be able, indeed forced, to follow
their own desires and preferences. This is what Durkheim calls
anomie. As the psychologist Jonathan Haidt points out:

> Complete freedom to pursue one's preferences may seem self-
> evidently good to many economists, but for Durkheim it's a recipe
> for misery and social decay. Durkheim thought that when people
> are left to their own devices, they can never satisfy their limitless
> acquisitiveness. Only by being a member of a group that imposes
> limits and sets standards for good behaviour can people achieve
> their desires and find satisfaction.

Humans cannot live happily in a world without value.

Durkheim's findings about suicide have been broadly supported
by modern research work. But his ideas go far wider than that.
They help to explain why many social indicators of well-being have
failed to keep pace with rapidly escalating increases in GDP per

capita in Western nations over the past few decades, or have even – as with rates of mental illness and depression – worsened significantly. They also cast new light by implication on the status of religion.

Different religions and indeed religion itself have been endlessly attacked in recent years by literary and scientific luminaries such as Christopher Hitchens, Richard Dawkins and Daniel Dennett, and especially so after the 9/11 terrorist atrocities. Regardless of the merits of their arguments – often rather overstated – these writers face a simple and central problem: religious observance remains robust in many countries around the world, including in the USA, where surveys suggest that more than 50 per cent of Americans consider religion to be very important in their lives. According to the anti-religionists, whatever the apparent instrumental value of religion may be, these people are being deluded on an epic scale, and this is itself the result of evolutionary processes that have gone disastrously wrong. For Dennett, religion is nothing less than a 'parasite'; for Dawkins, it is a 'virus' subject to mutation and natural selection, which forces its host to propagate it through the generations, hurting its host but ensuring its own survival.

Of course, some great evils have been done in the name of religion. The same is true of science – witness the effect of Nazi theories of eugenics and race. And it is worth noting that Durkheim also recognises that a moral community can be too strong, too binding in its norms and expectations, for its members or their neighbours to flourish. Not all religious observance is good for its practitioners and for its host society; there are many extreme religious sects, past and present, that show this. But the anti-religionists' view that billions of people are simply deluded is hardly compelling.

On an alternative view, however, it could simply be that moderate religious observance is good for individuals and good for societies, and that by and large they know it. A cluster of studies has found that religiously observant people have higher levels of well-being, health, longevity and happiness compared to control groups. They are less subject to alcohol abuse and depression. They deal with crises such as unemployment, serious illness, bereavement and divorce better. And the more people attend religious services, the more generous and charitable they become in general, and the more they participate in community activities. The point is not that the non-religious cannot do any and all of these things, and more; it is that in general they do not, or do less.

Religions work by bringing an ethos of shared endeavour to their members, integrating them socially into a moral community. To do this, they create shared habit, practice and ritual. The anthropologist Richard Sosis looked closely at the history of 200 communes, religious and secular, established in the USA in the nineteenth and twentieth centuries. He found that the religious communes lasted four times as long as the secular ones, and were half as likely to dissolve within the first five years of existence. Just 6 per cent of the secular communes were functioning after twenty years, as against nearly 40 per cent of the religious ones.

What made the difference? In the religious communes, the answer seemed to be their demands for self-sacrifice, through habits such as the renunciation of alcohol, fasting, and acceptance of a communal dress code or isolation from the outside world. In the secular communes, there was no such correlation. Sosis conjectured that sacrifices work most effectively when they are sacralized – that is, when the norms governing them are made holy and seen as subject to an external power such as a god or gods. Acts of self-sacrifice, and lesser communal activities like singing and chanting, become religious rituals which reduce internal conflict and increase commitment to collective goals, allowing the benefits of moral community to flow. Religious groups can then become larger and more extended, since they have the capacity to bind people together who may not be related or indeed have much else in common at all.

On this view, far from being viruses or parasites, religions are likely to have had evolutionary advantages for their members, as well as creating social capital for the communities around them. Moreover, the rituals, practices, customs and talismans which are so otiose and irrational to the scientific mind – and so unsuited to economic cost-benefit analysis – turn out to be precisely what create loyalty and community feeling, and thus what afford their members the benefits of health, well-being and resilience already described.

It appears, then, that sacred custom and ritual play a crucial role in the longevity and success of religious communities. But it is also striking that the emphasis from this emerging picture is less on revelation than on religions and moral communities as institutions. What matters is that humans as social animals should be able to develop among themselves habits, standards, practices, rules and moral codes to act as binding agents, which endow the world with value and so inhibit Durkheimian anomie and the adverse effects of too much individualism. Of course, this will hardly satisfy those of any religion who insist on the centrality of revelation, access to divine law and the truth of God's word. But it is where the evidence presently lies about the sources of human well-being.

What matters is to live in a moral community. But which one? After all, different moral communities may have very different moral codes. Based on field research in Orissa in India and the USA, the cultural psychologist Richard Shweder has identified three broad areas of moral difference, which he terms the ethic of autonomy, the ethic of community and the ethic of divinity. The *ethic of autonomy* is the morality of liberal individualism: it sees people as autonomous individuals seeking to satisfy their wants and needs, and it correspondingly emphasizes ideas of choice, procedural justice and rights. In such societies what matters is the right of people to express themselves without harm to others.

The *ethic of community* emphasizes institutions as entities in their own right, and sees people as members of institutions. It lays stress on interdependence, hierarchy, respect for others and duty. In such societies what matters is protection of institutions, including the social order itself, from external threat and individual selfishness. Finally, the *ethic of divinity* sees the world as sacred, and people as souls connected to an external order of things, which it is their duty to maintain. It emphasizes purity, sin, preservation, self-control and respect for the body. In such societies what matters is preserving the self and society from defilement and degradation.

Different people around the world are permeated to different degrees by these three kinds of moral community. Those from Western democracies largely fall into the first kind, the ethic of autonomy. But many other people around the world do not do so. Their basic cultural expectations and moral intuitions reflect very different sets of norms, emphasizing the communal and the social over the purely individual, and the sacred over the material. And even within Western countries the ethics of community and divinity are also present. The USA is, as we have seen, a highly individualistic society. But it is also one with extremely high rates of community service; and one whose citizens instinctively abhor any abuse of the national flag as a form of defilement, suggesting that it harbours a lingering ethic of divinity.

What matters to humans is not merely to live in societies which possess high social capital or personal linkages and institutional connections. It is that they should also be members of a moral community, living in a world not of anomie but of value and meaning.

This too is a deeply Burkean theme. Burke was no democrat, as we have seen. But, as with his hatred of slavery, all of his great 'international' campaigns – over America, India, Ireland and France – have at their core a deep belief in the importance of moral community, and a commitment to justice in response to the abuse of power. In the 'Speech on Conciliation', the American colonists are 'Englishmen . . . devoted to liberty according to English ideas, and on English principles'. When in his 'Speech on the Nabob of Arcot's Debts' (1785) Burke refers to 'our distressed fellow-citizens in India', he means Indians, not the men of the East India Company. In his speech against Warren Hastings of 16 February 1788, Burke inveighs against a 'geographical morality . . . once you cross the equinoctial line, all the virtues die . . . the laws of morality are the same everywhere; and actions that are stamped with the character of peculation, extortion, oppression and barbarity in England, are so in Asia, and the world over'.

In his *Letter to Sir Hercules Langrishe* of 1792, Burke's argument for Catholic emancipation in Ireland is grounded not just in prudence – the need to give the large Catholic majority a stake in society – but in indignation at the moral status of Catholics, 'without common interest, sympathy or connection'. And of course one of Burke's most basic criticisms of the French revolution is that it creates an 'armed doctrine' which threatens the entire international order between European nations.

Burke's emphasis on moral community has two fascinating corollaries. The first is his open and inclusive conception of empire, ultimately overthrown by events – by the American revolution, by union with Ireland in 1800 and by the growing insularity, religiosity and intolerance of the Raj in India – but of enduring interest as a contribution to the idea of 'soft power' today.

The second lies in Burke's awareness of the danger to moral community at home. In the present time, the research above strongly suggests that Burkean concerns about the excesses of liberal individualism are well founded. Yes, much of human behaviour is self-interested. But the standard view of people as greedy profit-maximizers, a view embedded in much of economics itself, systematically misunderstands how they behave, both individually and in the aggregate. Moreover, the evidence on money priming suggests that societies that emphasize financial success have the effect of making their members more greedy, more selfish and more individualistic. Indeed, for several decades at least, science itself seems to have been reinforcing a cultural process by which people in Western cultures are encouraged to see their own individualism as normal and right, regardless of its limitations, and to assume automatically that other people all think in the same way – or worse, to regard them as simply primitive if they do not.

But even empathy must have its limits, and modern research helps to explain why. The social order itself can be put at risk, and moral communities undermined, by human action. This is how Burke saw the revolution in France: first, as a determined attempt to destroy a society itself, thus imperilling the well-being of millions of people; and secondly, as an absolutely fundamental assault on a moral community of which he and much of European civilization were a part. For Burke as now for us, the collective wisdom of institutions is a vital component of social well-being. To lose that wisdom in disorder and revolution is for a society to become temporarily demented.

More broadly, this implies that the basic task of politics is simply to preserve social capital and moral community. Ideally, that requires virtuous leaders, who can both protect the social order and exemplify the community's moral norms through their actions.

However, the Burkean viewpoint goes still further. As we have seen, Burke follows Aristotle in holding that man is a *politikon zoon* or social animal. But the phrase 'social animal' captures only part of the meaning of the original Greek. Aristotle believed that the story of the cosmos is one of an unfolding energy, by which what is potential becomes actual. He argued that for humans that unfolding potential expresses itself in the capacity to deliberate publicly about the terms and purpose of their own self-governance. Humans thus have a unique capacity to reflect on and shape the nature of human society itself. The exercise of such a capacity – both how it is exercised and in its specific outcomes – is what gives definition to a society. It is what politics is.

For Aristotle the distinctive achievement of the Greek city-state or *polis* lay in the fact that it was the institution through which this human deliberative capability had been raised to its highest level. Burke's extraordinary further step is, through his theory and practice of party politics, to demonstrate a principled means by which such reflective deliberation can be extended outside a political class itself and into society as a whole. And he does this without sacrificing the virtues of expertise, diversity and long-term focus that characterize effective political decision-making at its best. In particular, Burke's distinctive notion of a 'partnership of the dead, the living and the yet to be born' preserves the institutional features, legacies and continuity of a well-ordered society against the claims of any current individual, group or generation. This is a profound philosophical achievement.

Self-consciousness in deliberation requires us to recognize that language itself is an institution, which can shape a society's understanding of value. This is a natural extension of Burke's earlier argument that the imposition of mathematical and scientific categories on human life always involves logical error. It implies that the jargonized language of economics and business should not be allowed to displace the language of value in human lives: that words like 'iteration', 'behaviour', 'agent', 'utility' and indeed 'social capital' should not be seen as synonyms for 'trust', 'conduct', 'person', 'happiness' and 'connection'. These ideas and those of loyalty, dignity and respect may not fit happily into economic models, but they carry with them vital norms and values which cannot be translated without loss of meaning, or even its abolition.

Burke's own rhetoric reflects this deep understanding, at several levels. Even as early as the *Enquiry* in 1757 he has a working theory of language, one that recognizes the powerful effect of abstract words like 'justice' or 'honour', which excite the emotions without any distinct understanding of what they mean. That is an insight he uses in his own speeches. And nearly forty years later, it is one that inspires his denunciation of the abstract ideas of the French revolution as mere slogans.

Moreover, Burke's awareness of other cultures, and his extraordinary capacity to immerse himself imaginatively in them, make him acutely sensitive to different sources of moral motivation. It is striking how his own thought combines insights from each of the three kinds of moral community described above: the ethic of autonomy in his celebration of personal liberty and mutual toleration, the ethic of community in his emphasis on allegiance and institutions, and the ethic of divinity in his insistence on the transcendent value of the social order itself. In effect, then, Burke has something important to say to members of each community, but he will never entirely please them. He is too diverse for the zealots. Like Walt Whitman in *Leaves of Grass* he is large, he contains multitudes.

But Burke's own speeches also embody an unceasing search for meaning and for ways to convey meaning. As Shakespeare deliberately plays with, breaks and steps outside Aristotle's three unities of time, place and action in his plays, so does Burke, his intellect fired by passion, play with, break and step outside the classical rules of rhetoric, with wild sweeps from the most elevated to the coarsest imagery in a few sentences. At times, as with his violent denunciation of Pitt during the Regency Crisis, the results are disastrous. At others, they are sublime.

For Burke, what ultimately gives meaning to the world, what enchants it, is that it is a providential gift from God. But this in turn fires and feeds off the extraordinary human capacity for recreative and empathic imagination. It is through imagination that we understand not merely what is but what could be, not merely the constraints but the potential, not merely limitation but aspiration. Where value is threatened by ego, by the 'ethics of vanity', by anomie, it is through imagination that we can recover it, re-enchant the world and restore the sense of moral community that allows humans to flourish.

In the final analysis, it is this insight, and this search for meaning, that unites Burke with the Lake poets. But the result is not what Keats, quoting Hazlitt, called the 'egotistical sublime' of

Wordsworth – that is, the monumental self unmoved by context or habit, whose inner dialogue allows it to disengage from the world. Nor yet is it Keats's own self-effacing 'negative capability', which holds the self at bay, as 'when a man is capable of being in uncertainties, mysteries, doubts, without any irritable reaching after fact and reason'. On the contrary, it is an extraordinary and distinctively Burkean imaginative engagement: a balance between ego and circumstance, between ambition and constraint, between individuality and society. Burke, the conservative, outdoes the Romantics and, for some at least, becomes their hero.

CONCLUSION

Burke Today

SO WHAT, TAKE HIM FOR ALL IN ALL, are we to make of Edmund Burke? Burke had his flaws, of course. He was proud, a creature of passion as well as intellect, and was sometimes overmastered by emotions of anger and pity which led him into political embarrassments. He could be bitter, obsessive, occasionally even vindictive. In a lifetime of speaking and writing on a vast range of subjects, he was far from absolutely consistent, and he would not have wanted to be. As his life went on, oppressed by debt, his youthful ambition yielding to disappointment amid the long grind of opposition politics, he became increasingly self-righteous and violent in his language. He wrote in his 'Speech on Conciliation' that 'It is ordained in the eternal constitution of things, that men of intemperate minds cannot be free. Their passions form their fetters.' So it often was with Burke himself.

Moreover, judged by conventional standards at least, Burke's political career was largely one of failure. He and his party failed to avert war between Britain and the American colonies. He failed to secure a conviction in the impeachment of Warren Hastings. His economical reforms and his efforts to address Irish and Catholic grievances were only partially successful. His pleas for a counter-revolutionary war against France were ignored. Over three decades in the House of Commons, he himself held office for under two years.

And some key aspects of Burke's thought may strike a modern audience as wrong, irrelevant or merely offensive. His emphasis on private property is often read simply as a defence of privilege and an attack on the poor. Political parties have rarely been held in lower public esteem, yet Burke insists on their importance. To many his intense dislike of atheism now appears out of touch. His belief in 'prejudice', habit and tradition is widely misunderstood. He has little of interest to say about women. And his opposition to the French revolution is often seen as hostility to change or innovation itself.

Yet as Burke himself ironically remarked, 'the conduct of a losing party never appears right: at least, it never can possess the only infallible criterion of wisdom to vulgar judgements – success'. When we see him in the round, a very different picture emerges. Here is a man who is warm, generous, charming, open and wise. His marriage to Jane was one of tender and loving regard, and his private life irreproachable at a time of considerable sexual licence. He was a devoted father and friend, who adored his family and supported his brother Richard and 'cousin Will' from a common purse for decades, despite their travails. He was highly sociable, had a wide correspondence, greatly enjoyed the theatre and was a founding member of the Club alongside Reynolds, Johnson and others. He was a lover of art, who enjoyed and added to the private collection he acquired with the purchase of Gregories. He supported the young Irish painter James Barry, and rescued the poet George Crabbe from poverty and the threat of debtors' prison. Fanny Burney, no mean observer of human nature, described her first impressions thus in 1782: 'He is tall, his figure is noble, his air commanding, his address graceful: his voice is clear, penetrating, sonorous, and powerful; his language is copious, various and eloquent; his manners are attractive, his conversation is delightful.'

Burke barely held political office, it is true. He is not like Pitt or Peel, both of them executive politicians whose stories are ones of achievement, for good or ill. No: Burke's is a story of ideas and dreams, a story told in his own and in the public imagination. It is a highly reflective enterprise, informed by vast self-education and demanding reflection on the part of the student of Burke if it is to be well understood. It addresses many audiences, at many levels. It is not simple, and so it is profoundly threatening to conventional thought and conventional categories, then and now. As Paine found to his horror, Burke is not a 'cluster' thinker, whose beliefs can be determined one from another by inference or from current fashions. On the contrary, he is a philosopher in action, and his philosophy, which anticipates many recent currents in post-Enlightenment thought, deserves far more attention than it has received of late.

Good politicians do not allow themselves to get too far ahead of public opinion. But Burke is not politic, and he is almost always ahead of public opinion. In his own time this was true of his great campaigns over America, Ireland, India and France. It was true of his struggle to restrain monarchical power, and it was true of his antipathy to slavery and capital punishment, and of his support for free markets.

What unites all of these positions is Burke's indomitable belief in ordered liberty, and in the right of humans to live their lives well and to enjoy the benefits of human society. Far from opposing change, Burke regards change as inevitable, and careful political reform as its natural and proper counterpart. Far from defending privilege, he saw a successful social order as the means by which individual talent and energy could find their just rewards. For him the function of politics is to allow these processes to take place to the benefit of society as a whole. This demands modesty, virtue and wisdom from political leaders. And as he put it in his 'Speech on a Bill for Repeal of the Marriage Act', 'If it should come to the last extremity, and to a contest of blood, God forbid! God forbid! – my part is taken; I would take my fate with the poor, and low, and feeble.'

But the counterpart of Burke's belief in freedom is his absolute detestation of the abuse of power. Contrary to some influential recent interpretations, Burke is not first and foremost a theorist of natural law; he is more empirical in spirit, indeed rooted in history, fact and circumstance. But for Burke it is a deep principle of natural law that no man shall be judge in his own cause. This is the source of what his biographer Conor Cruise O'Brien called the Great Melody, after W. B. Yeats: the theme that unifies and explains Burke's opposition to what he saw as oppressive British actions over the American colonies, the Irish Catholics and the peoples of India. The same theme inspires his critique of the Double Cabinet and the growing influence of the Crown. And it inspires his hatred of the subversive power of the French revolution.

Few people have seen the point more clearly, or expressed it more beautifully, than Winston Churchill. In his essay 'Consistency in Politics', he wrote:

On the one hand [Burke] is revealed as a foremost apostle of Liberty, on the other as the redoubtable champion of Authority. But a charge of political inconsistency applied to this life appears a mean and petty thing. History easily discerns the reasons and forces which actuated him, and the immense changes in the problems he was facing which evoked from the same profound mind and sincere spirit these entirely contrary manifestations. His soul revolted against tyranny, whether it appeared in the aspect of a domineering Monarch and a corrupt Court and Parliamentary system, or whether, mouthing the watch-words of a non-existent liberty, it towered up against him in the dictation of a brutal mob and wicked sect. No one can read the Burke of Liberty and the Burke of Authority without feeling that here was the same man pursuing the same ends, seeking the same ideals of society and Government, and defending them from assaults, now from one extreme, now from the other.

* * *

However, Edmund Burke is a politician not merely of his time but of ours. His ideas form a vast pool of wisdom from which we can still draw today. Indeed in many ways his lessons have been forgotten, to our great detriment. The time has come to learn them anew.

But first we need to face what some may see as a highly inconvenient truth. Edmund Burke was a conservative. Not a member of the Conservative party, not a neocon or a theocon, not a Thatcherite or a Reaganite – but a conservative nonetheless. Indeed, in many ways he was the first conservative, the founder: the first person who can properly lay claim to having forged conservatism as a distinctive body of political thought. This idea has been much disputed. After all, Burke never described himself as a conservative, and the term itself did not properly enter politics until several decades after his death. Indeed, in his own time Burke was a Whig, and the Whig party gave way in the nineteenth century to the Liberals, causing him to be claimed by many politicians of (classical) liberal inclination today. He was, to boot, a thoroughgoing advocate of many liberal measures of reform. So how can he be a conservative?

Political categories are not precisely defined, of course; there are often overlaps between them. As the Whig party slowly fragmented many Whigs, especially the followers of William Pitt, did not choose to join the Liberals. But there can be little doubt that Burke falls on the conservative side of the argument. As we have seen, liberalism – like its modern offshoot, libertarianism or neoliberalism – emphasizes the primacy of the individual; Burke emphasizes the importance of the social order. Liberalism sees freedom as the absence of impediment to the will; Burke sees freedom as ordered liberty. Liberalism believes above all in the power of reason; Burke believes in tradition, habit and 'prejudice'. Liberalism stresses universal principles; Burke stresses fact and circumstance. Liberalism is unimpressed by the past; Burke quarries it. Liberalism admires radical change; Burke detests it. The liberal will cannot be made the subject of duties; Burke insists upon them. The evidence is clear.

Burke is, then, the first conservative. But he has no monopoly on conservatism, and his own version has a strongly Whiggish flavour to it. It supports Parliament over the executive, and favours toleration. It emphasizes free economic and social institutions at every level and in every part of society, and it is deeply suspicious of great concentrations of power, be they those of the monarch, the East India Company or the modern state.

As a political creed, conservatism contains an inevitable tension between its leading principles, such as that between liberty and authority. Indeed, the thought that there can be no absolutely consistent worthwhile ethical theory is a rather Burkean insight, which has eluded some of the greatest moral philosophers. But it is easy to see why Burke's thought has fitted so naturally into the basic philosophy of the British Conservative party over the past 150 years. For in addition to its Whiggish roots, his emphasis on the social order and duty reaches out to Tory traditionalists, while his paternalist conviction that politics must help the whole of society engages those moved by concern for the least well off. Among the different Conservative party tribes, only the twentieth-century corporatists who believed in collective bargaining between capital and labour can derive no real sustenance from Burke. But the Conservatives' remarkable electoral success since the second Reform Act of 1867 has derived from building coalitions of voters, and this line of thought suggests that Burke's far-reaching ideas have been, whether recognized or not, at the heart of that success. And more than that, he gives conservatism a wide emotional pallet of sensibility and compassion, and so a capacity to understand and inspire all sections of society.

Yet Burke also clips the wings of many contemporary conservatives. In America, for example, it is often said that the Burkean tradition has been supplanted by three strands of modern conservatism: free-market, neoconservative and theoconservative or religious conservatism. All claim some adherence to Burke. But there can be little doubt that Burke would have rejected key features of all of them. Except in reaction to the most extreme necessity, his politics is one of moderation. He was an early supporter of free markets, but only within a strong context of personal probity, law, market norms and trust. He helped to establish modern conceptions of nationhood and national allegiance, but had the deepest respect for other cultures and rejected military adventures. He celebrated religious observance, but despised moral absolutism. Burke is an anti-ideologist, and he is so because he is a conservative.

We have seen in these pages how Burke is the first framer of the modern conception of a political party, as well as being a principal architect of the Rockingham Whigs, the first proto-political party. We have seen how he brings his thought together into a broadly coherent whole in the 1750s, how he develops and deploys it over a lifetime of political campaigning, and how in the 1790s he uses it to attack the romantic rationalism of Jean-Jacques Rousseau, and the moral and intellectual basis of the French revolution. We have seen how he is the first modern philosopher to treat the idea of society as a basic category within politics, indeed to locate political deliberation itself and its institutions within the human capacity to shape the social order.

We have seen how even after his death that same body of thought carries within it a devastating critique of liberal individualism in the modern era. And we have seen how Burkean ideas about human nature, well-being, society and institutions have received extraordinary support from recent research in social and evolutionary psychology and anthropology. Far from recent announcements of 'the death of conservatism', then, Burke gives us a vision of its future. In a world of shock-jocks, single-issue extremism and political fragmentation, it is a vision we may need.

But what about today? What can we learn from Burke today? I would suggest that there are six key lessons to be drawn.

The first is that extreme liberalism is now in crisis. Various disasters have gravely undermined conventional beliefs in the moral primacy of the individual, in the power of human reason alone to resolve political and economic problems, in the redemptive value of individual consumption, and in the capacity of unfettered individual freedom to deliver personal or social well-being. Not only that: there is evidence that liberal individualism may actively blind those living in many economically advanced and industrialized countries to the needs and nature of other countries and other peoples. It may even be true that extreme liberalism causes people to lose sight of the real social sources of human well-being and to become more selfish and individualistic, by priming them with ideas of financial success and celebrity.

But, as Burke shows us, the individual is not simply a compendium of wants, human happiness is not simply a matter of satisfying individual wants, and the purpose of politics is not to satisfy the interests of individuals living now: it is to preserve an evolving social order which meets the needs of generations past, present and future. The paradox of Burke's conservatism is thus that, properly understood, it is intrinsically modest, while extreme liberalism appears to promote arrogance and selfishness. Burke's conservatism constrains rampant individualism and the tyranny of the majority, while extreme liberalism threatens to worsen their effects. Indeed, Burke tempts us to the heretical thought that the route to a better politics may not be through yet more managerial claims – 'we can do it better' – but through a deep change of viewpoint.

Second, many of the recent disasters of liberalism arose from failures of policy and leadership which a Burkean perspective might well have been able to avoid. The White House under John F. Kennedy gathered together one of greatest assemblages of expertise ever seen in American politics, and they took their country into the Vietnam War. Western policy towards Russia in the 1990s was heavily economic in inspiration, focusing on currency convertibility and free-market institutions. It all but ignored the country's low levels of trust and social capital, and so actively assisted the loss of public assets to the new oligarchs. The Iraq and Afghan wars were launched without any detailed consideration of effective social reconstruction, and it took years to develop effective 'hearts and minds' approaches which respected local people and restrained the

insurgencies. Within the European Union, the new currency of the
euro was introduced as an elite project which deliberately ignored,
and ignores, longstanding public concerns about the huge differences in the societies of the various nations involved, and about
the legitimacy of the Union's own institutions. Burke would have
reminded those involved that a project which ultimately seeks to
abolish national identities and allegiances is likely to fail.

None of these great political actions was necessary; all ignored
local circumstances and the 'temper of the people'; and all were or
are proving to be disastrous in their effects. The same is true on a
smaller scale with the many melancholy case studies of social capital
destroyed by such things as out-of-town supermarkets and foolish
inner-city renewal projects. But a Burkean perspective allows us to
sense immediately what has gone wrong. It reminds us of the
institutional centrality of the city and the nation state. And more
deeply still, it offers an intellectual context within which to analyse
and understand the deeper currents of ethnic, religious or ideological allegiance.

Third, Burke offers an important but undervalued model of
political leadership. The purpose of politics for him is to preserve
and enhance the social order in the national interest. Leadership
begins in respect for the social order, and so in modesty. It demands
a close study of the people, indeed all of the people, and their institutions and 'manners'. It is therefore rooted in a sense of history, rather
than one of science. Burkean leaders believe in slow government.
They fear to sacrifice the interests of future generations at the altar
of present popularity. They do not regard politics as a subset of
economics, and are not obsessed with passing laws, interfering in
private concerns or tampering with working institutions. On the
contrary, they are reformers, drawing new ideas from experience
and tradition, not ideology or human invention; sceptical about
official expertise, radical schemes and ambitious government; cool
in spirit, consensual and practical; patriotic, but not dismissive
of the concerns of other countries and other ways of life; and

concerned to balance short-term redress with long-term improvement. Above all, a Burkean leader will insist on the common good, and the importance of public service and public duty.

Fourth, as we have seen, Burke was driven throughout his career by a hatred of excessive power, and the arbitrary use and abuse of power. In his own time, he regarded as his greatest achievement his campaign to restrain the influence, greed and self-dealing of the East India Company, and to insist on the accountability of private power to legitimate public authority. In the present era, he might well have seen the emergence of corporate and financial power in similar terms, as a kind of 'crony capitalism' in which much business activity has become divorced from the wider public interest, while executive pay has largely ceased to reflect personal achievement or collective performance. This is quite distinct from real capitalism and the proper functioning of free markets, wealth creation and entrepreneurship. By implication, Burke offers a profound critique of the market fundamentalism now prevalent in Western society. But he does so not from the left of the political spectrum, but from the right. A Burkean perspective would distinguish between conservative and liberal free markets. Understood conservatively, markets are not idolized, but treated as cultural artefacts mediated by trust and tradition. Capitalism becomes, not a one-size-fits-all ideology of consumption, but a spectrum of different models to be evaluated on their own merits.

But Burke would also note the extraordinary greed and self-dealing seen over the past decade by the modern nabobs of banking and finance in a series of cartels disguised as markets; the absence of much effective national regulation and supervision; the narrowing and fragmentation of political parties, and of their semi-public role within political deliberation; and the emergence in the USA of corporate 'super PACs' or Political Action Committees exploiting the constitutional protection of free speech to spend unlimited amounts of independent money on political campaigning. From a Burkean perspective, the effect of these developments is to unsettle a proper constitutional balance of powers, to exploit and exacerbate the extreme partisanship of modern American politics, and to push the USA towards a politics of redistribution mediated by corporate groups, rather than one inspired by a broader conception of social or economic benefit.

Fifth, Burke reminds us of the foundational importance of protecting representative government and the rule of law, as a bulwark against the abuse of power – whether that be corporate power or executive power within government itself. Today, the idea of democracy draws together countervailing principles, which balance and filter political participation. Power is separated out and allocated across different branches and levels of government; the legitimacy of the ballot is balanced by the legitimacy of constitutional procedure, transparency and established precedent; majorities have their say, but minority rights are protected. These are the lessons of Montesquieu and Madison – and of Burke himself.

There is much here of which Britain can be proud, in its own distinctive history and institutions. But every country is different, in its traditions, its values and its pathologies of government. There is no single one-size-fits-all model of democracy, but every genuine democracy relies on effective public deliberation, and in every genuine democracy political parties have a centrally important role. They have never been popular, and often rightly so. They are often reviled today, and often in need of reform. It is hard to see a future for them in a world of e-petitions, plebiscites, referenda, single-issue campaigning, tribal ideology, bureaucratic inertia and consumerism. Multi-party democracy is increasingly criticized as unstable and short-term by one-party states such as China, when the central paradox of China's own development is that it needs precisely the free and independent institutions it most distrusts. The truth is that good, stable government demands effective political parties. They are a vital contribution of Anglo-American statecraft, but they are under threat – and no workable alternative is in sight.

Finally, Burke provides a context within which to understand the loss and recovery of social value. His message is a vital and timeless insistence on the importance of human culture, in its widest sense. As a politician, he was devoted to an ideal of public service, and deplored the tendency to individual or generational arrogance, and the 'ethics of vanity'. His thought is imbued with the importance of history and memory, and an Orwellian detestation of those that would erase them. He insists on the importance of human connection and identity, and on manners, sentiment and 'prejudice', inherited and not invented, and embedded in social institutions and networks. He emphasizes the human self as an active social force, not the passive vehicle for happiness of the utilitarians, or the individual atom of much modern economics. For Burke, government itself cannot simply be a matter of utility and effectiveness. It must have some continuing purchase on our affections and allegiance.

But Burke also questions the present self-image of politics and the media, an empty post-modernism in which there is no truth, but only different kinds of narrative deployed in the service of power. Instead, he offers values and principles that do not change, the sanction of history and the moral authenticity of those willing to give up power to principle. He gives us again the lost language of politics: a language of honour, loyalty, duty and wisdom, which can never be adequately captured in any spreadsheet or economic model. And he highlights the importance of moderate religious observance and moral community as a source of shared norms, and the role of human creativity and imagination in re-enchanting the world and filling it with meaning. As the Western world wrestles with the possibility of an extended period of secular decline, as it seeks to derive public benefit from private vice and to reset its political and economic course, it is this vision of human possibility and renewed social value that may prove to be Burke's greatest legacy.

Notes

These notes generally list specific sources not mentioned in the text, readily identifiable online or cited in the Bibliography.

Introduction

1. Randolph Churchill on Disraeli: quoted in Weintraub, *Disraeli*.
2. Laski on Burke: Laski, *Political Thought in England from Locke to Bentham*.

Chapter 1: An Irishman Abroad, 1730–1759

1. Date of birth: Burke was born on New Year's Day in the old Julian Calendar, or 12 January in the Gregorian calendar adopted in 1752. His year of birth is uncertain. Traditionally it has been given as 1729, but this book follows F. P. Lock's dating of 1730.
2. Essay on Ireland in the 1740s: see *The Reformer*, 10 March 1748.
3. Gin and Judith Defour: see Dillon, *The Much-Lamented Death of Madame Geneva: The Eighteenth-Century Gin Craze*.
4. Illegitimacy and the 'first sexual revolution': see Dabhoiwala, *The Origins of Sex*, p. 204.
5. Dry-docked scholars: from the *Annual Register*, 1760, p. 206.
6. Perelman: see 'De Gustibus Ain't What Dey Used to Be', *New Yorker*, 18 April 1953.
7. Will Burke: see Burke's letter to Philip Francis, 9 June 1777, *Correspondence*, iii, p. 348.
8. Leo Strauss: see his *Natural Right and History*, final chapter.

Chapter 2: In and Out of Power, 1759–1774

1. Whigs and Tories: these terms, and their subdivisions and shifts in meaning, have been the subject of huge debate among

historians. Cf. J. G. A. Pocock's magisterial survey 'The Varieties of Whiggism from Exclusion to Reform', in his *Virtue, Commerce and History*.

2. Walpole in caricature: see Langford, *Walpole and the Robinocracy*.
3. Clubs: see Bingham, 'Clubs and Clubbability', in his *Dr Johnson and the Law and Other Essays on Johnson*; also Uglow, *Dr Johnson, his Club and Other Friends*.
4. House of Commons: see Thomas, *The House of Commons in the Eighteenth Century*.
5. Hats: Hats may not be worn in the chamber of the Commons today. Until 1998, however, MPs wishing to raise a point of order during a vote had to put on a hat to do so, and a collapsible top hat was kept close by for the purpose.
6. Hans Stanley: quoted in Pares, *King George III and the Politicians*, p. 14.
7. Gregories: see Lambert, *Edmund Burke of Beaconsfield*.
8. Wilkes: see Cash, *John Wilkes: The Scandalous Father of Civil Liberty*.
9. Double Cabinet: see Christie, *Myth and Reality in Late Eighteenth Century British Politics*, ch. 1.
10. Effect of Burke's speeches: see Harris, 'Publishing Parliamentary Oratory: The Case of Edmund Burke', *Parliamentary History* 26.1 (2007) 112–30.

Chapter 3: Ireland, America and King Mob, 1774–1780

1. Constituencies and elections: see Namier, *The Structure of Politics at the Accession of George III*; also O'Gorman, *Voters, Patrons and Parties*.
2. Yorkshire election of 1807: see Hague, *William Wilberforce*, ch. 14.
3. Charles James Fox: see Mitchell, *Charles James Fox*.
4. Gordon Riots: see Hibbert, *King Mob*, and Innes, *Inferior Politics*, ch. 7.

Chapter 4: India, Economical Reform and the King's Madness, 1780–1789

1. East India Company: see e.g. Robins, *The Corporation that Changed the World*.
2. Pitt: see Hague, *William Pitt the Younger*.
3. Hastings: see e.g. Trotter, *Warren Hastings: A Biography*; Bernstein, *Dawning of the Raj*.
4. Porphyria: see Richard Hift, Timothy Peters and Peter Meissner, 'A Review of the Clinical Presentation, Natural History and Inheritance of Variegate Porphyria: Its Implausibility as the Source of the "Royal Malady"', *Journal of Clinical Pathology* 65.3 (2012) 200–5.
5. Whig reactions to the King's madness: see Mitchell, *Charles James Fox and the Disintegration of the Whig Party*, ch. 4.
6. Burke as 'good old horse': Elliot, *Letters to a Prince, from a Man of Kent*.

Chapter 5: Reflecting on Revolution, 1789–1797

1. French revolution: see e.g. Doyle, *The Oxford History of the French Revolution*; Schama, *Citizens*.
2. Revolution Controversy: there is a comprehensive collection of sources in Butler (ed.), *Burke. Paine, Godwin, and the Revolution Controversy*.
3. Jacobins/Jacobinism: note that 'Jacobins' are quite different from 'Jacobites' – those who followed or believed in the right to rule of James II and his successors after James went into exile in 1688.
4. Burke and Fox: Mitchell gives a superb account of the decline in Burke and Fox's relationship, and its wider context, in *Charles James Fox and the Disintegration of the Whig Party*, chs 5 and 6.
5. *Appeal from the New to the Old Whigs*: as Pocock noted in 'The Varieties of Whiggism from Exclusion to Reform', Burke's usage

of the terms 'New Whig' and 'Old Whig' is not at all the same as that of modern historiography. This book stays with Burke's usage.

Chapter 6: Reputation, Reason and the Enlightenment Project

1. Disraeli and Peel: the story is told in Blake, *A History of the Conservative Party from Peel to Major*, Introduction.
2. Woodrow Wilson: 'Edmund Burke, the Man and his Times', from *Mere Literature*, reprinted in *Woodrow Wilson: Essential Writings and Speeches of the Scholar-President*.
3. Hazlitt and Burke: see Bromwich, *Hazlitt: The Mind of a Critic*, especially pp. 288ff.
4. Thomas Babington Macaulay, 'Southey's Colloquies', *Edinburgh Review* 50 (Jan. 1830) 528–9.
5. Paine's relationship with Burke: Copeland, *Edmund Burke: Six Essays*, ch. 5.
6. Paine's allegation of a 'masked pension': see Blakemore, *Intertextual War*, ch. 4.
7. 1757 essay on political parties: see Richard Bourke, 'Party, Parliament and Conquest in Newly Ascribed Burke Manuscripts', *Historical Journal* 55.3 (2012) 619–52. For a statement of previously accepted view, see O'Gorman, *Burke: His Political Philosophy*, p. 25.
8. Factions vs. parties: for eighteenth-century attitudes and debates on the relative merits of factions and parties, see Gunn, *Factions No More*.
9. 'His master's voice': see O'Gorman, *Burke: His Political Philosophy*, p. 26.
10. Rousseau and Burke: see Richard B. Sewall, 'Rousseau's Second Discourse in England from 1755 to 1762', *Philological Quarterly* 17.2 (Apr. 1938) 97–114.

Chapter 7: The Social Self

1. 'Who born for the Universe': 'Retaliation', by Oliver Goldsmith.
2. Absence of system: O'Gorman, *Edward Burke: His Political Philosophy*, p. 14.
3. Hume: P. F. Brownsey, 'Hume and the Social Contract', *Philosophical Quarterly* Vol. 28, No. 111 (Apr. 1978), pp. 132–48.
4. Adam Smith on Burke: see Bisset, *Life of Edmund Burke*, ii, p. 429.
5. Rousseau and the *Vindication*: Sewall, 'Rousseau's Second Discourse in England from 1755 to 1762'.
6. Warrior ethos: see Pocock, 'Introduction' to his edition of the *Reflections on the Revolution in France*, Hackett 1987. Some scholars including Sir Frank Kermode have read 'domination' as 'Domitian'; this book follows the usual reading.
7. Law of nature: Hobbes, *De Cive*.
8. Impact of William III: see Douglass North and Barry Weingast, 'Constitutions and Commitment: The Evolution of Institutions Governing Public Choice in Seventeenth Century England', *Journal of Economic History* 49.4 (1989) 803–32; cf. also Harford, *The Logic of Life* and Bingham, *This Little Britain*.

Chapter 8: Forging Modern Politics

1. This chapter owes a particular debt to Harvey Mansfield, *Statesmanship and Party Government: A Study of Burke and Bolingbroke*.
2. Exclusion Crisis: see e.g. Dillon, *The Last Revolution: 1688 and the Creation of the Modern World*.
3. Whigs and Tories: cf. Pocock, 'The Varieties of Whiggism from Exclusion to Reform'.
4. Horace Walpole on the Tories: *Memoirs of the Reign of King George III*, i, p. 192
5. Bute: see e.g. Pares, *King George III and the Politicians*, pp. 99ff.
6. Patriot King: it is worth noting that Bolingbroke also advocated

the need for a more systematic form of parliamentary opposition, or 'country party'.

7. Constitutional vs. democratic principles: see Lee Auspitz, 'A "Republican" View of Both Parties', *Public Interest* 67 (Spring 1982) 94–117.

8. Burke and Jefferson: see Copeland, *Edmund Burke: Six Essays*, ch. 5.

9. UK public spending in the late eighteenth century: see www.ukpublicspending.co.uk, after Mitchell, *British Historical Statistics*.

Chapter 9: The Rise of Liberal Individualism

1. Liberal individualism: similar ideas have been explored from a wide range of perspectives by thinkers such as, pre-eminently, Tocqueville (see below) and more recently C. B. Macpherson ('possessive individualism'), Roger Scruton and Alasdair MacIntyre. MacIntyre's account of liberal individualism in *After Virtue* and subsequent works, notably *Whose Justice? Which Rationality?*, appears to owe a good deal to Burke. It is unclear why MacIntyre is himself consistently hostile to Burke.

2. Matthew Parris: *The Times*, 30 June 2012.

3. Tocqueville and individualism: cf. *Democracy in America*, book 2, ch. 8, 'How the Americans combat individualism by the principle of self-interest rightly understood'. Tocqueville defines individualism as 'a calm and considered feeling which disposes each citizen to isolate himself from the mass of his fellows and withdraw into the circle of family and friends', and as such it poses a threat to society and to participatory government. The solution for him is 'self-interest rightly understood': this 'produces no great acts of self-sacrifice, but it suggests daily small acts of self-denial. By itself it cannot suffice to make a man virtuous; but it disciplines a number of persons in habits of regularity, temperance, moderation, foresight, self-command;

and if it does not lead men straight to virtue by the will, it gradually draws them in that direction by their habits.' Tocqueville cast himself as an adversary of Burke over the French revolution; see Gannett, *Tocqueville Unveiled*, ch. 4. But this is one of many points of overlap and continuity between them.

4. Moral choices and young people: see Smith, Christoffersen, Davidson and Herzog, *Lost in Transition: The Dark Side of Emerging Adulthood*.

5. J. S. Mill on man's nature in economics: see 'On the Definition of Political Economy', in *Essays on Some Unsettled Questions of Political Economy*.

6. Rationality: the large and rapidly growing critical literature on the nature and weaknesses of neoclassical economics includes Shleifer, *Inefficient Markets: An Introduction to Behavioral Finance*; or, more accessibly, Quiggin, *Zombie Economics*.

7. Burke's support for different revolutions: see Alfred Cobban, 'Edmund Burke and the Origins of the Theory of Nationality', *Cambridge Historical Journal* 2.1 (1926) 36–47.

8. Limits of expertise: see e.g. Tetlock, *Expert Political Judgement*.

9. Rationalism: compare the critique of rationalism in the twentieth century by the British philosopher Michael Oakeshott, in *Rationalism in Politics* and other works. This perhaps owes more to Burke than is generally recognized, including by Oakeshott himself.

Chapter 10: The Recovery of Value

1. Newcastle experiment: Melissa Bateson, Daniel Nettle and Gilbert Roberts, 'Cues of Being Watched Enhance Cooperation in a Real-World Setting', *Biology Letters* 2.3 (2006) 412–14.

2. Money primes: Kathleen Vohs, 'The Psychological Consequences of Money', *Science* 314.5802 (17 November 2006) 1154–6; Eugene Caruso, Kathleen Vohs, Brittani Baxter and Adam Waytz, 'Mere

Exposure to Money Increases Endorsement of Free-Market Systems and Social Inequality', *Journal of Experimental Psychology* Brief Report, 9 July 2012.

3. Behavioural economics: there is a huge literature here, but see e.g. Kahneman, Slovic and Tversky, *Judgement under Uncertainty*; Kahneman and Tversky, *Choices, Values and Frames*; and Kahneman, *Thinking, Fast and Slow*.

4. WEIRDness: see e.g. Joseph Henrich, Steven Heine and Ara Norenzayan, 'The Weirdest People in the World?', *Behavioural and Brain Sciences* 33.2–3 (June 2010) 61–83.

5. Attachment and structure: see Brooks, *The Social Animal*, p. 61. See also Roy F. Baumeister and Mark R. Leary, 'The Need to Belong: Desire for Interpersonal Attachments as a Fundamental Human Motivation', *Psychological Bulletin* 117.3 (1995) 497–529.

6. Neuroscience of compassion: see in particular the work of Jean Decety and collaborators, via http://home.uchicago.edu/~decety/jean_cv.html. E.g. 'A Social-Neuroscience Perspective on Empathy', *Current Directions in Psychological Science* 15.2 (2006) 54–8.

7. Volunteering: *The Health Benefits of Volunteering: A Review of Recent Research*, Corporation for National and Community Service 2007; also e.g. Luks and Payne, *The Healing Power of Doing Good*.

8. Language usage: see Hart and Risley, *Meaningful Differences in the Everyday Experience of Young American Children*.

9. Loss of social capital in Chicago: Loïc Wacquant and William Julius Wilson, 'The Cost of Racial and Class Exclusion in the Inner City', *Annals of the American Academy of Political and Social Science* 501 (Jan. 1989) 8–25.

10. Negative social capital: Alejandro Portes, 'Social Capital: Its Origins and Applications in Modern Sociology', *Annual Review of Sociology* 24 (1998), pp. 1–24.

11. Durkheim and suicide: Durkheim, *On Suicide*; Haidt, *The Righteous Mind*.

12. Modern explanations of suicide: Richard Eckersley and Keith Dear, 'Cultural Correlates of Youth Suicide', *Social Science & Medicine* 55.11 (Dec. 2002) 1891–1904.

13. Hitchens, Dawkins, Dennett: see works cited in the Bibliography.

14. Communes in eighteenth- and nineteenth-century America: Richard Sosis, 'Religion and Intragroup Cooperation: Preliminary Results of a Comparative Analysis of Utopian Communities', *Cross-Cultural Research* 34.1 (2000) 70–87.

15. Types of religious community: Richard Shweder, Nancy Much, Manmohan Mahapatra and Lawrence Park, 'The "Big Three" of Morality (Autonomy, Community, Divinity) and the "Big Three" Explanations of Suffering', 1997, reprinted in Shweder, *Why Do Men Barbeque? Recipes for Cultural Psychology.*

16. Benefits of religious observance: see e.g. David Myers, 'The Funds, Friends, and Faith of Happy People', *American Psychologist* 55.1 (2000) 56–67.

17. Burke's rhetoric: see Chris Reid, 'Burke as Rhetorician and Orator', in Dwan and Insole (eds), *The Cambridge Companion to Burke*, Harris, *op. cit.*, and the works by Bullard and Reid in the Bibliography.

Conclusion: Burke Today

1. Euro: see Marsh, *The Euro: The Battle for the New Global Currency.*

2. Alleged death of conservatism: see Tanenhaus, *The Death of Conservatism.*

3. Corporate power: see e.g. Monks, *Corpocracy: How CEOs and the Business Roundtable Hijacked the World's Greatest Wealth Machine . . . And How to Get It Back.*

4. State of US politics: see Mann and Ornstein, *It's Even Worse than It Looks.*

5. Different conceptions of free markets: see Norman, 'Conservative Free Markets, and the Case for Real Capitalism'.

Select Bibliography

This Bibliography lists both works cited and those of general interest relating to Burke's life, times and thought, and their influence and interpretation.

Works by Burke

Correspondence, ed. Thomas Copeland et al., 10 vols, Cambridge University Press 1958–78

Works, 8 vols, Bohn's British Classics, London 1854–89

Writings and Speeches, ed. Paul Langford et al., 8 vols to date, Oxford University Press 1981–

Biographies of Burke

Stanley Ayling, *Edmund Burke: His Life and Opinions*, John Murray 1988

Robert Bisset, *The Life of Edmund Burke*, 2 vols, London 1800

Carl Cone, *Burke and the Nature of Politics*, University of Kentucky Press 1957 and 1964

Russell Kirk, *Edmund Burke: A Genius Reconsidered*, Arlington House 1967

Paul Langford, 'Edmund Burke', *Dictionary of National Biography*

F. P. Lock, *Edmund Burke*, 2 vols, Oxford University Press 1998 and 2006

C. B. Macpherson, *Burke*, Oxford University Press 1980

Philip Magnus, *Edmund Burke*, John Murray 1939

John Morley, *Burke*, Macmillan 1888

Robert Murray, *Edmund Burke: A Biography*, Oxford University Press 1931

Conor Cruise O'Brien, *The Great Melody*, University of Chicago Press 1992

James Prior, *Memoir of the Life and Character of the Right Hon. Edmund Burke*, Philadelphia 1825

Nicholas K. Robinson, *Edmund Burke: A Life in Caricature*, Yale University Press 1996

Other works

Jeremy Bernstein, *Dawning of the Raj*, Aurum Press 2000

Paul Bew, *Ireland: The Politics of Enmity 1789–2006*, Oxford University Press 2007

Harry Bingham, *This Little Britain*, Fourth Estate 2007

Tom Bingham, *Dr Johnson and the Law and Other Essays on Johnson*, Inner Temple and Dr Johnson's House Trust 2010

Tom Bingham, *The Rule of Law*, Penguin 2010

Robert Blake, *A History of the Conservative Party from Peel to Major*, Heinemann 1997

Steven Blakemore, *Intertextual War*, Associated University Presses 1997

David Bromwich, *Hazlitt: The Mind of a Critic*, Oxford University Press 1983

David Bromwich, *On Empire, Liberty and Reform: Speeches and Letters of Edmund Burke*, Yale University Press 2000

David Brooks, *The Social Animal*, Random House 2011

Paddy Bullard, *Edmund Burke and the Art of Rhetoric*, Cambridge University Press 2011

Ian Buruma, *Anglomania: A European Love Affair*, Vintage Books 2000

Geoffrey Butler, *The Tory Tradition*, Conservative Political Centre 1957

Marilyn Butler (ed.), *Burke. Paine, Godwin, and the Revolution Controversy*, Cambridge University Press 1984

Herbert Butterfield, *George III and the Historians*, Collins 1957

Arthur Cash, *John Wilkes: The Scandalous Father of Civil Liberty*, Yale University Press 2006

Ian Christie, *Myth and Reality in Late Eighteenth Century British Politics*, Macmillan 1970

Alfred Cobban, *Edmund Burke and the Revolt against the Eighteenth Century*, Allen and Unwin 1929

Linda Colley, *In Defiance of Oligarchy: The Tory Party 1714–60*, Cambridge University Press 1982

Thomas Copeland, *Edmund Burke: Six Essays*, Jonathan Cape 1950

J. C. Curwen, *Observations on the State of Ireland*, 1818

Faramerz Dabhoiwala, *The Origins of Sex*, Allen Lane 2012

Richard Dawkins, *The God Delusion*, Bantam 2006

Daniel Dennett, *Breaking the Spell: Religion as a Natural Phenomenon*, Allen Lane 2006

Patrick Dillon, *The Last Revolution: 1688 and the Creation of the Modern World*, Jonathan Cape 2006

Patrick Dillon, *The Much-Lamented Death of Madam Geneva: The Eighteenth-Century Gin Craze*, Headline Books 2002

Sean Patrick Donlan, *Edmund Burke's Irish Identities*, Irish Academic Press 2007

William Doyle, *The Oxford History of the French Revolution*, Oxford University Press 2002

Emile Durkheim, *On Suicide*, Penguin 2006

David Dwan and Christopher Insole (eds), *The Cambridge Companion to Burke*, Cambridge University Press 2012

Gilbert Elliot, *Letters to a Prince, from a Man of Kent*, 1789

Amanda Foreman, *Georgiana, Duchess of Devonshire*, Random House 1998

Robert T. Gannett Jr, *Tocqueville Unveiled*, University of Chicago Press 2003

Luke Gibbons, *Edmund Burke and Ireland*, Cambridge University Press 2003

J. A. W. Gunn, *Factions No More: Attitudes to Party in Government and Opposition in Eighteenth-Century England*, Frank Cass 1972

William Hague, *William Pitt the Younger*, HarperCollins 2004

William Hague, *William Wilberforce*, HarperCollins 2007

Jonathan Haidt, *The Righteous Mind*, Allen Lane 2012

Tim Harford, *The Logic of Life*, Little, Brown 2008

Ian Harris, 'Edmund Burke', entry in *Stanford Encyclopaedia of Philosophy*

Robin Harris, *The Conservatives: A History*, Transworld 2011

Betty Hart and Todd Risley, *Meaningful Differences in the Everyday Experience of Young American Children*, Brookes Publishing 1995

Christopher Hibbert, *King Mob*, Longman 1958

Christopher Hitchens, *God is Not Great: How Religions Poisons Everything*, Atlantic 2007

Thomas Hobbes, *De Cive* ('On the Citizen'), ed. R. Tuck and M. Silverthorne, Cambridge University Press 1998

Joanna Innes, *Inferior Politics*, Oxford University Press 2009

Daniel Kahneman, *Thinking, Fast and Slow*, Farrar, Straus & Giroux 2011

Daniel Kahneman, Paul Slovic and Amos Tversky, *Judgement under Uncertainty*, Cambridge University Press 1982

Daniel Kahneman and Amos Tversky, *Choices, Values and Frames*, Cambridge University Press 2000

Elizabeth R. Lambert, *Edmund Burke of Beaconsfield*, University of Delaware Press 2003

Paul Langford, *A Polite and Commercial People*, Oxford University Press 1994

Paul Langford, *Walpole and the Robinocracy*, Chadwyck-Healey 1986

Harold Laski, *Political Thought in England from Locke to Bentham*, Holt 1920

W. E. H. Lecky, *A History of England in the Eighteenth Century*, 8 vols, 1878–90

Allan Luks and Peggy Payne, *The Healing Power of Doing Good*, iUniverse.com 2001

Jim McCue, *Edmund Burke and our Present Discontents*, Claridge Press 1997

John James McGregor, *A New Picture of Dublin*, 1821

Alasdair MacIntyre, *After Virtue*, Duckworth 1981

Alasdair MacIntyre, *Whose Justice? Which Rationality?*, Duckworth 1996

C. B. Macpherson, *The Political Theory of Possessive Individualism*, Clarendon Press 1965.

Thomas Mann and Norman Ornstein, *It's Even Worse than It Looks*, Basic Books 2012

Harvey Mansfield, *Statesmanship and Party Government: A Study of Burke and Bolingbroke*, University of Chicago Press 1965

David Marsh, *The Euro: The Battle for the New Global Currency*, Yale University Press 2009

J. S. Mill, *Essays on Some Unsettled Questions of Political Economy*, 1829–30

B. R. Mitchell, *British Historical Statistics*, Cambridge University Press 1988 (revised edn 2011)

L. G. Mitchell, *Charles James Fox*, Penguin 1997

L. G. Mitchell, *Charles James Fox and the Disintegration of the Whig Party*, Oxford University Press 1971

Robert A. G. Monks, *Corpocracy: How CEOs and the Business Roundtable Hijacked the World's Greatest Wealth Machine . . . And How to Get It Back*, John Wiley 2007

Thomas Moore, *Memoirs of the Life of the Right Honourable Richard Brinsley Sheridan*, 1824

Lewis Namier, *England in the Age of the American Revolution*, Macmillan 1930

Lewis Namier, *The Structure of Politics at the Accession of George III*, Macmillan 1929

Jesse Norman (ed.), *The Achievement of Michael Oakeshott*, Duckworth 1992

Jesse Norman, *The Big Society*, University of Buckingham Press 2010

Jesse Norman, 'Conservative Free Markets, and the Case for Real Capitalism', www.jessenorman.com

Michael Oakeshott, *Rationalism in Politics*, revised edn, ed. T. Fuller, Liberty Press 1991

Frank O'Gorman, *Edmund Burke: His Political Philosophy*, Allen & Unwin 1973

Frank O'Gorman, *The Emergence of the British Two-Party System 1760–1832*, Edward Arnold 1982

Frank O'Gorman, *Voters, Patrons and Parties*, Oxford University Press 1989

Noël O'Sullivan, *Conservatism*, Everyman 1976

Mark Pagel, *Wired for Culture: The Natural History of Human Cooperation*, Allen Lane 2012

Richard Pares, *King George III and the Politicians*, Oxford University Press 1953

Nicholas Penny, *Reynolds: Catalogue of a Royal Academy of Arts Exhibition*, Weidenfeld & Nicolson 1986

J. G. A. Pocock, *Virtue, Commerce and History*, Cambridge University Press 1985

Robert Putnam, *Bowling Alone*, Simon & Schuster 2000

John Quiggin, *Zombie Economics*, Princeton University Press 2010

Christopher Reid, *Edmund Burke and the Practice of Political Writing*, Gill & Macmillan 1985

Nick Robins, *The Corporation that Changed the World*, Pluto Press 2006

Simon Schama, *Citizens*, Knopf 1989

Roger Scruton, *The Meaning of Conservatism*, Penguin 1980

Andrei Shleifer, *Inefficient Markets: An Introduction to Behavioral Finance*, Oxford University Press 2000

Richard Shweder, *Why Do Men Barbeque? Recipes for Cultural Psychology*, Harvard University Press 2003

Christian Smith, Kari Christoffersen, Hilary Davidson and Patricia Snell Herzog, *Lost in Transition: The Dark Side of Emerging Adulthood*, Oxford University Press 2011

Leo Strauss, *Natural Right and History*, University of Chicago Press 1965

Andrew Sullivan, *The Conservative Soul*, HarperCollins 2006

Sam Tanenhaus, *The Death of Conservatism*, Random House 2009

Philip E. Tetlock, *Expert Political Judgement*, Princeton University Press 2006

P. D. G. Thomas, *The House of Commons in the Eighteenth Century*, Oxford University Press 1971

Lionel James Trotter, *Warren Hastings: A Biography*, London 1878

Jenny Uglow, *Dr Johnson, his Club and Other Friends*, National Portrait Gallery 1998

Various, *Dictionary of National Biography*, Oxford University Press 1885–

Horace Walpole, *Memoirs of the Reign of King George III*, ed. G. F. R. Barker, 4 vols, 1894

Stanley Weintraub, *Disraeli*, Hamish Hamilton 1993

Woodrow Wilson, *Essential Writings and Speeches of the Scholar-President*, ed. Mario R. DiNunzio, New York University Press 2006

Acknowledgements

IN WRITING THIS BOOK I am acutely conscious of how much I owe to a vast number of other people.

In addition to relying on the primary research of Burke's biographers, and others listed in the Bibliography, I have benefited enormously from the assistance of many current professional historians and Burke scholars. These include Paul Bew, Richard Bourke, Paddy Bullard, Stephen Farrell, Patrick Geoghegan, Ian Harris, Tristram Hunt, Eamon O'Flahertie and Chris Reid, all of whom commented – sometimes at length – on an early draft. Several also generously shared published and unpublished work with me. Needless to say, none is responsible for any mistakes or errors of interpretation that remain.

I am also very grateful to Richard Bourke for giving me early sight of his important article on three newly attributed Burke essays, and in particular the 1757 essay on political parties, published in the *Historical Journal*. Patrick Geoghegan was a very generous host on a visit I paid to Trinity College Dublin, and Catherine Gilltrap kindly showed me the College's wonderful portrait of Burke.

A brilliant array of other friends have taken the time to read and comment on early drafts. These include Lee Auspitz, Terence Kealey, Danny Kruger, Andrew Lilico, Bob Monks and Peter Oborne. Matt Ridley gently corrected key aspects of an early version of Chapter 10. Nicholas Penny helped me to understand Joshua Reynolds far better. Sid Blumenthal shared some insights from his forthcoming biography of Abraham Lincoln. Lee and Kate Auspitz hosted a memorable dinner with that doyen of Burke scholarship, Harvey Mansfield. I have greatly enjoyed and learned much from the writings of Roger Scruton on conservatism, Burke and many other topics.

I have discussed Burke and his ideas in many forums over the past few years. Three stand out: a talk at the London School of Economics opposite a great Burkean, Maurice Glasman; a seminar at All Souls College, Oxford, at which Joanna Innes gamely tried to put me right on Burke and commerce; and a fascinating colloquium on Magna Carta and its influence hosted by the Liberty Fund. I thank them all.

This book would not have seen the light of day at all without the enthusiasm and support of my agent, Caroline Michel, or the publishing skills and energy of Martin Redfern and Stephen Guise at HarperCollins and – copyeditor supreme – Peter James; and Lara Heimert and Katy O'Donnell at Basic Books. I am hugely obliged to my staff in Hereford and at Westminster – Tom Hirons, Gill Rivers, Wendy Robertson, Rosanna Turner, Jemima Warren and Amy Woolfson – whose professionalism allowed me to combine my parliamentary and constituency work with the writing of this book.

I ran out of expressions of love and gratitude to my wife, Kate, and our children, Sam, Nell and Noah, many years ago.

This book is dedicated to my colleagues in the House of Commons; and to the mixed and disembodied genius of the British constitution.

Hereford, January 2013

Index

NOTE: Works and speeches by Edmund Burke (EB) appear directly under title; works by others under author's name

Action Committees, 287; *see also* America

utilitarianism, 242–3, 247, 262

van der Post, Sir Laurens, 259
Verney, Ralph, 2nd Earl: friendship with Will Burke, 47; as EB's patron, 48–9, 56; lends money to EB, 58–9; financial difficulties, 71–2, 108; supports Will Burke, 72
Vietnam War, 285
Vindication of Natural Society, A (EB), 23–5, 31, 34, 188, 190, 198, 212
Vohs, Kathleen, 261
Voltaire, François Marie Arouet, 35, 83, 187; *Philosophical Letters*, 186

Wacquant, Loïc and William Julius Wilson, 267
Walpole, Horace, 141, 220
Walpole, Sir Robert, 37–42, 94
Warton, Thomas, 46
Washington, George, 226
Wendover, Buckinghamshire, 48–50, 71
Wentworth Woodhouse (house), Yorkshire, 56
Westminster Hall, 128–30
Whigs: beginnings and principles, 37, 218; 'supremacy', 38; Rockingham and, 56, 145; and Wilkes, 63; in Brooks's club, 113; reaction to EB's *Reflections*, 142; support

constitutional monarchy, 145; EB appeals for reversion to old principles, 147–8; break up and join Pitt's ministry, 152, 155, 282; posthumous view of EB, 174; name, 218–19; as predecessors of Liberals, 282; *see also* Liberal party
Whiteboys (Irish group), 42
Whitman, Walt: *Leaves of Grass*, 276
Wilberforce, William, 75, 99
Wilde, Oscar, 83
Wilkes, John, 60–5, 67; *Essay on Woman* (attrib.), 62
William II (Rufus), King, 128
William III (of Orange), King, 11, 37, 87, 136, 205, 211
Wilson, Woodrow, 4, 174–5
Wimpole Street, London, 33–4
Windham, William, 158
Wollstonecraft, Mary, 28; *A Vindication of the Rights of Men*, 141; *A Vindication of the Rights of Women*, 141
women: EB's view and treatment of, 13, 28, 279
Wordsworth, William, 175–6, 276
Works (EB; posthumous publication), 172
Wraxall, Sir Nathaniel, 96
Wren, Sir Christopher, 50
Wyvill, Christopher, 92

Yeats, William Butler, 2, 256, 281
Yorktown: British defeat (1781), 111
Young, Arthur, 68